*The Nation
in Crisis:
1828–1865*

# The Structure of American History

DAVIS R. B. ROSS, ALDEN T. VAUGHAN,
AND JOHN B. DUFF, EDITORS

VOLUME I
*Colonial America: 1607–1763*
VOLUME II
*Forging the Nation: 1763–1828*
VOLUME III
*The Nation in Crisis: 1828–1865*
VOLUME IV
*The Emergence of Modern America: 1865–1900*
VOLUME V
*Progress, War, and Reaction: 1900–1933*
VOLUME VI
*Recent America: 1933 to the Present*

# The Nation in Crisis: 1828–1865

*edited by* **Davis R. B. Ross**
COLUMBIA UNIVERSITY

**Alden T. Vaughan**
COLUMBIA UNIVERSITY

**John B. Duff**
SETON HALL UNIVERSITY

THOMAS Y. CROWELL COMPANY

NEW YORK · ESTABLISHED 1834

COPYRIGHT © 1970 BY
THOMAS Y. CROWELL COMPANY, INC.
ALL RIGHTS RESERVED

Except for use in a review, the reproduction or utilization of this work in any form or by any electronic, mechanical, or other means, now known or hereafter invented, including photocopying and recording, and in any information storage and retrieval system is forbidden without the written permission of the publisher.

L. C. Card 78-101951

*Series design by Barbara Kohn Isaac*

Manufactured in the United States of America

# Preface

*The Structure of American History* is designed to introduce undergraduate students of United States history and interested general readers to the variety and richness of our historical literature. The six volumes in the series offer selections from the writings of major historians whose books have stood the test of time or whose work, though recent, has met with unusual acclaim. Some of the selections deal with political history, some with diplomatic, some with economic, and others with social; all however offer thoughtful and provocative interpretations of the American past.

The volumes, with seven substantial selections in each, cover the following chronological periods:

    I. Colonial America: 1607–1763
   II. Forging the Nation: 1763–1828
  III. The Nation in Crisis: 1828–1865
  IV. The Emergence of Modern America: 1865–1900
   V. Progress, War, and Reaction: 1900–1933
  VI. Recent America: 1933 to the Present

Each volume opens with a general introduction to the period as a whole, in which we have suggested major themes that give coherence to the era and have outlined briefly the direction of past and recent scholarship. An editors' introduction precedes each selection; in these we have not sought to tell the reader what he is about to encounter but rather to identify the selection's author, establish its historical setting, and provide its historiographical context. Finally, a short bibliographical essay follows each selection, in which the reader is introduced to a wide range of related literature.

Several criteria guided us in our choice of readings: the distinction of the author, the significance of his interpretation, the high literary quality of his style. Because we conceived of the series as a supplement to, rather than a substitute for, the reading usually assigned in college-level survey courses, we have tried to avoid material that merely expands in detail the coverage offered in the traditional textbooks; we have sought, instead, selections from works that shed new light and raise new questions, or at the very least provide a kind of reading experience not customarily encountered in traditional assignments. For, at bottom, *The Structure of American History* stems from the editors' conviction that the great works of historical writing should not be reserved for the graduate student or the professional scholar but should be made available to those readers who can perhaps best benefit from an early encounter with Francis Parkman, Samuel Eliot Morison, Allan Nevins, Oscar Handlin, and their peers. We want college students to know from the outset that the stuff of history is neither the textbook nor the latest article in a scholarly journal. What has often inspired us, as teachers and writers of history, and what we hope will inspire students and lay readers, is history written by the great practitioners of the art: men who have written with vigor and grace the results of their own meticulous research and meditation.

In order to make our selections as extensive as possible, we have, with reluctance, omitted all footnotes. We urge readers to remember that the authority of each historian rests largely on the documentation he offers in support of his statements, and that readers who wish to investigate the evidence on which a historian has based his argument should refer to the original published version—cited on the first page of each selection. Readers are also reminded that many of the books recommended in the bibliographical notes appended to each selection are obtainable in paperback editions. We have refrained from indicating which volumes are currently in paper for the list of paperbacks grows too rapidly. We refer those interested to R. R. Bowker Company, *Paperbound Books in Print,* available at the counter of most bookstores.

D.R.B.R.<br>
A.T.V.<br>
J.B.D.

# Contents

| | |
|---|---:|
| Introduction | 1 |
| The New West, 1820–1830 | 3 |
|     FREDERICK JACKSON TURNER | |
| Radicals and Workers in the Age of Jackson | 33 |
|     ARTHUR M. SCHLESINGER, JR. | |
| The Socialization of Christianity | 76 |
|     HENRY STEELE COMMAGER | |
| Slavery and Personality | 107 |
|     STANLEY ELKINS | |
| The Dred Scott Decision | 144 |
|     ALLAN NEVINS | |
| Lincoln the Liberal Statesman | 185 |
|     JAMES G. RANDALL | |
| The War Ends | 221 |
|     BRUCE CATTON | |

# *Introduction*

The American Civil War (1861–1865) casts its shadow in time both forward and backward. As early as 1820 Thomas Jefferson, reflecting on the reopened slavery controversy during the debate over the Missouri Compromise, had written that like "a fire bell in the night" it had awakened him and filled him with terror. When President Jackson delivered his Farewell Address seventeen years later, he too spoke somberly of the divisions that threatened to tear American society asunder. Old Hickory warned Americans of conflicts spawned by irresponsible enthusiasts, the abolitionists, and by unprincipled men of wealth, the monied class. Neither statesman was unique in his time; the intensity and rapidity of changes in America's political institutions, economy, boundaries, and values made many ponder the future with alarm. Events corresponded with feelings: the Bank War, the 1837 depression, the Texas question, the war with Mexico, and the fateful series of conflicts in the 1850's led directly to a domestic, fratricidal war. The era from 1828 to 1865 was indeed a time of crisis and challenge.

If both Jefferson and Jackson at times saw through the glass darkly, more often they were optimistic. Both believed that the large majority of Americans was not only virtuous, but also reasonable. With nature's bounty so richly bestowed upon the United States and with republican values providing the bedrock of American faith, the future often seemed bright. Again events reinforced attitudes: the successful extension of white manhood suffrage; the numerous additions of territory and the rounding out of national boundaries; the flourishing economy, characterized by advances in textile, carpet, and food processing manufactures, as well as by the astounding success of American clipper ships in the competition for world trade; the completion of canals and railways; and the unmistakable manifestation of national strength with military success over Mexico. The era from 1828 to 1865 was indeed a time of accomplishment and opportunity.

Crisis and challenge, accomplishment and opportunity. As with all epochs, 1828–1865 demonstrated American ambivalences. Tensions permeated society, with freedom versus slavery, nationalism versus sectionalism, idealism versus compromise, and industrialism versus agrarianism providing the leading issues of the period. Society did not settle them all; but try it did, as reform movements emerged in unprecedented abundance, espousing causes as fundamental as abolition, as frivolous as sabbatarianism. And many of the debates of the day linger on to our own time, reflected in historians' preoccupation with the problems and personalities of the antebellum era. Scholars have waged verbal wars, for example, about the nature, extent, and significance of the "Jacksonian Revolution," about the moral and economic aspects of slavery, and about the causes of the Civil War—historiographic struggles that will undoubtedly continue as long as Americans find democracy and union to be basic values.

# The New West, 1820–1830

## Frederick Jackson Turner

No historian has influenced American historical thought more than Frederick Jackson Turner (1861–1932). Born and raised on the Wisconsin frontier, Turner appropriately is best known for his frontier theory. In a famous address before the American Historical Association in 1893 (and as developed in other essays), Turner informed his professional colleagues and the general public that the golden age of the frontier had ended. The 1890 census results had disclosed that the nation's frontier had finally been exhausted; it was now time to assess the influence of the frontier on American life. Turner questioned the then current theories about the European origins of American institutions and values. He argued that a distinctive American civilization had emerged in American forests: European immigrants and their descendants, forced to abandon Old World customs when faced with the simple yet rigorous exigencies of wilderness life, assumed new habits, beliefs, and institutions. The frontiersman emerged, as Hector St. John Crèvecoeur had noted a century earlier, a "new man." Democracy, Turner asserted, had not found roots in the forests of Germany and then been transplanted westward

*Source:* Frederick Jackson Turner, *The Rise of the New West, 1820–1830* (New York: Harper Bros., 1906), pp. 67–110.

to the New World; rather, its origins lay on the American frontier. So too with such values as nationalism, individualism, and restlessness.

Turner explained that cheap land lured men and women westward in successive waves. Initially, the hostile environment reduced life to near-primitivism, stripping away the veneers of civilization. But this stage was followed by one in which the settlers developed cooperative habits, such as building bridges, roads, and log cabins, as well as fighting Indians—these habits in turn encouraged democratic procedures. Yet even as the frontier made communities democratic, it also promoted individual self-reliance and placed a premium on each person's practical worth rather than on his inherited class status; again, faced with enormous obstacles, frontier groups looked to the national government for aid and protection, making them more nationalistic than others; and finally, the presence of even more land on the horizon kept the frontiersman eager to press on and careless about his current holding, leading to mobility and wastefulness.

Despite an indifferent reception in 1893, for the next forty years—while Turner labored first at the University of Wisconsin until 1910; then at Harvard University to 1924; and finally as a research associate at the Huntington Library at San Marino, California, until his death in 1932—the Turner thesis remained ascendant. The American Historical Association by the 1920's was dubbed "One Big Turner *Verein*." Turnerians had gone far beyond the master in making claims for the frontier. The thesis fit the national mood. The closing of the frontier presented some groups with an argument for overseas economic expansion; continued American development made the extension of American political and economic institutions imperative. Others, discomfited by the responsibilities inherent in America's emergence as a world power, found the emphasis of the frontier thesis on the American origins of democracy a handy excuse not to become more responsibly involved in international affairs; such involvement would endanger the purity of the American experiment. Then, too, it possessed contemporary relevance, explaining in a large measure the painful shift from an agricultural to an industrial society. Turner's writings sometimes reflected a nostalgia for the virile, individualistic, agrarian, and domestic past, compounded with a gloomy prognosis of an industrial future in which America would slide into state collectivism and proletarian unrest.

Not surprisingly, a reaction set in. The 1930's marked the beginning of a full-scale assault on the thesis. Two general reasons explain the attacks: the 1929 stock-market crash and the ensuing great depression dramatized the industrial and urban nature of American problems so that a thesis deeply rooted in agrarian and rural causation no longer seemed persuasive. Equally important, the long domination of one general theory of the American past inevitably brought a counter-pendulum swing; a new generation could not resist the urge to write its own history. Factors such as urbanism, immigration, and business corporations, to name but three, were shown to have played key roles in shaping the American past. Turner's thesis, especially in the hands of his zealous followers, failed to take these elements into account.

Critics pointed to Turner's imprecision in using the term "frontier." At times he seemed to speak of a specific geographical location, at others he spoke of a process, and at still others he used the term poetically to evoke a cluster of values that he personally associated with the West. Even where he had been most precise, as with his assertion that the frontier acted as a "safety valve," dampening urban radicalism by draining surplus workers from the industrially depressed East, Turner met criticism. Clearly, migration westward took place during times of prosperity, not depression, and the proletariat in urban areas earned too little even to get to the frontier, let alone to be able to afford the high costs of setting up a homestead once there. And for the urban poor, unused to farming or ranching, the West offered no feasible escape. Instead, the bulk of internal migration in the late nineteenth century flowed to the cities. Thus the safety valve worked in reverse, attracting discontented farmers to cities, lessening the extent and intensity of agrarian unrest. Other observers showed that when westerners enacted "democratic" constitutions, almost universally they had borrowed from charters already in force in the East. Still others, upset by Turner's apparent suggestion that a near-primitivism existed on the frontier, argued that new settlers brought with them their own cultural baggage, manifesting itself in the literary societies, libraries, and traveling drama companies that flourished on each of the successive frontiers. Comparison of other frontier experiences with the American experience revealed that the frontier alone could not explain the extent of or the devotion to democracy. For example, French Canada and Siberian Russia failed to produce the same democratic intensity.

After such an assault, what remained? Virtually all of Turner's poesy has been shorn from modern scholars' views of the frontier. Instead neo-Turnerians have tried to define the term with greater verbal accuracy, separating the frontier as a geographical location from the frontier as a process. Even while doing this, they still adhere to the notion that plural meanings of the word are valuable in describing such a complex phenomenon. In addition, although the "safety valve" may not have worked as Turner suggested, scholars recently have reaffirmed the frontier's sociopsychological and macroeconomic impact: Americans believed that "free" land offered an escape from onerous industrial surroundings, if not for themselves, then for their children; the abundance of landed resources did help to maintain the relatively high American wage structure. Also, since each Western community had to go through the political constitution-making stage, experimentation in forms and refinements of democratic processes resulted.

Lastly, the neo-Turnerians have scaled down the claims of the hypothesis. It does not explain everything, they admit, but is rather an important ingredient in analyzing the American past. As a result, the present-day defenders maintain that the American frontier (as a place abundant in material resources, with a sparse population, and adjacent to unsettled portions of the continent) provided individuals with extraordinary opportunities to improve their economic and social lot by their efforts alone. Individuals and their institutions were altered in the process, the extent and direction of change depending upon the heritage that the individual brought with him and the flexibility of the sociopolitical system out of which he came and which still embraced the frontier area. In brief, the frontier experience in America deepened and enhanced a preexisting Anglo-Saxon cultural heritage of democracy and freedom. One can neither focus entirely on the frontier to explain American life nor ignore it altogether.

It is unfortunate that Turner's public reputation stems chiefly from his 1893 address. What he had tentatively advanced in the name of scientific inquiry and hypothesis became crystallized as a hard and fast thesis by his supporters and critics alike. This has obscured the variety of his contributions to historical knowledge and techniques. He was more than a spinner of poetical generalities. In the selection that follows from the only book-length historical study he completed, Turner proves his mastery of narrative and analysis. To be sure, the glint of the frontier shines through the discussion; yet Turner recognizes other forces, particularly sectionalism, in his account of America during the period 1820–1830. *The Rise of the New West*, published as part of the multi-volumed *American Nation* series, remains a classic.

The rise of the new west was the most significant fact in American history in the years immediately following the War of 1812. Ever since the beginnings of colonization on the Atlantic coast a frontier of settlement had advanced, cutting into the forest, pushing back the Indian, and steadily widening the area of civilization in its rear. There had been a west even in early colonial days; but then it lay close to the coast. By the middle of the eighteenth century the west was to be found beyond tide-water, advancing towards the Alleghany Mountains. When this barrier was crossed and the lands on the other side of the mountains were won, in the days of the Revolution, a new and greater west, more influential on the nation's destiny, was created.

The men of the "Western Waters" or the "Western World," as they loved to call themselves, developed under conditions of separation from the older settlements and from Europe. The lands, practically free, in this vast area not only attracted the settler, but furnished opportunity for all men to hew out their own careers. The wilderness ever opened a gate of escape to the poor, the discontented, and the oppressed. If social conditions tended to crystallize in the east, beyond the Alleghanies there was freedom. Grappling with new problems, under these conditions, the society that spread into this region developed inventiveness and resourcefulness; the restraints of custom were broken, and new activities, new lines of growth, new institutions were produced. Mr. Bryce has well declared that "the West is the most American part of America.... What Europe is to Asia, what England is to the rest of Europe, what America is to England, that the Western States and Territories are to the Atlantic States." The American spirit—the traits that have come to be recognized as the most characteristic—was developed in the new commonwealths that sprang into life beyond the seaboard. In these new western lands Americans achieved a boldness of conception of the country's destiny and democracy. The ideal of the west was its emphasis upon the worth and possibilities of the common man, its belief in the right of every man to rise to the full measure of his own nature, under conditions of social mobility. Western democracy was no theorists's dream. It came, stark and strong and full of life, from the American forest.

The time had now come when this section was to make itself felt as a dominant force in American life. Already it had shown its influence upon the older sections. By its competition, by its attractions for settlers, it reacted on the east and gave added impulse to the democratic movement in New England and New York. The struggle of Baltimore, New York City, and Philadelphia for the rising commerce of the interior was a potent factor in the development of the middle region. In the south the spread of the cotton-plant and the new form which slavery took were phases of the westward movement of the plantation. The discontent of the old south is partly explained by the migration of her citizens to the west and the Alleghanies. The future of the south lay in its affiliation to the Cotton Kingdom of the lower states which were rising on the plains of the Gulf of Mexico.

Rightly to understand the power which the new west was to exert upon the economic and political life of the nation in the years between 1820 and 1830, it is necessary to consider somewhat fully the statistics of growth in western population and industry.

The western states ranked with the middle region and the south in respect to population. Between 1812 and 1821 six new western commonwealths were added to the Union: Louisiana (1812), Indiana (1816), Mississippi (1817), Illinois (1818), Alabama (1819), and Missouri (1821). In the decade from 1820 to 1830, these states, with their older sisters, Kentucky, Tennessee, and Ohio, increased their population from 2,217,000 to nearly 3,700,000, a gain of about a million and a half in the decade. The percentages of increase in these new communities tell a striking story. Even the older states of the group grew steadily. Kentucky, with 22 per cent., Louisiana, with 41, and Tennessee and Ohio, each with 61, were increasing much faster than New England and the south, outside of Maine and Georgia. But for the newer communities the percentages of gain are still more significant: Mississippi, 81 per cent.; Alabama, 142; Indiana, 133; and Illinois, 185. The population of Ohio, which hardly more than a generation before was "fresh, untouched, unbounded, magnificent wilderness," was now nearly a million, surpassing the combined population of Massachusetts and Connecticut.

A new section has arisen and was growing at such a rate that a description of it in any single year would be falsified before it could be published. Nor is the whole strength of the western element revealed by these figures. In order to estimate the weight of the western population in 1830, we must add six hundred thousand souls in the western half of New York, three hundred thousand in the interior counties of Pennsylvania, and over two hundred thousand in the trans-Alleghany counties of Virginia, making an aggregate of four million six hundred thousand. Fully to reckon the forces of backwoods democracy, moreover, we should include a large fraction of the interior population of Maine, New Hampshire, and Vermont, North Carolina, and Georgia, and northern New York. All of these regions were to be influenced by the ideals of democratic rule which were springing up in the Mississippi Valley.

In voting-power the western states alone—to say nothing of the interior districts of the older states—were even more important than the figures for population indicate. The west itself had, under the apportionment of 1822, forty-seven out of the two hundred and thirteen members of the House of Representatives, while in the Senate its representation was eighteen out of forty-eight—more than that of any other section. Clearly, here was a region to be reckoned with; its economic interests, its ideals, and its political leaders were certain to have a powerful, if not a controlling, voice in the councils of the nation.

At the close of the War of 1812 the west had much homogeneity. Parts of Kentucky, Tennessee, and Ohio had been settled so many years that they no longer presented typical western conditions; but in most of its area the west then was occupied by pioneer farmers and stock-raisers, eking out their larder and getting peltries by hunting, and raising only a small surplus for market. By 1830, however, industrial differentiation between the northern and southern portions of the Mississippi Valley was clearly marked. The northwest was changing to a land of farmers and town-builders, anxious for a market for their grain and cattle; while the southwest was becoming increasingly a cotton-raising section, swayed by the same impulses in respect to staple exports as those which governed the southern seaboard. Economically, the northern portion of the valley tended to connect itself with the middle states, while the southern portion came into increasingly intimate connection with the south. Nevertheless, it would be a radical mistake not to deal with the west as a separate region, for, with all these differences within itself, it possessed a fundamental unity in its social structure and its democratic ideals, and at times, in no uncertain way, it showed a consciousness of its separate existence.

In occupying the Mississippi Valley the American people colonized a region far surpassing in area the territory of the old thirteen states. The movement was, indeed, but the continuation of the advance of the frontier which had begun in the earliest days of American colonization. The existence of a great body of land, offered at so low a price as to be practically free, inevitably drew population towards the west. When wild lands sold for two dollars an acre, and, indeed, could be occupied by squatters almost without molestation, it was certain that settlers would seek them instead of paying twenty to fifty dollars an acre for farms that lay not much farther to the east—particularly when the western lands were more fertile. The introduction of the steamboat on the western waters in 1811, moreover, soon revolutionized transportation conditions in the West. At the beginning of the period of which we are treating, steamers were ascending the Mississippi and the Missouri, as well as the Ohio and its tributaries. Between the close of the War of 1812 and 1830, moreover, the Indian title was extinguished to vast regions in the west. Half of Michigan was opened to settlement; the northwestern quarter of Ohio was freed; in Indiana and Illinois (more than half of which had been Indian country prior to 1816) all but a comparatively small region of undesired prairie lands south of Lake Michigan was ceded; almost the whole state of Missouri was freed from its Indian title; and, in the Gulf region, at the close of the decade, the Indians held but two isolated islands of territory, one in western Georgia and eastern Alabama, and the other in northern and central Mississippi. These ceded regions were the fruit of the victories of William Henry Harrison in the northwest, and of Andrew Jackson in the Gulf region. They were, in effect, conquered provinces, just opened to colonization.

The maps of the United States census, giving the distribution of population in 1810, 1820, and 1830, exhibit clearly the effects of the defeat of the Indians, and show the areas that were occupied in these years. In 1810 settlement beyond the mountains was almost limited to a zone along the Ohio River and its tributaries, the Cumberland and the Tennessee. In the southwest, the vicinity of Mobile showed sparse settlement, chiefly survivals of the Spanish and English occupation; and, along the fluvial lands of the eastern bank of the lower Mississipi, in the Natchez region, as well as in the old province of Louisiana, there was a considerable area occupied by planters.

By 1820 the effects of the War of 1812 and the rising tide of westward migration became manifest. Pioneers spread along the river-courses of the northwest well up to the Indian boundary. The zone of settlement along the Ohio ascended the Missouri, in the rush to the Boone's Lick country, towards the centre of the present state. From the settlements of middle Tennessee a pioneer farming area reached southward to connect with the settlements of Mobile, and the latter became conterminous with those of the lower Mississippi.

By 1830 large portions of these Indian lands, which were ceded between 1817 and 1829, received the same type of colonization. The unoccupied lands in Indiana and Illinois were prairie country, then deemed unsuited for settlement because of the lack of wood and drinking-water. It was the hardwoods that had been taken up in the northwest, and, for the most part, the tracts a little back from the unhealthful bottom-lands, but in close proximity to the rivers, which were the only means of transportation before the building of good roads. A new island of settlement appeared in the northwestern portion of Illinois and the adjacent regions of Wisconsin and Iowa, due to the opening of the lead-mines. Along the Missouri Valley and in the Gulf region the areas possessed in 1820 increased in density of population. Georgia spread her settlers into the Indian lands, which she had so recently secured by threatening a rupture with the United States.

Translated into terms of human activity, these shaded areas, encroaching on the blank spaces of the map, meant much for the map, meant much for the history of the United States. Even in the northwest, which we shall first describe, they represent, in the main, the migration of southern people. New England, after the distress following the War of 1812 and the hard winter of 1816–1817, had sent many settlers into western New York and Ohio; the Western Reserve had increased in population by the immigration of Connecticut people; Pennsylvania and New Jersey had sent colonists to southern and central Ohio, with Cincinnati as the commercial centre. In Ohio the settlers of middle-state origin were decidedly more numerous than those from the south, and New England's share was distinctly smaller than that of the south. In the Ohio legislature in 1822 there were thirty-eight members of middle-state birth, thirty-three of southern (including Kentucky), and twenty-five of New England. But Kentucky and Tennessee (now sufficiently settled to need larger and cheaper farms for the rising generation), together with the up-country of the south, contributed the mass of the pioneer colonists to most of the Mississippi Valley prior to 1830. Of course, a large fraction of these came from the Scotch-Irish and German stock that in the first half of the eighteenth century passed from Pennsylvania along the Great Valley to the up-country of the south. Indiana, so late as 1850, showed but ten thousand natives of New England, and twice as many persons of southern as of middle states origin. In the history of Indiana, North Carolina contributed a large fraction of the population, giving to it its "Hoosier" as well as much of its Quaker stock. Illinois in this period had but a sprinkling of New-Englanders, engaged in business in the little towns. The southern stock, including settlers from Kentucky and Tennessee, was the preponderant class. The Illinois legislature for 1833 contained fifty-eight from the south (including Kentucky and Tennessee), nineteen from the middle states, and only four from New England. Missouri's population was chiefly Kentuckians and Tennesseeans.

The leaders of this southern element came, in considerable measure, from well-to-do classes, who migrated to improve their conditions in the freer opportunities of a new country. Land speculation, the opportunity of political preferment, and the advantages which these growing communities brought to practioners of the law combined to attract men of this class. Many of them, as we shall see, brought their slaves with them, under the systems of indenture which made this possible. Missouri, especially, was sought by planters with their slaves.

But it was the poorer whites, the more democratic, non-slave-holding element of the south, which furnished the great bulk of the settlers north of the Ohio. Prior to the close of the decade the same farmer type was in possession of large parts of the Gulf region, whither, through the whole of our period, the slave-holding planters came in increasing numbers.

Two of the families which left Kentucky for the newer country in these years will illustrate the movement. The Lincoln family had reached that state by migration from the north with the stream of backwoodsmen which bore along with it the Calhouns and the Boones. Abraham Lincoln was born in a hilly, barren portion of Kentucky in 1809. In 1816, when Lincoln was a boy of seven, his father, a poor carpenter, took his family across the Ohio on a raft, with a capital consisting of his kit of tools and several hundred gallons of whiskey. In Indiana he hewed a path into the forest to a new home in the southern part of the state, where for a year the family lived in a "half-faced camp," or open shed of poles, clearing their land. In the hardships of the pioneer life Lincoln's mother died, as did many another frontier woman. In 1830 Lincoln was a tall, strapping youth, six feet four inches in height, able to sink his axe deeper than other men into the opposing forest. At that time his father moved to the Sangamon country of Illinois with the rush of land-seekers into that new and popular region. Near the home of Lincoln in Kentucky was born, in 1808, Jefferson Davis, whose father, shortly before the War of 1812, went with the stream of southward movers to Louisiana and then to Mississippi. Davis's brothers fought under Jackson in the War of 1812, and the family became typical planters of the Gulf region.

Meanwhile, the roads that led to the Ohio Valley were followed by an increasing tide of settlers from the east. "Old America seems to be breaking up, and moving westward," wrote Morris Birkbeck in 1817, as he passed on the National Road through Pennsylvania. "We are seldom out of sight, as we travel on this grand track, towards the Ohio, of family groups, behind and before us. . . . A small waggon (so light that you might almost carry it, yet strong enough to bear a good load of bedding, utensils and provisions, and a swarm of young citizens,—and to sustain marvellous shocks in its passage over these rocky heights) with two small horses; sometimes a cow or two, comprises their all; excepting a little store of hard-earned cash for the land office of the district, where they may obtain a title for as many acres as they possess half-dollars, being one fourth of the purchase-money. The waggon has a tilt, or cover, made of a sheet, or perhaps a blanket. The family are seen before, behind, or within the vehicle, according to the road or the weather, or perhaps the spirits of the party. . . . A cart and single horse frequently affords the means of transfer, sometimes a horse and pack-saddle. Often the back of the poor pilgrim bears all his effects, and his wife follows, naked-footed, bending under the hopes of the family."

The southerners who came by land along the many bad roads through Tennessee and Kentucky usually travelled with heavy, long-bodied wagons, drawn by four or six horses. These family groups, crowding roads and fords, marching towards the sunset, with the canvas-covered wagon, ancestor of the prairie-schooner of the later times, were typical of the overland migration. The poorer classes travelled on foot, sometimes carrying their entire effects in a cart drawn by themselves. Those of more means took horses, cattle, and sheep, and sometimes set their household goods by wagon or by steamboat up the Mississippi.

The routes of travel to the western country were numerous. Prior to the opening of the Erie Canal the New England element either passed along the Mohawk and the Genesee turnpike to Lake Erie, or crossed the Hudson and followed the line of the Catskill turnpike to the headwaters of the Allegheny, or, by way of Boston, took ship to New York, Philadelphia, or Baltimore, in order to follow a more southerly route. In Pennsylvania the principal route was the old road which, in a general way, followed the line that Forbes had cut in the French and Indian War from Philadelphia to Pittsburgh by way of Lancaster and Bedford. By this time the road had been made a turnpike through a large portion of its course. From Baltimore the traveller followed a turnpike to Cumberland, on the Potomac, where began the old National Road across the mountains to Wheeling, on the Ohio, with branches leading to Pittsburgh. This became one of the great arteries of western migration and commerce, connecting, as it did at its eastern end, with the Shenandoah Valley, and thus affording access to the Ohio for large areas of Virginia. Other routes lay through the passes of the Alleghanies, easily reached from the divide between the waters of North Carolina and of West Virginia. Saluda Gap, in northwestern South Carolina, led the way to the great valley of eastern Tennessee. In Tennessee and Kentucky many routes passed to the Ohio in the region of Cincinnati or Louisville.

When the settler arrived at the waters of the Ohio, he either took a steamboat or placed his possessions on a flatboat, or ark, and floated down the river to his destination. From the upper waters of the Allegheny many emigrants took advantage of the lumber-rafts, which were constructed from the pine forests of southwestern New York, to float to the Ohio with themselves and their belongings. With the advent of the steamboat these older modes of navigation were, to a considerable extent, superseded. But navigation on the Great Lakes had not sufficiently advanced to afford opportunity for any considerable movement of settlement, by this route, beyond Lake Erie.

In the course of the decade the cost of reaching the west varied greatly with the decrease in the transportation rates brought about by the competition of the Erie Canal, the improvement of the turnpikes, and the development of steamboat navigation. The expense of the long overland journey from New England, prior to the opening of the Erie Canal, made it extremely difficult for those without any capital to reach the west. The stage rates on the Pennsylvania turnpike and the old National Road, prior to the opening of the Erie Canal, were about five or six dollars a hundred-weight from Philadelphia or Baltimore to the Ohio River; the individual was regarded as so much freight. To most of the movers, who drove their own teams and camped by the wayside, however, the actual expense was simply that of providing food for themselves and their horses on the road. The cost of moving by land a few years later is illustrated by the case of a Maryland family, consisting of fifteen persons, of whom five were slaves. They travelled about twenty miles a day, with a four-horse wagon, three hundred miles, to Wheeling, at an expense of seventy-five dollars. The expense of travelling by stage and steamboat from Philadelphia to St. Louis at the close of the decade was about fifty-five dollars for one person; or by steamboat from New Orleans to St. Louis, thirty dollars, including food and lodging. For deck-passage, without food or lodging, the charge was only eight dollars. In 1823 the cost of passage from Cincinnati to New Orleans by steamboat was twenty-five dollars; from New Orleans to Cincinnati, fifty dollars. In the early thirties one could go from New Orleans to Pittsburgh, as cabin passenger, for from thirty-five to forty-five dollars.

Arrived at the nearest point to his destination on the Ohio, the emigrant either cut out a road to his new home or pushed up some tributary of that river in a keel-boat. If he was one of the poorer classes, he became a squatter on the public lands, trusting to find in the profits of his farming the means of paying for his land. Not uncommonly, after clearing the land, he sold his improvements to the actual purchaser, under the customary usage or by pre-emption laws. With the money thus secured he would purchase new land in a remoter area, and thus establish himself as an independent land-owner. Under the credit system which existed at the opening of the period, the settler purchased his land in quantities of not less than one hundred and sixty acres at two dollars per acre, by a cash payment of fifty cents per acre and the rest in instalments running over a period of four years; but by the new law of 1820 the settler was permitted to buy as small a tract as eighty acres from the government at a minimum price of a dollar and a quarter per acre, without credit. The price of labor in the towns along the Ohio, coupled with the low cost of provisions, made it possible for even a poor day-laborer from the East to accumulate the necessary amount to make his land-purchase.

Having in this way settled down either as a squatter or as a land-owner, the pioneer proceeded to hew out a clearing in the midst of the forest. Commonly he had selected his lands with reference to the value of the soil, as indicated by the character of the hardwoods, but this meant that the labor of clearing was the more severe in good soil. Under the sturdy strokes of his axe the light of day was let into the little circle of cleared ground. With the aid of his neighbors, called together under the social attractions of a "raising," with its inevitable accompaniment of whiskey and a "frolic," he erected his log-cabin. "America," wrote Birkbeck, "was bred in a cabin."

Having secured a foothold, the settler next proceeded to "girdle" or "deaden" an additional forest area, preparatory to his farming operations. This consisted in cutting a ring through the bark around the lower portion of the trunk, to prevent the sap from rising. In a short time the withered branches were ready for burning, and in the midst of the stumps the first crop of corn and vegetables was planted. Often the settler did not even burn the girdled trees, but planted his crop under the dead foliage.

In regions nearer to the east, as in western New York, it was sometimes possible to repay a large portion of the cost of clearing by the sale of pot and pearl ashes extracted from the logs, which were brought together into huge piles for burning. This was accomplished by a "log-rolling," under the united efforts of the neighbors, as in the case of the "raising." More commonly in the west the logs were wasted by burning, except such as were split into rails, which, laid one above another, made the zigzag "worm-fences" for the protection of the fields of the pioneer.

When a clearing was sold to a later comer, fifty or sixty dollars, in addition to the government price of land, was commonly charged for forty acres, enclosed and partly cleared. It was estimated that the cost of a farm of three hundred and twenty acres at the edge of the prairie in Illinois, at this time, would be divided as follows: for one hundred and sixty acres of prairie, two hundred dollars; for fencing it into four forty-acre fields with rail-fences, one hundred and sixty dollars; for breaking it up with a plough, two dollars per acre, or three hundred and twenty dollars; eighty acres of timber land and eighty acres of pasture prairie, two hundred dollars. Thus, with cabins, stables, etc., it cost a little over a thousand dollars to secure an improved farm of three hundred and twenty acres. But the mass of the early settlers were too poor to afford such an outlay, and were either squatters within a little clearing, or owners of eighty acres, which they hoped to increase by subsequent purchase. Since they worked with the labor of their own hands and that of their sons, the cash outlay was practically limited to the original cost of the lands and articles of husbandry. The cost of an Indiana farm of eighty acres of land, with two horses, two or three cows, a few hogs and sheep, and farming utensils, was estimated at about four hundred dollars.

The peculiar skill required of the axeman who entered the hardwood forests, together with readiness to undergo the privations of the life, made the backwoodsman in a sense an expert engaged in a special calling. Frequently he was the descendant of generations of pioneers, who, on successive frontiers, from the neighborhood of the Atlantic coast towards the interior, had cut and burned the forest, fought the Indians, and pushed forward the line of civilization. He bore the marks of the struggle in his face, made sallow by living in the shade of the forest, "shut from the common air," and in a constitution often racked by malarial fever. Dirt and squalor were too frequently found in the squatter's cabin, and education and the refinements of life were denied to him. Often shiftless and indolent, in the intervals between his tasks of forest-felling he was fonder of hunting than of a settled agricultural life. With his rifle he eked out his sustenance, and the peltries furnished him a little ready cash. His few cattle grazed in the surrounding forest, and his hogs fed on its mast.

The backwoodsman of this type represented the outer edge of the advance of civilization. Where settlement was closer, co-operative activity possible, and little villages, with the mill and retail stores, existed, conditions of life were ameliorated, and a better type of pioneer was found. Into such regions circuit-riders and wandering preachers carried the beginnings of church organization, and schools were started. But the frontiersmen proper constituted a moving class, ever ready to sell out their clearings in order to press on to a new frontier, where game more abounded, soil was reported to be better, and where the forest furnished a welcome retreat from the uncongenial encroachments of civilization. If, however, he was thrifty and forehanded, the backwoodsman remained on his clearing, improving his farm and sharing in the change from wilderness life.

Behind the type of the backwoodsman came the type of the pioneer farmer. Equipped with a little capital, he often, as we have seen, purchased the clearing, and thus avoided some of the initial hardships of pioneer life. In the course of a few years, as saw-mills were erected, frame-houses took the place of the log-cabins; the rough clearing, with its stumps, gave way to well-tilled fields; orchards were planted; live-stock roamed over the enlarged clearing; and an agricultural surplus was ready for export. Soon the adventurous speculator offered corner lots in a new town-site, and the rude beginnings of a city were seen.

Thus western occupation advanced in a series of waves: the Indian was sought by the fur-trader; the fur-trader was followed by the frontiersman, whose live-stock exploited the natural grasses and the acorns of the forest; next came the wave of primitive agriculture, followed by more intensive farming and city life. All the stages of social development went on under the eye of the traveller as he passed from the frontier towards the east. Such were the forces which were steadily pushing their way into the American wilderness, as they had pushed for generations.

While thus the frontier folk spread north of the Ohio and up the Missouri, a different movement was in progress in the Gulf region of the west. In the beginning precisely the same type of occupation was to be seen: the poorer classes of southern emigrants cut out their clearings along rivers that flowed to the Gulf and to the lower Mississippi, and, with the opening of this decade, went in increasing numbers into Texas, where enterprising Americans secured concessions from the Mexican government.

Almost all of the most recently occupied area was but thinly settled. It represented the movement of the backwoodsman, with axe and rifle, advancing to the conquest of the forest. But closer to the old settlements a more highly developed agriculture was to be seen. Hodgson, in 1821, describes plantations in northern Alabama in lands ceded by the Indians in 1818. Though settled less than two years, there were within a few miles five schools and four places of worship One plantation had one hundred acres in cotton and one hundred and ten in corn, although a year and half before it was wilderness.

But while this population of log-cabin pioneers was entering the Gulf plains, caravans of slave-holding planters were advancing from the seaboard to the occupation of the cotton-lands of the same region. As the free farmers of the interior had been replaced in the upland country of the south by the slave-holding planters, so now the frontiersmen of the southwest were pushed back from the more fertile lands into the pine hills and barrens. Not only was the pioneer unable to refuse the higher price which was offered him for his clearing, but, in the competitive bidding of the public land sales, the wealthier planter secured the desirable soils. Social forces worked to the same end. When the pioneer invited his slave-holding neighbor to a "raising," it grated on his sense of the fitness of things to have the guest appear with gloves, directing the gang of slaves which he contributed to the function. Little by little, therefore, the old pioneer life tended to retreat to the less desirable lands, leaving the slave-holder in possession of the rich "buck-shot" soils that spread over central Alabama and Mississippi and the fat alluvium that lined the eastern bank of the Mississippi. Even to-day the counties of dense negro population reveal the results of this movement of segregation.

By the side of the picture of the advance of the pioneer farmer, bearing his household goods in his canvas-covered wagon to his new home across the Ohio, must therefore be placed the picture of the southern planter crossing through the forests of western Georgia, Alabama, and Mississippi, or passing over the free state of Illinois to the Missouri Valley, in his family carriage, with servants, packs of hunting-dogs, and a train of slaves, their nightly camp-fires lighting up the wilderness where so recently the Indian hunter had held possession.

But this new society had a characteristic western flavor. The old patriarchal type of slavery along the seaboard was modified by the western conditions in the midst of which the slave-holding interest was now lodged. Planters, as well as pioneer farmers, were exploiting the wilderness and building a new society under characteristic western influences. Rude strength, a certain coarseness of life, and aggressiveness characterized this society, as it did the whole of the Mississippi Valley. Slavery furnished a new ingredient for western forces to act upon. The system took on a more commercial tinge: the plantation had to be cleared and made profitable as a purely business enterprise.

The slaves were purchased in considerable numbers from the older states instead of being inherited in the family. Slave-dealers passed to the southwest, with their coffles of negroes brought from the outworn lands of the old south. It was estimated in 1832 that Virginia annually exported six thousand slaves for sale to other states. An English traveller reported in 1823 that every year from ten to fifteen thousand slaves were sold from the states of Delaware, Maryland, and Virginia, and sent to the south. At the same time, illicit importation of slaves through New Orleans reached an amount estimated at from ten to fifteen thousand a year. It was not until the next decade that this incoming tide of slaves reached its height, but by 1830 it was clearly marked and was already transforming the southwest. Mississippi doubled the number of her slaves in the decade, and Alabama nearly trebled hers. In the same period the number of slaves of Maryland, Virginia, and North Carolina increased but slightly.

As the discussion of the south has already made clear, the explanation of this transformation of the southwest into a region of slave-holding planters lies in the spread of cotton into the Gulf plains. In 1811 this region raised but five million pounds of cotton; ten years later its product was sixty million pounds; and in 1826 its fields were white with a crop of over one hundred and fifty million pounds. It soon oustripped the seaboard south. Alabama, which had practically no cotton crop in 1811, and only ten million pounds in 1821, had in 1834 eighty-five million pounds, a larger crop than either South Carolina or Georgia.

Soon after 1830 the differences between the northern and southern portions of the Mississippi Valley were still further accentuated. (1) From New York and New England came a tide of settlement, in the thirties, which followed the Erie Canal and the Great Lakes, and began to occupy the prairie lands which had been avoided by the southern axe-men. This region then became an extension of the greater New England already to be seen in New York. (2) The southern pioneers in the northwest formed a transitional zone between this northern area and the slave states south of the Ohio. (3) In the Gulf plains a greater south was in process of formation, but by no means completely established. As yet it was a mixture of pioneer and planter, slave and free, profoundly affected by its western traits. The different states of the south were steadily sending in bands of colonists. In Alabama, for example, the Georgians settled, as a rule, in the east; the Tennesseeans, moving from the great bend of the Tennessee River, were attracted to the northern and middle section; and the Virginians and Carolinians went to the west and southwest, following the bottom-lands near the rivers.

By 1820 the west had developed the beginnings of many of the cities which have since ruled over the region. Buffalo and Detroit were hardly more than villages until the close of this period. They waited for the rise of steam navigation on the Great Lakes and for the opening of the prairies. Cleveland, also, was but a hamlet during most of the decade; but by 1830 the construction of the canal connecting the Cuyahoga with the Scioto increased its prosperity, and its harbor began to profit by its natural advantages. Chicago and Milwaukee were mere fur-trading stations in the Indian country. Pittsburgh, at the head of the Ohio, was losing its old pre-eminence as the gateway to the west, but was finding recompense in the development of its manufactures. By 1830 its population was about twelve thousand. Foundries, rolling-mills, nail-factories, steam-engine shops, and distilleries were busily at work, and the city, dingy with the smoke of soft coal, was already dubbed the "young Manchester" or the "Birmingham" of America. By 1830 Wheeling had intercepted much of the overland trade and travel to the Ohio, profiting by the old National Road and the wagon trade from Baltimore.

Cincinnati was rapidly rising to the position of the "Queen City of the West." Situated where the river reached with a great bend towards the interior of the northwest, in the rich farming country between the two Miamis, and opposite the Licking River, it was the commercial centre of a vast and fertile region of Ohio and Kentucky; and by 1830, with a population of nearly twenty-five thousand souls, it was the largest city of the west, with the exception of New Orleans. The centre of steamboat-building, it also received extensive imports of goods from the east and exported the surplus crops of Ohio and adjacent parts of Kentucky. Its principal industry, however, was pork-packing, from which it won the name of "Porkopolis." Louisville, at the falls of the Ohio, was an important place of transshipment, and the export centre for large quantities of tobacco. There were considerable manufactures of rope and bagging, products of the Kentucky hemp-fields; and new cotton and woollen factories were struggling for existence. St. Louis occupied a unique position, as the entrepôt of the important fur-trade of the upper Mississippi and the vast water system of the Missouri, as well as the outfitting-point for the Missouri settlements. It was the capital of the far west, and the commercial centre for Illinois. Its population at the close of the decade was about six thousand.

Only a few villages lay along the Mississippi below St. Louis until the traveller reached New Orleans, the emporium of the whole Mississippi Valley. As yet the direct effect of the Erie Canal was chiefly limited to the state of New York. The great bulk of western exports passed down the tributaries of the Mississippi to this city, which was, therefore, the centre of foreign exports for the valley, as well as the port from which the coastwise trade in the products of the whole interior departed. In 1830 its population was nearly fifty thousand.

The rise of an agricultural surplus was transforming the west and preparing a new influence in the nation. It was this surplus and the demand for markets that developed the cities just mentioned. As they grew, the price of land in their neighborhood increased; roads radiated into the surrounding country; and farmers, whose crops had been almost worthless from the lack of transportation facilities, now found it possible to market their surplus at a small profit. While the west was thus learning the advantages of a home market, the extension of cotton and sugar cultivation in the south and southwest gave it a new and valuable market. More and more, the planters came to rely upon the northwest for their food supplies and for the mules and horses for their fields. Cotton became the engrossing interest of the plantation belt, and, while the full effects of this differentiation of industry did not appear in the decade of this volume, the beginnings were already visible. In 1835, Pitkin reckoned the value of the domestic and foreign exports of the interior as far in excess of the whole exports of the United States in 1790. Within forty years the development of the interior had brought about the economic independence of the United States.

During most of the decade the merchandise to supply the interior was brought laboriously across the mountains by the Pennsylvania turnpikes and the old National Road; or, in the case of especially heavy freight, was carried along the Atlantic coast into the Gulf and up the Mississippi and Ohio by steamboats. The cost of transportation in the wagon trade from Philadelphia to Pittsburgh and Baltimore to Wheeling placed a heavy tax upon the consumer. In 1817 the freight charge from Philadelphia to Pittsburgh was sometimes as high as seven to ten dollars a hundredweight; a few years later it became from four to six dollars; and in 1823 it had fallen to three dollars. It took a month to wagon merchandise from Baltimore to central Ohio. Transportation companies, running four-horse freight wagons, conducted a regular business on these turnpikes between the eastern and western states. In 1820 over three thousand wagons ran between Philadelphia and Pittsburgh, transporting merchandise valued at about eighteen million dollars annually.

The construction of the National Road reduced freight rates to nearly one-half what they were at the close of the War of 1812; and the introduction of steam navigation from New Orleans up the Mississippi cut water-rates by that route to one-third of the former charge. Nevertheless, there was a crying need for internal improvements, and particularly for canals, to provide an outlet for the increasing products of the west. "Even in the country where I reside, not eighty miles from tidewater," said Tucker, of Virginia, in 1818, "it takes the farmer one bushel of wheat to pay the expense of carrying two to a seaport town."

The bulk of the crop, as compared with its value, practically prevented transportation by land farther than a hundred miles. It is this that helps to explain the attention which the interior first gave to making whiskey and raising live-stock; the former carried the crop in a small bulk with high value, while the live-stock could walk to a market. Until after the War of 1812, the cattle of the Ohio Valley were driven to the seaboard, chiefly to Philadelphia or Baltimore. Travellers were astonished to see on the highway droves of four or five thousand hogs, going to an eastern market. It was estimated that over a hundred thousand hogs were driven east annually from Kentucky alone. Kentucky hog-drivers also passed into Tennessee, Virginia, and the Carolinas with their droves. The swine lived on the nuts and acorns of the forest; thus they were peculiarly suited to pioneer conditions. At first the cattle were taken to the plantations of the Potomac to fatten for Baltimore and Philadelphia, much in the same way that, in recent times, the cattle of the Great Plains are brought to the feeding-grounds in the corn belt of Kansas, Nebraska, and Iowa. Towards the close of the decade, however, the feeding-grounds shifted into Ohio, and the pork-packing industry, as we have seen, found its centre at Cincinnati, the most important source of supply for the hams and bacon and salt port which passed down the

Mississippi to furnish a large share of the plantation food. From Kentucky and the rest of the Ohio Valley droves of mules and horses passed through the Tennessee Valley to the south to supply the plantations. Statistics at Cumberland Gap for 1828 gave the value of live-stock passing the turnpike gate there at $1,167,000. Senator Hayne, of South Carolina, declared that in 1824 the south was supplied from the west, through Saluda Gap, with live-stock, horses, cattle, and hogs to the amount of over a million dollars a year.

But the outlet from the west over the roads to the east and south was but a subordinate element in the internal commerce. Down the Mississippi floated a multitude of heavily freighted craft: lumber rafts from the Allegheny, the old-time arks, with cattle, flour, and bacon, hay-boats, keel-boats, and skiffs, all mingled with the steamboats which plied the western waters. Flatboatmen, raftsmen, and deck-hands constituted a turbulent and reckless population, living on the country through which they passed, fighting and drinking in true "half-horse, half-alligator" style. Prior to the steamboat, all of the commerce from New Orleans to the upper country was carried on in about twenty barges, averaging a hundred tons each, and making one trip a year. Although the steamboat did not drive out the other craft, it revolutionized the commerce of the river. Whereas it had taken the keel-boats thirty to forty days to descend from Louisville to New Orleans, and about ninety days to ascend the fifteen hundred miles of navigation by poling and warping up-stream, the steamboat had shortened the time, by 1822, to seven days down and sixteen days up. As the steamboats ascended the various tributaries of the Mississippi to gather the products of the growing west, the pioneers came more and more to realize the importance of the invention. They resented the idea of the monopoly which Fulton and Livingston wished to enforce prior to the decision of Chief Justice Marshall, in the case of Gibbons *vs.* Ogden—a decision of vital interest to the whole interior.

They saw in the steamboat a symbol of their own development. A writer in the *Western Monthly Review* unconsciously expressed the very spirit of the self-contented, hustling, materialistic west in these words: "An Atlantic cit, who talks of us under the name of backwoodsmen, would not believe, that such fairy structures of oriental gorgeousness and splendor, as the Washington, the Florida, the Walk in the Water, the Lady of the Lake, etc. etc., had ever existed in the imaginative brain of a romancer, much less, that they were actually in existence, rushing down the Mississippi, as on the wings of the wind, or plowing up between the forests, and walking against the mighty current 'as things of life,' bearing speculators, merchants, dandies, fine ladies, every thing real, and every thing affected, in the form of humanity, with pianos, and stocks of novels, and cards, and dice, and flirting, and love-making, and drinking, and champaigne, and on the deck, perhaps, three hundred fellows, who have seen alligators, and neither fear whiskey, nor gun-powder. A steamboat, coming from New Orleans, brings to the remotest villages of our streams, and the very doors of the cabins, a little Paris, a section of Broadway, or a slice of Philadelphia, to ferment in the minds of our young people, the innate propensity for fashions and finery. Within a day's journey of us, three distinct canals are in respectable progress towards completion.... Cincinnati will soon be the centre of the 'celestial empire,' as the Chinese say; and instead of encountering the storms, the sea sickness, and dangers of a passage from the gulf of Mexico to the Atlantic, whenever the Erie canal shall be completed, the opulent southern planters will take their families, their dogs and parrots, through a world of forests, from New Orleans to New York, giving us a call by the way. When they are more acquainted with us, their voyage will often terminate here."

By 1830 the produce which reached New Orleans from the Mississippi Valley amounted to about twenty-six million dollars. In 1822 three million dollars' worth of goods was estimated to have passed the Falls of the Ohio on the way to market, representing much of the surplus of the Ohio Valley. Of this, pork amounted to $1,000,000 in value; flour to $900,000; tobacco to $600,000; and whiskey to $500,000. The inventory of products reveals the Mississippi Valley as a vast colonial society, producing the raw materials of a simple and primitive agriculture. The beginnings of manufacture in the cities, however, promised to bring about a movement for industrial independence in the west. In spite of evidences of growing wealth, there was such a decline in agricultural prices that, for the farmer who did not live on the highways of commerce, it was almost unprofitable to raise wheat for the market.

An Ohio pioneer of this time relates that at the beginning of the decade fifty cents a bushel was a great price for wheat at the river; and as two horses and a man were required for four days to make the journey of thirty-five miles to the Ohio, in good weather, with thirty-five or forty bushels of wheat, and a great deal longer if the roads were bad, it was not to be expected that the farmer could realize more than twenty-five cents in cash for it. But there was no sale for it in cash. The nominal price for it in trade was usually thirty cents. When wheat brought twenty-five cents a bushel in Illinois in 1825, it sold at over eighty cents in Petersburg, Virginia, and flour was six dollars a barrel at Charleston, South Carolina.

These are the economic conditions that assist in understanding the political attitude of western leaders like Henry Clay and Andrew Jackson. The cry of the east for protection to infant industries was swelled by the little cities of the west, and the demand for a home market found its strongest support beyond the Alleghanies. Internal improvements and lower rates of transportation were essential to the prosperity of the westerners. Largely a debtor class, in need of capital, credit, and an expansion of the currency, they resented attempts to restrain the reckless state banking which their optimism fostered.

But the political ideals and actions of the west are explained by social quite as much as by economic forces. It was certain that this society, where equality and individualism flourished, where assertive democracy was supreme, where impatience with the old order of things was a ruling passion, would demand control of the government, would resent the rule of the trained statesmen and official classes, and would fight nominations by congressional caucus and the continuance of presidential dynasties. Besides its susceptibility to change, the west had generated, from its Indian fighting, forest-felling, and expansion, a belligerency and a largeness of outlook with regard to the nation's territorial destiny. As the pioneer, widening the ring-wall of his clearing in the midst of the stumps and marshes of the wilderness, had a vision of the lofty buildings and crowded streets of a future city, so the west as a whole developed ideals of the future of the common man, and of the grandeur and expansion of the nation.

The west was too new a section to have developed educational facilities to any large extent. The pioneers' poverty, as well as the traditions of the southern interior from which they so largely came, discouraged extensive expenditures for public schools. In Kentucky and Tennessee the more prosperous planters had private tutors, often New England collegians, for their children. For example, Amos Kendall, later postmaster-general, was tutor in Henry Clay's family. So-called colleges were numerous, some of them fairly good. In 1830 a writer made a survey of higher education in the whole western country and reported twenty-eight institutions, with seven hundred and sixty-six graduates and fourteen hundred and thirty undergraduates. Less than forty thousand volumes were recorded in the college and "social" libraries of the entire Mississippi Valley. Very few students went from the west to eastern colleges; but the foundations of public education had been laid in the land grants for common schools and universities. For the present this fund was generally misappropriated and wasted, or worse. Nevertheless, the ideal of a democratic education was held up in the first constitution of Indiana, making it the duty of the legislature to provide for "a general system of education, ascending in a regular graduation from township schools to a State university, wherein tuition shall be gratis, and equally open to all."

Literature did not flourish in the west, although the newspaper press followed closely after the retreating savage; many short-lived periodicals were founded, and writers like Timothy Flint and James Hall were not devoid of literary ability. Lexington, in Kentucky, and Cincinnati made rival claims to be the "Athens of the West." In religion, the west was partial to those denominations which prevailed in the democratic portions of the older sections. Baptists, Methodists, and Presbyterians took the lead.

The religious life of the west frequently expressed itself in the form of emotional gatherings, in the camp-meetings and the revivals, where the rude, unlettered, but deeply religious backwoods preachers moved their large audiences with warnings of the wrath of God. Muscular Christianity was personified in the circuit-rider, who, with his saddle-bags and Bible, threaded the dreary trails through the forest from settlement to settlement. From the responsiveness of the west to religious excitement, it was easy to perceive that here was a region capable of being swayed in large masses by enthusiasm. These traits of the camp-meeting were manifested later in political campaigns.

Thus this society beyond the mountains, recruited from all the older states and bound together by the Mississippi, constituted a region swayed for the most part by common impulses. By the march of the westerners away from their native states to the public domain of the nation, and by their organization as territories of the United States, they lost that state particularism which distinguished many of the old commonwealths of the coast. The section was nationalistic and democratic to the core. The west admired the self-made man and was ready to follow its hero with the enthusiasm of a section more responsive to personality than to the programmes of trained statesmen. It was a self-confident section, believing in its right to share in government, and troubled by no doubts of its capacity to rule.

## For Further Reading

The reader will find Turner's key essays on the frontier in his *Frontier in American History* (1920). The most recent updating and reapplication of Turner's ideas (and a bibliographic guide) is Ray Allen Billington, *America's Frontier*

*Heritage* (1966). Although there is no full-scale biography, the following essays give valuable and sympathetic insights into Turner the man and the historian: Carl Becker's "Frederick Jackson Turner" in his *Everyman His Own Historian* (1935); Merle Curti's brief biographical sketch of Turner in O. Lawrence Burnette, Jr., comp., *Wisconsin Witness to Frederick Jackson Turner* (1961); Avery Craven's "Frederick Jackson Turner" in William T. Hutchinson, ed., *Marcus W. Jernegan Essays in American Historiography* (1937); Wilbur R. Jacobs, "Frederick Jackson Turner," *The American West* (Winter 1964), vol. I; Lee Benson, *Turner and Beard* (1960); and Richard Hofstadter, *The Progressive Historians: Turner, Beard, Parrington* (1968).

Ray Allen Billington is general editor of a projected, ambitious series of volumes on frontier history; some of these, in addition to Billington's own contribution mentioned above, have been published: Douglas E. Leach, *The Northern Colonial Frontier, 1607–1763* (1966); Jack M. Sosin, *The Revolutionary Frontier, 1763–1783* (1967); Rodman Paul, *Mining Frontiers of the Far West, 1848–1880* (1963); Oscar O. Winther, *The Transportation Frontier: Trans-Mississippi West, 1865–1890* (1964), and Gilbert C. Fite, *The Farmer's Frontier 1865–1900* (1966). Two handy collections of essays give the flavor of the controversy over Turner's thesis: George Rogers Taylor, ed., *The Turner Thesis* (rev. ed., 1956), and Ray Allen Billington, ed., *The Frontier Thesis* (1966).

# Radicals and Workers in the Age of Jackson

## Arthur M. Schlesinger, Jr.

*W*as Andrew Jackson a democrat or a Tennessee aristocrat interested only in his personal glory; an unreconstructed agrarian or a spokesman for the rising capitalistic entrepreneurs; a wise chief executive acting with vision on the important issues facing his administration or an ignorant man reacting impulsively, guided only by his personal prejudices? What did he represent: a symbol for his time, embodying the values of his fellow Americans or merely a clever politician who manipulated sectional and class interests to achieve electoral success; a bringer of democratic reform or an exploiter of an already triumphant institutional change? What were his contributions to American life: the reclaimer for the office of the President its proper leadership function or the usurper and aggrandizer of executive power; the destroyer of a banking institution that catered only to the privileged classes or the perpetrator of economic collapse and banking anarchy; the agent causing desirable rotation of civil servants or the creator of a corrupt political spoils system? Historians have long debated these and other

*Source:* Arthur M. Schlesinger, Jr., *The Age of Jackson* (Boston: Little, Brown and Company, 1945), pp. 201–209, 306–321, 334–349. Copyright 1945 by Arthur M. Schlesinger, Jr. Reprinted by permission of the publisher.

questions basic to an assessment of the man and his times. Even the convenience of dubbing the period 1828–1840 as "the Age of Jackson" has been questioned; some prefer the label "the Age of Egalitarianism."

During the nineteenth century, it proved difficult to consider Jackson objectively; historical perspective suffered as America underwent the successive convulsions of territorial expansion, economic development, popularization of the electoral process, excitation of moral fervor in the crusade against slavery, civil war, and tremendous industrial growth. The Great Man theory—or, its obverse, the Devil thesis—was a handy device for historians seeking to perceive meaning and order in a chaotic past. Thus James Parton, in a three-volume biography of the Old Hero published in 1860, admitted that Jackson was a real hero in his time, yet belabored his subject for perverting the ideals of the Founding Fathers by introducing the spoils system. William Graham Sumner, an apostle of hard currency and conservative banking practices, writing in 1882, indicted Jackson's destruction of the bank for the paper money "evils" that beset post-Civil War America.

The first four decades of the twentieth century spawned even more controversial interpretations of Jackson and his period. Vernon L. Parrington and Charles A. Beard, writing during the progressive era, saw Jackson as the champion of the common man smiting the entrenched monied classes, much as they viewed contemporary reformers, such as Robert LaFollette and Theodore Roosevelt, as attacking predators of wealth. Still others in the 1930's projected the New Deal back into the Jacksonian period.

Perhaps the most celebrated effort to establish kinship between the Jacksonian and Rooseveltian revolutions came from the pen of Arthur M. Schlesinger, Jr., with his *Age of Jackson* (1945). The book's immediate success was not surprising. Schlesinger had been reared in scholarly surroundings: his father, a professor at Harvard University, had reached the front rank of American social historians; and his mother, Elizabeth Bancroft Schlesinger, was related to George Bancroft, the eminent nineteenth-century historian. Like Parrington and Beard before him, Schlesinger portrayed the period 1828–1860 in class terms: capital versus labor. Schlesinger saw the struggle in ideological terms that paralleled those of his contemporary America. Democracy, in both the 1830's and the 1930's, had triumphed insofar as it had allowed for the peaceful settlement of social tensions.

As a historical work *The Age of Jackson* combines a brilliant narrative and interpretative style. In the opening chapters Schlesinger dramatizes the transition from John Quincy Adams to Jackson; explains the mixed politico-economic heritage of Hamilton and Jefferson; describes the nature of Western, Eastern, and Southern discontent in the 1820's; provides vignettes of Old Hickory's supporters and opponents; and traces the course of the central political issue of the age, the Bank War, through its many permutations among politicians, businessmen, and—most important—workers, especially the Locofocos in the Eastern states. Schlesinger then proceeds to deal with Jacksonian democracy in topical terms. The following passages—on Locofocoism, Jacksonian democracy as an intellectual movement, and its relation to industrialism—capture the essence of Schlesinger's interpretative techniques: a wide coverage of historical sources, an engaging wit, and a closely reasoned exposition. They also underscore his emphasis on Eastern workingmen's influence on the character of the Jacksonian era.

Schlesinger's work has stimulated other controversies. Critics have attacked his Eastern, urban, and labor emphases. Some have suggested that laborers acted on immediate and local issues, often ignoring national questions. Others have located the lines of cleavage in Jackson's time as existing between the rising entrepreneurs and those who already had risen. Still others have found that Jackson's opponents, the Whigs, exhibited the same characteristics and drew their support from the same coalition as did the Democrats. Finally, scholars have more recently argued that it is more fruitful to analyze Jackson in terms of what he represented as a symbol or an image to his fellow Americans than to become bemired in straightening out the political issues. Hence John William Ward has cast Jackson as the symbol to Americans of how they wished to view themselves—as products of Will, Nature, and Providence; and Marvin Meyers has suggested Jackson was the key figure in an American "persuasion"—the sometimes backward-looking response of a society in the midst of flux.

*P*ennsylvania had to orient its political conflicts about the problems of industrialism nearly to the same extent as Massachusetts and New York. Philadelphia, the home of Nicholas Biddle and the United States Bank, was also the home of America's first city central labor union, in 1827, and of the first Workingmen's party the next year. The contrast between the Greek temple on Chestnut Street and the slums which so appalled Mathew Carey provided a background against which the Bank War raged with unusual intensity.

But the Bank was resourceful and had many ways of circumventing opposition. The leading spokesman of the Philadelphia Workingmen's party of 1828–1831 was Stephen Simpson, a political careerist in his early forties, formerly a cashier in Stephen Girard's bank and for many years a journalist. An "original" Jackson man as early as 1822, he failed of his expected reward in 1829 and turned against the administration, emerging in the fall of 1830 as nominee for Congress on the Federal ticket. (Federalism still lingered in Philadelphia, even then a main backwater of American politics.) He also obtained the Workingmen's endorsement. He was beaten; but his political intuitions were aroused, as when a pioneer lifts his nose at the whiff of game, and he turned to writing a book which would insinuate himself into the confidence of the growing labor movement.

The result was a curious volume, published in Philadelphia in 1831, entitled *The Working Man's Manual*. Simpson was not without ability, and he developed some of the leading motifs of the Workingmen's agitation more ably than their own writers had yet succeeded in doing. The book appealed powerfully to the fears of social degradation, declaring that the "children of toil" had been depressed to a point where they were "as much shunned in society, as if they were leprous convicts just emerged from loathsome cells." It dealt effectively with the economic foundations of inequality and set forth the case against the paper credit system along good hard-money lines.

But midway through the book Simpson suddenly began to reach astonishing conclusions, coming out for internal improvements, for the protective tariff, indeed for the entire American System ("what can be more noble, laudable, and virtuous?"), and arguing vigorously in an appendix for the United States Bank. This abrupt change of heart was probably not unrelated to the acceptance by Simpson, early in 1831, of the editorship of the conservative *Pennsylvania Whig*. In July he joined with other "original Jackson men" in renouncing the administration at a public ceremony for its hostility to the American System. He completed his expiation in 1832 by writing a laudatory biography of the banker Girard. The wind had changed, and the smell of game was coming from another direction.

Those whom the Bank could not seduce, it sought to annihilate. When Roberts Vaux, philanthropist and prison reformer, one of Philadelphia's best-loved citizens, declared against the Bank, "an edict of social extermination," as an observer described it, "was forthwith registered against him." Friends abandoned him, and attempts were even made to expel him from various literary and philanthropic societies, some of which he had helped found. When Charles Jared Ingersoll, another foe of the Bank, proposed a friend for the American Philosophical Society, the candidate was vengefully blackballed; and Richard Rush, Secretary of the Treasury under John Quincy Adams, son of Benjamin Rush and himself a distinguished lawyer, was blackballed by the Philosophical Society in the autumn of 1833 for the acknowledged reason that he approved General Jackson's paper on the removal of the deposits. A few years later, when Rush returned from settling the Smithsonian bequest in London, he found that old friends still shunned him, and in his own family only one brother maintained close relations with him.

Philadelphia forgave slowly. In 1839 when a Philadelphia firm published Walter Savage Landor's *Pericles and Aspasia,* it carefully omitted the dedicatory ode with which the author began the second volume, "To General Andrew Jackson. President of the United States."

> . . . How rare the sight, how grand!
> Behold the golden scales of Justice stand
> Self-balanced in a mailed hand. . . .

Yet the pressure of General Jackson was as much a natural fact as the pressure of Philadelphia, and, in some respects, more effective. Biddle had cagily relied as much as possible on Pennsylvania Democrats in the campaign for recharter. Senator G. M. Dallas was scheduled to manage the fight in the upper house; and Charles Jared Ingersoll represented the Bank in some of its negotiations with the government. But the veto made them think a second time, and when the smoke of battle cleared both had hurried over to the Jackson camp. Dallas was little more than a party wheelhorse, but the brilliant, erratic and charming Ingersoll, with his quizzical smile, his close-cropped brown hair, his elastic step, provided after 1833 consistent leadership in the fight against corporations and paper money. Unfortunately his judgment was not equal to his abilities, and he never quite commanded the influence which his talent and experience should have given him.

Henry D. Gilpin was another intellectual converted to the Jacksonian cause. A slender man, wearing gold-rimmed spectacles, thiry-two years old in 1833, he was a good lawyer with a cultivated background and literary inclinations. For six years he edited the *Atlantic Souvenir,* an annual, and he was later to become president of the Pennsylvania Academy of Fine Arts. As government director of the Bank, he learned its character at first hand, becoming profoundly convinced that corporations were the "great question of the time in morals as much as politics." Along with Ingersoll, Rush and a few others, he braved the displeasure of his class to associate with radicals, trade-unionists, Democratic politicians and other disreputable characters. An intimate friend of Van Buren and of George Bancroft, he kept them informed of the progress of radical democracy in Pennsylvania.

Late in 1833 the Philadelphia labor movement began to revive, and by 1836 the Trades' Union of the City and Council of Philadelphia claimed about fifty societies and more than ten thousand members. Its leaders were John Ferral, a handloom weaver, for many years a tireless champion of labor interests, and William English, an ambitious and unreliable journeyman shoemaker. English's impassioned oratory gave the movement a radical and intransigent tone. "The war waged by capital against labour is co-existent with capital itself," he declared at the Union celebration on July 4, 1835.

> In all ages, in all countries, capital has been used as a never-failing means of obtaining power, and the oppression and impoverishment of the productive classes are the certain consequences of such a combination.
>
> The history of the world is but a history of the wrongs practised by privileged wealth upon oppressed poverty. Even in this country, this boasted land of liberty, has the omnipotence of wealth . . . rendered the condition of the labourer little better than that of the slave.

In a lively sheet called *The Radical Reformer and Working Man's Advocate,* Thomas Brothers, an English radical and disciple of Cobbett, come to examine the experiment of democracy, sought to rally labor behind the cause of hard money.

From the first the Union was active in politics. The Bank War mobilized labor, and the *Pennsylvanian* of Philadelphia, organ of the progressive Democrats, acknowledged the alliance by defending the right to organize and even supporting strikes for a ten-hour day. H. D. Gilpin was in correspondence with English and Ferral, as well as Ely Moore; and Charles Jared Ingersoll, as counsel for the Philadelphia plasterers in 1836, won their acquittal in one of the cases which helped end the application of the doctrine of criminal conspiracy to labor organizations.

The boom of 1834–1835 caused the same split in the Pennsylvania Democratic party as in New York and Massachusetts. The progressive wing favored Henry A. Muhlenberg, the leading radical in the Pennsylvania delegation in Congress, over George Wolf, the conservative Democratic Governor, and finally ran him on a separate ticket. In their view, the state-banking system had to be reformed along hard-money lines or "the great object to be attained in putting down the Bank of the United States . . . will not be accomplished." In Philadelphia the Muhlenberg ticket, supported by the *Pennsylvanian* and by the labor leaders, included William English as nominee for the state Senate, and Thomas Hogan, another union man, for the Assembly. The conservative candidate, Ritner, romped in because of the split Democratic vote; but the schism plainly showed the determination of the radical wing. As in New York and Massachusetts, the progressives were fighting to force their views on the whole state party.

This was the pattern of Locofocoism. In every state, the reckless expansion of banking facilities provoked widespread popular disgust; and Locofocoism, the expression of that disgust, accordingly was strongest in the states where issues of currency and incorporation were most vital. It was thus an *Eastern* movement, designed to meet *Eastern* economic difficulties, preoccupied with fears to which the West was largely indifferent. As Locofocoism began more and more to shape the policy of the administration, that policy departed increasingly from the desires of the West.

Jackson's original Western support, it has been pointed out, sprang from the glowing enthusiasm for the Hero of New Orleans and was largely uninformed by ideas, beyond a vague impression that the General was a friend of the American System. His first administration then produced a series of decisions, almost every one of which was basically unpopular on the frontier, even if none could harm Jackson's invincible personal position. The Maysville veto weakened the administration through most of the West. In Michigan and Illinois, indeed, the Democrats ignored its message and far exceeded the Whigs in their passion for internal improvements; in general, the Western Democrats favored a spendthrift policy no less than the Whigs. The tariff was not an urgent question in the thirties, except in connection with nullification, but the Western Democrats resisted the free-trade tendencies of radical Democrats in the East and South (and of Jackson). As for the Bank, Jackson had to allow his hard-money aims to be misunderstood in the West, where the important anti-Bank sentiment came from the desire to liberate credit and paper money from Eastern control; in other words, he was largely supported by people who regarded the veto as an inflationary rather than a deflationary action. None of these decisions was demanded by the West, and none, save the misinterpreted war against the Bank, won its zealous backing.

The unveiling of the hard-money program during the second term brought the conflict into the open. Caring much more for self-determination and home rule than for economic democracy, most of the Western politicians found it hard to go along with the President on the currency question. Either they left the party, like White, Bell and Eaton, or gave the hard-money policy halfhearted support nationally while ignoring the question within their states, like Lewis Cass and Richard M. Johnson.

When Western Democrats did advocate Locofoco positions, they did so in many cases for motives which the great social fluidity of the West rendered highly temporary and accidental. The case of Franklin Plummer of Mississippi, who gave probably the most radical speech delivered by a Westerner in Congress during Jackson's presidency, is in this respect instructive.

Rising in the House near the end of the panic session, Plummer launched into a harangue on the Workingmen's party. He set forth the familiar platform—"the leading measures advocated by that despised party of which I have the honor of being an humble member"—and went on to assail at great length "this American banking system, this rag-money system, this system of legalized monopolies, which makes the rich richer and the poor poorer." Jackson he admired, and he would stick with the administration: "I will not go against the party until the party goes against the principles of the workingmen." But he denounced the Democratic organization and stated ingeniously the Workingmen's case against politics in general.

There were two classes in society, he said, one subsisting by labor, the other by law. The second, and smaller, class, by its control of the government, systematically deprived the larger class of the products of its labor. But the smaller class, the aristocracy, was itself separated into two groups, "the ins and the outs." The outs always appeal to the voters by attacking the misdeeds of those in power; but when the people respond by raising them to power, they "laugh at their credulity, and continue, and even increase, those abuses which they have been elected to correct. . . . The gamblers alternately win, while the great mass of the people, who pay the fiddler and other expenses of carrying on the operation, have not even a solitary chance in the game." The Bank issue, Plummer declared, was the only issue disputed by the aristocracy in which the masses had any real interest.

Plummer was a New Englander who had emigrated to Mississippi. A glib man, with an entertaining flow of language and the shrewdness of a Yankee peddler, he became a first-class jury lawyer and a great political favorite. A contemporary reported that he was "as a cross-road and stump orator unequalled—as a bush-whacker and log-cabin electioneerer unrivalled." On one campaign Plummer, canvassing the district with his competitor, stopped at a farm for noon dinner. His rival took the occasion to commend himself to the farmer's wife by kissing her little girl and praising her beauty; "but she was completely carried away when she saw Plummer pick up her wee toddling boy, lay it gently across his lap, turn over its little petticoat, and go to *hunting red bugs!* 'They are powerful bad,' said Plummer, 'and mighty hard on babies.' She was enchanted, and never forgot that tender hearted Congressman."

The small farmers of the pine woods of eastern Mississippi sent Plummer to Congress in 1828. In 1832 he was opposed by the nominal Jackson organization but won anyway; hence his lofty attitude toward established parties. But Plummer was too good a vote getter to be wasted on the Workingmen. In 1835 the bankers of Natchez invited him to town, gave him banquets, loaned him twenty-five thousand dollars and encouraged him to run for Senator. Plummer bought a barouche, hired a servant in livery and started out on a campaign. He had betrayed himself, of course, and failing in the election he somehow lost his nerve, sinking out of politics and dying an obscure drunkard in Jackson in 1847.

The rise and fall of Plummer showed the temptations which surrounded radicalism on the frontier. An unstable society, with extremes of poverty and wealth, but with easy access to riches and a quick turnover in the composition of the aristocracy, might produce a brief, frenetic and opportunistic radicalism; but it was not likely to produce radicalism which was serious, unbribable and consistent. Such men as Plummer would denounce riches loudly enough, but were always ready to change their tune should the next speculation prove successful.

There were certainly leaders in the West dedicated to the principles of democracy—men like Moses Dawson, Thomas Morris, Benjamin Tappan and William Allen in Ohio, Robert Dale Owen now serving as a Democrat in the legislature of Indiana, Kingsley Bingham in Michigan, Polk and William Carroll in Tennessee, Benton in Missouri—but even their ideas and solutions were largely borrowed from the East. In the thirties this radical group was strongest in Ohio, which most approximated the economic conditions of the East and actually underwent its own version of the Locofoco schism in 1836. In the forties, as the dominion of the new finance crept westward, the radical Democrats grew stronger, and Locofoco ideas played a vital and sometimes dominating role in the state constitutional conventions of that and the next decade.

But the East remained the source of the effective expression of Jacksonian radicalism, and Eastern ideas rose to supremacy in Washington as Jacksonianism changed from an agitation into a program. (The test of this would come when Jacksonian measures were presented to the West without the magic of Andrew Jackson.) The East simply had the consistent and bitter experience which alone could serve as a crucible of radicalism.

The great illusion of historians of the frontier has been that social equality produces economic egalitarianism. In fact, the demand for economic equality is generally born out of conditions of social inequality, and becomes the more passionate, deeply felt and specific as the inequality becomes more rigid. The actual existence of equal opportunities is likely to diminish the vigilance with which they are guarded, and to stimulate the race for power and privilege. The fur capitalists of St. Louis and the land speculators of Mississippi were as characteristic of the West as Andrew Jackson.

The Jacksonian revolution rested on premises which the struggles of the thirties hammered together into a kind of practical social philosophy. The outline of this way of thinking about society was clear. It was stated and restated, as we have seen, on every level of political discourse from presidential messages to stump speeches, from newspaper editorials to private letters. It provided the intellectual background without which the party battles of the day cannot be understood.

The Jacksonians believed that there was a deep-rooted conflict in society between the "producing" and "non-producing" classes—the farmers and laborers, on the one hand, and the business community on the other. The business community was considered to hold high cards in this conflict through its network of banks and corporations, its control of education and the press, above all, its power over the state: it was therefore able to strip the working classes of the fruits of their labor. "Those who produce all wealth," said Amos Kendall, "are themselves left poor. They see principalities extending and palaces built around them, without being aware that the entire expense is a tax upon themselves."

If they wished to preserve their liberty, the producing classes would have to unite against the movement "to make the rich richer and the potent more powerful." Constitutional prescriptions and political promises afforded no sure protection. "We have heretofore been too disregardful of the fact," observed William M. Gouge, "that social order is quite as dependent on the laws which regulate the distribution of wealth, as on political organization." The program now was to resist every attempt to concentrate wealth and power further in a single class. Since free elections do not annihilate the opposition, the fight would be unceasing. "The struggle for power," said C. C. Cambreleng, "is as eternal as the division of society. A defeat cannot destroy the boundary which perpetually separates the democracy from the aristocracy."

The specific problem was to control the power of the capitalistic groups, mainly Eastern, for the benefit of the noncapitalist groups, farmers and laboring men, East, West and South. The basic Jacksonian ideas came naturally enough from the East, which best understood the nature of business power and reacted most sharply against it. The legend that Jacksonian democracy was the explosion of the frontier, lifting into the government some violent men filled with rustic prejudices against big business, does not explain the facts, which were somewhat more complex. Jacksonian democracy was rather a second American phase of that enduring struggle between the business community and the rest of society which is the guarantee of freedom in a liberal capitalist state.

Like any social philosophy, Jacksonian democracy drew on several intellectual traditions. Basically, it was a revival of Jeffersonianism, but the Jeffersonian inheritance was strengthened by the infusion of fresh influences; notably the antimonopolistic tradition, formulated primarily by Adam Smith and expounded in America by Gouge, Leggett, Sedgwick, Cambreleng; and the pro-labor tradition, formulated primarily by William Cobbett and expounded by G. H. Evans, Ely Moore, John Ferral.

The inspiration of Jeffersonianism was so all-pervading and fundamental for its every aspect that Jacksonian democracy can be properly regarded as a somewhat more hard-headed and determined version of Jeffersonian democracy. But it is easy to understate the differences. Jefferson himself, though widely revered and quoted, had no personal influence on any of the leading Jacksonians save perhaps Van Buren. Madison and Monroe were accorded still more vague and perfunctory homage. The radical Jeffersonians, Taylor, Randolph and Macon, who had regarded the reign of Virginia as almost an era of betrayal, were much more vivid in the minds of the Jacksonians.

Yet even Taylor's contributions to the later period have been exaggerated. His great work, the *Inquiry into the Principles and Policy of the Government of the United States,* published in 1814 just before the Madisonian surrender, had no significant contemporary vogue except among the faithful; and its difficult style, baffling organization and interminable length prevented it ever from gaining wide currency. By Jackson's presidency it was long out of print. In 1835 it was reported unobtainable in New York and to be procured only "with great difficulty" in Virginia. There is little trace of its peculiar terminology in the Jacksonian literature.

While the *Inquiry* properly endured as the most brilliant discussion of the foundations of democracy, many of its details were in fact obsolete by 1830. It was oriented to an important degree around the use of the national debt as the mechanism of aristocracy; in Jackson's day the debt had been extinguished but the aristocracy remained. Moreover, Taylor's arguments against executive power, against the party system and for a revivified militia had lost their point for the Jacksonians. George Bancroft voiced a widely felt need when he called, in 1834, for a general work on American society. "Where doubts arise upon any point relating to the business of government," one radical wrote in response, "no dependence can be placed upon any treatise that has yet appeared which professes to discuss this subject. You must draw upon your own resources, you must think,—and think alone."

The obsolescence of Taylor was caused by the enormous change in the face of America. The period of conservative supremacy from 1816 to 1828 had irrevocably destroyed the agricultural paradise, and the Jacksonians were accommodating the insights of Jefferson to the new concrete situations.

This process of readjustment involved a moderately thorough overhauling of favorite Jeffersonian doctrines.

The central Jeffersonian hope had been a nation of small freeholders, each acquiring thereby so much moral probity, economic security and political independence as to render unnecessary any invasion of the rights or liberties of others. The basis of such a society, as Jefferson clearly recognized, was agriculture and handicraft. What was the status of the Jeffersonian hope now that it was clear that, at best, agriculture must share the future with industry and finance?

Orestes A. Brownson exhausted one possibility in his essay on "The Laboring Classes." He reaffirmed the Jeffersonian demand: "we ask that every man become an independent proprietor, possessing enough of the goods of this world, to be able by his own moderate industry to provide for the wants of his body." But what, in practice, would this mean? As Brownson acknowledged years later, his plan would have "broken up the whole modern commercial system, prostrated the great industries, . . . and thrown the mass of the people back on the land to get their living by agricultural and mechanical pursuits." Merely to state its consequences was to prove its futility. The dominion of the small freeholder was at an end.

The new industrialism had to be accepted: banks, mills, factories, industrial capital, industrial labor. These were all distasteful realities for orthodox Jeffersonians, and, not least, the propertyless workers. "The mobs of great cities," Jefferson had said, "add just so much to the support of pure government, as sores do to the strength of the human body." The very ferocity of his images expressed the violence of his feelings. "When we get piled upon one another in large cities, as in Europe," he told Madison, "we shall become corrupt as in Europe, and go to eating one another as they do there." It was a universal sentiment among his followers. "No man should live," Nathaniel Macon used to say, "where he can hear his neighbour's dog bark."

Yet the plain political necessity of winning the labor vote obliged a change of mood. Slowly, with some embarrassment, the Jeffersonian preferences for the common man were enlarged to take in the city workers. In 1833 the *New York Evening Post,* declaring that, if anywhere, a large city of mixed population would display the evils of universal suffrage, asked if this had been the case in New York and answered: No. Amasa Walker set out the same year to prove that "great cities are not *necessarily,* as the proverb says, 'great sores'," and looked forward cheerily to the day when they would be "great fountains of healthful moral influence, sending forth streams that shall fertilize and bless the land." The elder Theodore Sedgwick added that the cause of the bad reputation of cities was economic: "it is the sleeping in garrets and cellars; the living in holes and dens; in dirty, unpaved, unlighted streets, without the accommodations of wells, cisterns, baths, and other means of cleanliness and health"—clear up this situation, and cities will be all right.

Jackson himself never betrayed any of Jefferson's revulsion to industrialism. He was, for example, deeply interested by the mills of Lowell in 1833, and his inquiries respecting hours, wages and production showed, observers reported, "that the subject of domestic manufacturers had previously engaged his attentive observation." His presidential allusions to the "producing classes" always included the workingmen of the cities.

The acceptance of the propertyless laboring classes involved a retreat from one of the strongest Jeffersonian positions. John Taylor's distinction between "natural" and "artificial" property had enabled the Jeffersonians to enlist the moral and emotional resources contained in the notion of property. They could claim to be the protectors of property rights, while the business community, by despoiling the producers of the fruits of their labor, were the enemies of property. Yet, this distinction, if it were to have other than a metaphorical existence, had to rest on the dominance of agriculture and small handicraft. The proceeds of the labor of a farmer, or a blacksmith, could be measured with some exactness; but who could say what the "just" fruits of labor were for a girl whose labor consisted in one small operation in the total process of manufacturing cotton cloth? In what sense could propertyless people be deprived of their property?

Taylor had repeatedly warned that "fictitious" property would seek to win over "real" property by posing as the champion of all property against the mob. Now that the Democrats were the party, not only of small holders, but of propertyless workers, the conservative pose seemed more plausible. The Whigs diligently set forth to make every attack on "fictitious" capital an attack on all property rights. "The philosophy that denounces accumulation," said Edward Everett, "is the philosophy of barbarism." The outcry over monopoly, added Henry Clay, is "but a new form of attacking the rights of property. A man may not use his property in what form he pleases, even if sanctioned by the laws of the community in which he lives, without being denounced as a monopolist."

The Whigs slowly won the battle. The discovery of the courts that a corporation was really a person completed their victory. By 1843 William S. Wait could strike the Jeffersonian flag: "'Security to property' no longer means security to the citizen in the possession of his moderate competency, but security to him who monopolizes thousands—security to a few, who may live in luxury and ease upon the blood and sweat of many."

Jacksonians now tended to exalt human rights as a counterweight to property rights. The Whigs, charged Frank Blair, were seeking such an extension of "the rights of property as to swallow up and annihilate those of persons"; the Democratic party would "do all in its power to preserve and defend them." "We believe property should be held subordinate to man, and not man to property," said Orestes A. Brownson; "and therefore that it is always lawful to make such modifications of its constitution as the good of Humanity requires." The early decisions of Roger B. Taney's court helped establish the priority of the public welfare. But the Democrats had surrendered an important ideological bastion. The right to property provided a sturdy foundation for liberalism, while talk of human rights too often might end up in sentimentality or blood.

In several respects, then, the Jacksonians revised the Jeffersonian faith for America. They moderated that side of Jeffersonianism which talked of agricultural virtue, independent proprietors, "natural" property, abolition of industrialism, and expanded immensely that side which talked of economic equality, the laboring classes, human rights and the control of industrialism. This readjustment enabled the Jacksonians to attack economic problems which had baffled and defeated the Jeffersonians. It made for a greater realism, and was accompanied by a general toughening of the basic Jeffersonian conceptions. While the loss of "property" was serious, both symbolically and intellectually, this notion had been for most Jeffersonians somewhat submerged next to the romantic image of the free and virtuous cultivator; and the Jacksonians grew much more insistent about theories of capitalist alienation. Where, for the Jeffersonians, the tensions of class conflict tended to dissolve in vague generalizations about the democracy and the aristocracy, many Jacksonians would have agreed with A. H. Wood's remark, "It is in vain to talk of Aristocracy and Democracy—these terms are too variable and indeterminate to convey adequate ideas of the present opposing interests; the division is between the rich and the poor—the warfare is between them."

This greater realism was due, in the main, to the passage of time. The fears of Jefferson were now actualities. One handled fears by exorcism, but actualities by adjustment. For the Jeffersonians, mistrust of banks and corporations was chiefly a matter of theory; for the Jacksonians, it was a matter of experience. The contrast between the scintillating metaphors of John Taylor and the sober detail of William M. Gouge expressed the difference. Jefferson rejected the Industrial Revolution and sought to perpetuate the smiling society which preceded it (at least, so the philosopher; facts compelled the President toward a different policy), while Jackson, accepting industrialism as an ineradicable and even useful part of the economic landscape, sought rather to control it. Jeffersonian democracy looked wistfully back toward a past slipping further every minute into the mists of memory, while Jacksonian democracy came straightforwardly to grips with a rough and unlovely present.

The interlude saw also the gradual unfolding of certain consequences of the democratic dogma which had not been so clear to the previous generation. Though theoretically aware of the relation between political and economic power, the Jeffersonians had been occupied, chiefly, with establishing political equality. This was their mission, and they had little time to grapple with the economic questions.

But the very assertion of political equality raised inevitably the whole range of problems involved in poverty and class conflict. How could political equality mean anything without relative economic equality among the classes of the country? This question engaged the Jacksonians. As Orestes A. Brownson said, "A Loco-foco is a Jeffersonian Democrat, who having realized political equality, passed through one phase of the revolution, now passes on to another, and attempts the realization of social equality, so that the actual condition of men in society shall be in harmony with their acknowledged rights as citizens." This gap between Jeffersonian and Jacksonian democracy enabled men like John Quincy Adams, Henry Clay, Joseph Story and many others, who had been honest Jeffersonians, to balk at the economic extremities to which Jackson proposed to lead them.

The Jacksonians thus opened irrevocably the economic question, which the Jeffersonians had only touched halfheartedly. Yet, while they clarified these economic implications of democracy, the Jacksonians were no more successful than their predecessors in resolving certain political ambiguities. Of these, two were outstanding—the problem of the virtue of majorities, and the problem of the evil of government. Since the Jacksonians made useful explorations of these issues after 1840, they will be reserved for later discussion.

A second source of inspiration for the Jacksonians was the libertarian economic thought stirred up by Adam Smith and *The Wealth of Nations*. Believers in the myth of Adam Smith, as expounded by present-day publicists both of the right and of the left, may find this singular; but the real Adam Smith was rich in ammunition for the Jacksonians, as for any foe of business manipulation of the state.

*The Wealth of Nations* quietly, precisely and implacably attacked the alliance of government and business, showing how monopoly retarded the economic growth of nations and promoted the exploitation of the people. It was, in effect, a criticism of the kind of mercantilist policy which, in modified form, Hamilton had instituted in the Federalist program of the seventeen-nineties. Smith's classic argument against monopoly appealed strongly to the Jacksonians, and his distinction between productive and unproductive labor converged with the Jacksonian distinction between the producers and the nonproducers. They adopted his labor theory of value, in preference to the physiocratic doctrine which argued that value originated exclusively in land, and toward which Jefferson leaned. Smith's currency views were on the moderate hard-money line, favoring the suppression of notes under five pounds. And, contrary to the Adam Smith of folklore, the real Smith had no objection to government intervention which would protect, not exploit, the nation. "Those exertions of the natural liberty of a few individuals," he wrote, discussing the question of banking control, "which might endanger the security of the whole society, are, and ought to be, restrained by the laws of all governments; of the most free, as well as of the most despotical." His advocacy of education and his general hope for the well-being of the farming and laboring classes further recommended him to the Jacksonians.

In many respects, Adam Smith formulated on the economic level the same sentiments which Jefferson put into glowing moral and political language. Jefferson himself thought *The Wealth of Nations* "the best book extant" on economic questions. The translation of J. B. Say's popularization of Smith increased the currency of laissez-faire doctrine. The little village of Stockbridge in Massachusetts was a particular center of free-trade thought. When Theodore Sedgwick observed of Adam Smith in 1838, "His voice has been ringing in the world's ears for sixty years, but it is only now in the United States that he is listened to, reverenced, and followed," the credit for this awakening went in great part to himself. His missionary efforts converted William Cullen Bryant, David Dudley Field and Theodore Sedgwick, Jr., and its was doubtless from Bryant that the previously nonpolitical Leggett got his introduction to *The Wealth of Nations.*

Leggett's brand of radicalism consisted almost entirely in a vigorous and unsparing effort to apply the doctrine of Adam Smith to the emerging corporate society. "If we analyze the nature and essence of free governments," Leggett wrote, "we shall find that they are more or less free in proportion to the absence of *monopolies.*" From this central conviction stemmed his denunciation of the Bank, of the paper system and of the exclusive character of corporate grants. The *Evening Post* remained under Bryant's editorship the most consistently able organ of free-trade opinion. The radical wing of New York Democrats were the special advocates of *laissez faire.* C. C. Cambreleng, defending the Jacksonian program from the charge of agrarianism, once exclaimed indignantly in the House, "Were Franklin and Jefferson agrarians, sir? Was Adam Smith an agrarian?" Colonel Samuel Young was a student of Smith and Say, as well as of Bentham, and the original Locofocos were free traders of the most doctrinaire sort.

The basic economic conception, which Adam Smith shared with Jefferson, was of a "natural order of things," that, once cleared of monopolistic clogs, would function to the greatest good of the greatest number. This conception, for all its apparent clarity, soon turned out to be packed with ambiguities. Free enterprise might mean, as with Leggett, a fighting belief in the virtue of competition, or it might mean, as with present-day conservatives, a fighting belief in the evil of government intervention. The battles of the Jackson era showed how these two interpretations of *laissez faire* were to come into increasing conflict.

The Jacksonians, vigorously in the first camp, had no hesitation in advocating government intervention in order to restore competition. In any case, their conception of the "natural order"—the region in which government was obligated not to interfere—included the right of the workingman to the full proceeds of his labor. Government, said Van Buren, should always be administered so as to insure to the laboring classes "a full enjoyment of the fruits of their industry."

> Left to itself, and free from the blighting influence of partial legislation, monopolies, congregated wealth, and interested combinations, the compensation of labor will always preserve this salutary relation. It is only when the natural order of society is disturbed by one or other of these causes, that the wages of labor become inadequate.

The prescription of free enterprise thus became government action to destroy the "blighting influence of partial legislation, monopolies, congregated wealth, and interested combinations" in the interests of the "natural order of society."

But the language of Adam Smith, as a result of its origin in a critique of mercantilism as government policy, lent itself also to attacks on government intervention. The presidency of Jackson had begun to reduce the conservative enthusiasm, in the manner of Hamilton, for state interference, and the business community commenced now to purloin the phrases of *laissez faire*. By 1888 E. M. Shepard, a Grover Cleveland Democrat, could dedicate a biography of Van Buren to the thesis that Van Buren was a thoroughgoing foe of government intervention—a thesis which required the total omission of such measures as the order establishing the ten-hour day.

In the end, business altogether captured the phrases of *laissez faire* and used them more or less ruthlessly in defense of monopoly, even coupling them with arguments for the protective tariff, a juxtaposition which would at least have given earlier conservatives a decent sense of embarrassment. Adam Smith himself doubted whether large businessmen really believed in free competition. The sequel confirmed his doubts. The irony was that the slogans of free trade, which he developed in order to destroy monopoly, should end up as its bulwark.

A third important stimulus to the Jacksonians was the foaming tide of social revolt in Britain, reaching them primarily through the writings of William Cobbett. As the "Peter Porcupine" of Federalist journalism, Cobbett had been an early object of Jeffersonian wrath. But, on returning to Britain after some years in America, Cobbett discovered that the conservative values he had been so stalwartly defending were rapidly disappearing before the smoky ravages of industrialism. He gave splendid and angry expression to the hatred of independent workingmen for the impending degradation, and his fluent, robust, abusive prose created a new political consciousness among the common people of Britain.

A vehement advocate of the rights of workers to the full fruits of their industry, and a savage enemy of the new financial aristocracy, he found a rapt audience in America, especially in the labor movement. *Paper against Gold*, reprinted in New York in 1834, helped the hard-money campaign. William H. Hale of New York, the author of *Useful Knowledge for the Producers of Wealth*, and Thomas Brothers, the editor of the *Radical Reformer* of Philadelphia, were perhaps his leading disciples, but his unquenchable vitality inspired the whole radical wing.

Cobbett on his part watched events across the Atlantic with immense enthusiasm. Jackson's fight against the Bank stirred him to the inordinate conclusion that Jackson was "the bravest and greatest man now living in this world, or that ever has lived in this world, as far as my knowledge extends." He wrote a life of Jackson (or rather interpolated characteristic comments into a reprint of Eaton's book), and even issued an abridged version of Gouge's *Paper Money*, under the title of *The Curse of Paper-Money and Banking*. He addressed superb open letters to the American President, and his admiration for "the greatest soldier and the greatest statesman whose name has ever yet appeared upon the records of valour and of wisdom" never faltered.

Yet, with all his passion for social justice, Cobbett talked very little about democracy. He seemed almost to feel—and his American followers had similar overtones—that, if the speculators, rag barons and capitalists were thrown out, and the lower classes instituted in power, the main problems of society would be solved. His gusty idealization of the British yeoman, redolent of beef and beer, led him away from theories of class balance into implications of class infallibility, almost at times leaning from democracy toward socialism. These were but shadings, and in his American disciples shades of shadings. Yet George H. Evans, John Commerford, John Ferral and the early labor leaders seemed to regard democracy as more protective doctrine than good in itself. In power they might have acted little differently—if toward different ends—from Daniel Webster and Nicholas Biddle.

The radical democrats had a definite conception of their relation to history. From the Jeffersonian analysis, fortified by the insights of Adam Smith and Cobbett, they sketched out an interpretation of modern times which gave meaning and status to the Jacksonian struggles.

Power, said the Jacksonians, goes with property. In the Middle Ages the feudal nobility held power in society through its monopoly of land under feudal tenure. The overthrow of feudalism, with the rise of new forms of property, marked the first step in the long march toward freedom. The struggle was carried on by the rising business community—"commercial, or business capital, against landed capital; merchants, traders, manufacturers, artizans, against the owners of the soil, the great landed nobility." It lasted from the close of the twelfth century to the Whig Revolution of 1688 in Britain.

The aristocracy of capital thus destroyed the aristocracy of land. The business classes here performed their vital role in the drama of liberty. The victory over feudalism, as the *Democratic Review* put it, "opened the way for the entrance of the democratic principle into the Government." But the business community gained from this exploit an undeserved reputation as the champion of liberty. Its real motive had been to establish itself in power, not to free mankind; to found government on property, not on the equal rights of the people. "I know perfectly well what I am saying," cried George Bancroft, "and I assert expressly, and challenge contradiction, that in all the history of the world there is not to be found an instance of a commercial community establishing rules for self-government upon democratic principles." "It is a mistake to suppose commerce favorable to liberty," added Fenimore Cooper. "Its tendency is to a monied aristocracy." "Instead of setting man free," said Amos Kendall, it has "only increased the number of his masters."

The next great blow for liberty was the American Revolution, "effected not in favor of men in classes; . . . but in favor of men." But the work of Hamilton halted the march of democracy. "He established the money power," wrote Van Buren, "upon precisely the same foundations upon which it had been raised in England." The subsequent history of the United States was the struggle to overthrow the Hamiltonian policy and fulfill the ideals of the Revolution.

What of the future? The Jacksonians were sublimely confident: history was on their side. "It is now for the yeomanry and the mechanics to march at the head of civilization," said Bancroft. "The merchants and the lawyers, that is, the moneyed interest broke up feudalism. The day for the multitude has now dawned." "All classes, each in turn, have possessed the government," exclaimed Brownson; "and the time has come for all predominance of class to end; for Man, the People to rule."

This was not simply a national movement. It was a movement of all people, everywhere, against their masters, and the Jacksonians watched with keen interest the stirrings of revolt abroad. Jackson and his cabinet joined in the celebrations in Washington which followed the Revolution of 1830 in France; and Van Buren, as Secretary of State, ordered the new government informed that the American people were "universally and enthusiastically in favor of that change, and of the principle upon which it was effected." (The Whigs, on the other hand, in spite of Clay's support of national revolutions in Greece and South America, remained significantly lukewarm.) Lamennais, the eloquent voice of French popular aspirations, was read in Jacksonian circles. The *Paroles d'un Croyant* influenced Orestes A. Brownson, and in 1839 *Le Livre du Peuple* was published in Boston under the title of *The People's Own Book,* translated by Nathaniel Greene, postmaster of Boston, brother of Charles Gordon Greene of the *Post* and intimate of David Henshaw.

Democrats followed with similar enthusiasm the progress of the Reform Bill in England, while the Whigs sympathized with the Tories. The Chartist uprisings at the end of the decade were greeted with delight by the Democratic press. British reformers returned this interest. Not only Cobbett and Savage Landor but the veteran radical Jeremy Bentham observed Jackson's administration with approval. Bentham, a friend of John Quincy Adams, had been disappointed at the triumph in 1828 of this military hero; but early in 1830, as he huddled by his hissing steam radiator, he heard read aloud Jackson's first message to Congress. The old man was highly pleased to discover greater agreement with the new President than with the old. Later he wrote that lengthy and cryptic memorandum entitled *Anti-Senatica,* intended to aid Jackson in the problems of his administration.

Jacksonians everywhere had this faith in the international significance of their fight. For this reason, as well as from a desire to capture their votes, Democratic leaders made special appeals to newly naturalized citizens. Where many Whigs tended to oppose immigration and demand sanctions against it, Democrats welcomed the newcomers with open arms and attacked the nativist agitation. The United States must remain a refuge from tyranny. "The capitalist class," said Samuel J. Tilden, "has banded together all over the world and organized the *modern dynasty of associated wealth,* which maintains an unquestioned ascendency over most of the civilized portions of our race." America was the proving-ground of democracy, and it was the mission of American Democrats to exhibit to the world the glories of government by the people. They were on the spearhead of history. They would not be denied. "With the friends of freedom throughout the world," declared Theophilus Fisk, "let us be co-workers." "The People of the World," cried Fanny Wright, "have but one Cause."

From the start of the century, first in banking and insurance, then in transportation, canals, bridges, turnpikes, then in manufacturing, the corporation was gradually becoming the dominant form of economic organization. The generation of Jackson was the first to face large-scale adjustment to this new economic mechanism. For owners and large investors, the adjustment presented no particular problem. But those on the outside had a feeling of deep misgiving which was less an economic or political than a moral protest: it was basically a sense of shock.

Economic life before the corporation, at least according to the prevalent conceptions, was more or less controlled by a feeling of mutual responsibility among the persons concerned. Economic relationships were generally personal—between master and workman laboring together in the same shop, between buyer and seller living together in the same village. The very character of this relation produced some restraints upon the tendency of the master to exploit the workman, or of the seller to cheat the buyer. Reciprocal confidence was necessarily the keynote of a system so much dominated by personal relations. Business and private affairs were governed by much the same ethical code.

But industrialism brought the growing depersonalization of economic life. With the increase in size of the labor force, the master was further and further removed from his workmen, till the head of a factory could have only the most tenuous community of feeling with his men. With the development of manufacturing and improved means of distribution, the seller lost all contact with the buyer, and feelings of responsibility to the consumer inevitably diminished. The expansion of investment tended to bring on absentee ownership, with the divorce of ownership and management; and the rise of cities enfeebled the paternal sentiments with which many capitalists had regarded their workers in towns and villages. Slowly the vital economic relationships were becoming impersonal, passing out of the control of a personal moral code. Slowly private morality and business morality grew apart. Slowly the commercial community developed a collection of devices and ceremonials which enabled businessmen to set aside the ethic which ruled their private life and personal relations.

Of these devices the most dramatic and generally intelligible was the corporation. For a people still yearning for an economy dominated by individual responsibility, still under the spell of the Jeffersonian dream, the corporation had one outstanding characteristic: its moral irresponsibility. "Corporations have neither bodies to be kicked, nor souls to be damned," went a favorite aphorism. Beyond good and evil, insensible to argument or appeal, they symbolized the mounting independence of the new economy from the restraints and scruples of personal life.

"As directors of a company," wrote William M. Gouge, "men will sanction actions of which they would scorn to be guilty in their private capacity. A crime which would press heavily on the conscience of one man, becomes quite endurable when divided among many." Even businessmen could not deny the accusation. "Corporations will do what individuals would not dare to do," exclaimed Peter C. Brooks, the wealthiest man in Boston. "—Where the dishonesty is the work of *all* the Members, every *one* can say with Macbeth in the murder of Banquo 'thou canst not say *I* did it.'" It is difficult to exaggerate the frequency with which the corporation was condemned as a technique for the stilling of conscience. "These artificial creatures," said a committee of the Massachusetts legislature, ". . . unlike individual employers, are not chastened and restrained in their dealings with the laborers, by human sympathy and direct personal responsibility to conscience and to the bar of public opinion."

In 1840 Amos Kendall urged the inculcation of the belief that "there is but one code of morals for private and public affairs." His very concern was a confession that two codes existed. The new economy had burst the bonds of the old personal morality, and the consequences were fundamental for the whole Jeffersonian tradition.

As long as individual responsibility existed in the economic system, as long as a single code more or less governed business and personal life, the Jeffersonians were right, and that government was best which governed least. But these were the moral characteristics of a society of small freeholds, as Jefferson well understood. When the economy became too complex to admit of much personal responsibility, when ownership became attenuated and liability limited and diffused, when impersonality began to dominate the system and produce irresponsibility, when, in short, economic life began to throw off the control of personal scruple, then government had to extend its function in order to preserve the ties which hold society together. The history of government intervention is thus a history of the growing ineffectiveness of private conscience as a means of social control. With private conscience powerless, the only alternative to tyranny or anarchy was the growth of the public conscience, and the natural expression of the public conscience was the democratic government.

In spite of the Jeffersonian inhibitions, then, the Jacksonians were forced to intervene in the affairs of business. Their ultimate aim was to safeguard the equitable distribution of property which they felt alone could sustain democracy, but this effort inevitably required a battle against the concentration of wealth and power in a single class.

The most conspicuous form of corporation was the bank, and, according to Jacksonian economic theory, no institution played a more important role in transferring wealth from the producing class to the accumulators. The hard-money policy was, of course, primarily designed to reduce the power and increase the stability of the paper system. Within the states, Jacksonians developed various types of structural control: periodic supervision, compulsory publicity, requirements of a broad specie basis for circulation and discounts. These proposals, however innocent in appearance, often provoked bitter resistance. In Massachusetts in 1840 a Whig committee rebuked a proposal that banks be required to keep ten per cent of their capital in specie as a measure which would "palpably 'violate the contract' made by the Legislature with the banks, and essentially 'alter and impair their rights.'" But in the end most such reforms won reluctant acceptance.

The main Jacksonian proposal, however, was to attack the monopoly character of banking by enacting general laws of incorporation; and this reform was quickly adapted for the whole corporate system. Incorporation by special charter had little to recommend it, except for people who already had their own charters and wanted to keep out competitors. It was a prolific source of legislative corruption as well as a system of special privilege hardly consistent with democracy; and it created banks and corporations in response to political pressure rather than to economic need. The radical Democrats thus advocated free banking, at least for the functions of discount and deposit (along with sharp limitation and prospective abolition of the power of note issue), instead of the uneconomic and undemocratic banking monopoly. Similarly, they favored general laws of incorporation which would extend corporate exemption to all business groups satisfying certain requirements, instead of limiting it, on a basis of legal "monopoly," to those able to cajole, bully or bribe state legislatures.

The movement toward general laws was assisted by the development, from the experience of the early land companies, of the private business association, an organization midway between the corporation and the simple partnership. In some aspects, the general laws were a recognition of the power and usefulness of the business association, giving it status before the courts and bestowing on it the few legal privileges of corporations which it had not yet gained.

In 1836 Henry Edwards, the Democratic Governor of Connecticut, called for a general law of incorporation, and in 1837 the legislature passed the Hinsdale Act, the first modern corporation law. In the next few years other states passed limited general laws. The question was agitated by the radicals in the legislatures, brought up at state constitutional conventions, blared out in crowded halls at election time and set forth with homely illustrations on the hustings. After the Civil War general laws became customary, and today they are so universal that it is hard to conceive of any other system. They constitute a direct legacy from Jacksonian democracy.

The fate of the Jacksonian economic legislation was that common historical irony: it on the whole promoted the very ends it was intended to defeat. The general laws sprinkled holy water on corporations, cleansing them of the legal status of monopoly and sending them forth as the benevolent agencies of free competition. A series of court decisions, arising out of the New York general banking law of 1838, concluded that pre–general-law corporations were legally the same as those created under the new dispensation. Even the onetime "monopoly" was thereby transmuted into a laissez-faire corporation and endowed with new prestige and virtue. Capitalism, in the end, gained a new moral force from the incorporation laws.

Yet the fact that the Jacksonian program was eventually beneficial to economic enterprise does not mean that the business world was astute enough to recognize this in advance. In fact, businessmen fought the Jacksonian program bitterly, step by step, and indulged in interminable wails of calamity and disaster. Taney's opinion in the Charles River Bridge case, for example, was clearly more responsive to the necessities of capitalistic expansion than Story's, which would have held back the development of transportation for years. Yet businessmen of the day agreed with Story and denounced Taney as a radical.

One inference from this episode is perhaps that the mass of businessmen did not really want free competition. They might accept it in principle, but in practice they were likely to be seduced by the fatal allure of monopoly. Many in Jackson's day were excluded from the immediate benefits of the system of special charters. Some had been themselves thwarted in getting a charter by the efforts of richer and more influential persons, already in the business, to preserve their monopoly. Some even tried to beat the system by forming private business associations. Yet they thought always in terms of the special charter and its special advantages, fascinated perhaps by the lurking expectation that someday they could employ those advantages to frustrate potential competitors. Rather than abandon this dream, they steadfastly opposed the antimonopoly policy of Jackson, just as in other times they have resented attempts by rival capitalists or by government action to restore competition in some field from which it has been driven. While the business community finally succeeded in capturing the symbols of free enterprise and used them as incantations against government interference, it largely disregarded them as principles of its own behavior.

The fact that the Jacksonian policy benefited business enterprise does not mean that, even in its own terms, it was a failure. No legislative program could have been enacted which would not eventually have been mastered by the overpowering energies of the new capitalism. Moreover, the Jacksonians had no intention of restricting honest enterprise. They had too strong a conviction of the relation between economic diversity and political freedom; their aim was rather to preserve capitalism and keep the government out of the hands of the capitalists. "Commerce is entitled to a complete and efficient protection in all its legal rights," as Fenimore Cooper put it, "but the moment it presumes to control . . . it should be frowned on, and rebuked." This sentiment was universal among the Jacksonians. "We must protect these merchants," exclaimed George Bancroft, "but not be governed by them." "We do not assail property," declared Samuel J. Tilden, "we merely deny it political power." For a time, the Jacksonian economic policy, by broadening the field of competitive enterprise, admirably served these purposes.

The frontal attack on capitalist domination had to be supported by the full mobilization of the noncapitalist groups. The Jeffersonian tradition had already rallied the farmers and the artisans. But the Jeffersonians, no less than the Federalists, looked on industrial labor as an element, fortunately small, to be regarded with mistrust and abhorrence. Without property the working classes of great cities must be without independence, factious and corrupt, the prey of demagogues and tyrants. This analysis may not have been altogether inaccurate, but neither the Jeffersonians nor especially the Federalists accompanied it by serious attempts to prevent the new industrialism from spawning the class whose influence they so much feared.

The class thus grew, for all the disapproval of the old parties, and eventually its power commanded recognition. Jacksonian democracy acted on this new political fact. Class consciousness was much greater a century ago than people imagine who believe it was invented in the Great Depression. Jacksonian speeches roused it, much Jacksonian legislation was based on it, the Jacksonian press appealed to it. Democratic papers opened their columns to the defense of trade-unionism, printed reports of union meetings and assailed the enemies of labor organization. Such Democratic politicians as Charles Jared Ingersoll and John Worth Edmonds defended unions in the courts against charges of criminal conspiracy. Robert Rantoul, Jr., the brilliant and ambitious Massachusetts Democrat, won labor's greatest legal victory by his argument in the famous case of *Commonwealth v. Hunt.*

In October, 1840, Hunt and others, members of the Boston Bootmakers' Society, were on trial in the Boston municipal court for combining to compel master bootmakers to employ only union men. The testimony, including that of master bootmakers, disclosed that the union had improved the quality and efficiency of the work, and Rantoul sought to show that the English common law under which the men were indicted had no status in a Massachusetts court. Judge Peter Oxenbridge Thacher conceded in his charge to the jury that it was lawful for the defendants to refuse individually to work for a master who employed nonunion workmen; but "if they combined together to control, by force of numbers, the employment of other persons, ... I consider that both the means and the object were violations of law." If unions were allowed to continue, "all industry and enterprise would be suspended, and all property would become insecure. ... A frightful despotism would soon be erected on the ruins of this free and happy commonwealth." Judge Thacher's juries were not in the habit of defying him, and this one returned a verdict of guilty in two hours and ten minutes.

The case was promptly appealed to the state Supreme Court, where in the March term, 1842, Rantoul assailed the indictment as defective "because each of the defendants had a right to do that which is charged against them jointly." The decision was handed down by Lemuel Shaw, Chief Justice of the court. While also a former Federalist, Shaw was not, like

Thacher, blinded by party preferences to the facts of life. He had no particular sympathy for democracy, but he had a very real sense of the imperatives of change. "The strength of that great judge," observed Justice Oliver Wendell Holmes, "lay in an accurate appreciation of the requirements of the community whose officer he was. . . . few have lived who were his equals in their understanding of the grounds of public policy to which all laws must ultimately be referred."

Shaw pointed out that two different questions were involved: the legality of the combination, and the legality of its methods. On the first point he accepted Rantoul's argument: a combination could not be criminal unless the actual object of that combination were criminal. On the second point Shaw, noting that the means proposed was the refusal to work for a master employing nonunion labor, declared, "We cannot perceive, that it is criminal for men to agree together to exercise their own acknowledged rights, in such a manner as best to subserve their own interests."

Shaw's decision aroused considerable protest. "Startling and not sound," exclaimed Francis Lieber, adding that in the case of trade-unions "we know to what insufferable social tyranny, to what evil habits and fearful crimes they lead." But, though Shaw's justification of strikes for the closed shop did not gain must acceptance, the basic legality of unions *per se* was thereafter substantially established. The death knell was sounded for indictments of unions as criminal conspiracies.

The debate over unionism exhibited another aspect of the struggle for *laissez faire*. From the first, conservatism had rested part of its case on the ground that unions interrupted the freedom of trade. As early as 1832 Judge Thacher had declared that the law must protect "in full extent, the principle of equal and fair competition. If individuals may combine together, to gain an unfair advantage over others, it would violate this principle." Chief Justice Savage of New York, in his decision in the case of the Geneva bootmakers, indulged in similar invocations of free trade. "It is important to the best interests of society that the price of labor be left to regulate itself," he said. ". . . Competition is the life of trade."

Yet these doctrines immediately caused contradictions if they were applied only to unions and not to corporations. What, for example, of the policy of Hamilton? What of the United States Bank? For men like Thacher and Savage, who rejected the broad application, free competition was obviously an exorcism, not a faith.

In any case, the very principles could yield arguments quite as cogent on the other side. As that ardent apostle of *laissez faire*, William Leggett, put it, "We are for leaving trade free; and the right to combine is an indispensable attribute of its freedom." (Unlike some Jacksonians, Leggett was willing to extend this right to business as well as to labor.) John Worth Edmond's argument in the case of the Hudson shoemakers rested on a thoroughgoing free-trade position. And Judge Lemuel Shaw, who had not deserted the free-trade convictions of his trading forebears, supposed his defense of unions to come as inevitably from his principles as Thacher doubtless supposed the reverse. "It is through . . . competition," he said, "that the best interests of trade and industry are promoted"— almost the same words as Chief Justice Savage's, and leading to almost exactly opposite conclusions.

It was becoming clear that people could prove anything from the maxims of free trade, including even (what would have most shocked Adam Smith) the transcendent virtue of monopoly.

The Democrats also supported the workingmen's struggle for a shorter day. The average length of the working day in Lowell in 1845 varied from eleven hours and twenty-four minutes in December and January to thirteen hours and thirty-one minutes in April—ordinarily from sunrise to sunset. In the eighteen-thirties labor organizations raised the cry for reduction, and radical Democrats took it up with enthusiasm. An ardent young Jacksonian named Ben Butler carried on the agitation in the very shadow of the mills, where workers hardly dared attend protest meetings for fear of discharge and the black list, which would prevent their employment by other large corporations.

Van Buren's executive order of 1840 gave the movement

official blessing. In Massachusetts in the next fifteen years Democrats several times presented ten-hour laws to the legislature. But the proposals were killed by Whig committees, like the one which visited Lowell in 1845 and returned "fully satisfied, that the order, decorum, and general appearance of things in and about the mills, could not be improved by any suggestion of theirs, or by any act of the Legislature." This was a mild expression of conservative disapproval. In other moods Whigs denounced the ten-hour movement as "one of the worst deformities in their deformed code. To work only ten hours in summer and eight hours in winter is to waste life." But the ten-hour campaign flourished during the forties and fifties, to the cordial applause of the radical Democrats.

Another part of the Jacksonian effort sought to guarantee the political rights of labor. Having gained the ballot, the workingman now faced the problem of making sure he voted as he pleased. Employers not seldom threatened to discharge those who dared vote the radical ticket, and Fenimore Cooper reported that he had heard this practice openly defended. As late as 1850 in Massachusetts the chairman of the Whig state central committee sent a circular to prominent Whigs, asking them to use their influence over their employees in the coming election. The superintendent of the Boott Mills in Lowell obligingly replied that he would fire every man who voted the ten-hour ticket.

The fight to make the labor vote effective took several forms. In Massachusetts, where the state Senate was based on property rather than population, the Democrats tried sporadically to revise the method of apportionment. They were unsuccessful till 1853. They also urged ballot reform. David Henshaw in 1829 fought through to the state Supreme Court a suit which resulted in securing legal recognition for the printed ballot, the first step toward uniform ballots, and from 1849 Amasa Walker led a campaign for the adoption of the secret ballot. The secret-ballot law eventually enacted by a liberal legislature was repealed by the Whigs in 1853 on the ground that it "insulted the manliness and independence of the laboring men." The Democratic movement to reduce the poll tax similarly produced the ingenious Whig theory that the lower classes would consider themselves degraded by such an action. The Democrats sought further to repeal the sunset law, which made it hard for a workingman to vote by closing the polls at sunset. As a party they remained constantly receptive to projects for improving and protecting the suffrage.

Yet the radical Democrats never committed the fallacy of resting everything on political mechanisms. The pervading insight of the Jacksonians into the relation of democarcy and a wide distribution of property kept them from tumbling into excessive optimism over minor reforms. Security of the vote would help the laboring class, but their vital need was economic independence, and the best way of elevating labor was to enact the economic program of the radical Democracy.

The problem of labor for the Jacksonians, then, consisted in mobilizing the votes of the workingmen to support a policy which would increase their share in the national income. In their attempt to preserve the economic base of labor action they had a potent ally—the public domain in the West. The broad expanse across green forests and illimitable prairies and fertile plains offered inviting refuge to the discontented and underprivileged of the East; and the greater the number drawn to the frontier from the settled states, the higher the wages and the easier the life for those who stayed behind.

Both new states and old thus benefited from the migration to the cheap lands beyond the Alleghenies. "The West, the Paradise of the Poor," a writer called it in the *Democratic Review*. "It forms a practical corrective of the evils caused by the tendency of property to accumulate in large masses." "If some of our cities are not like Birmingham and Manchester," said George Bancroft, "it is owing not to our legislation, but to the happy accident of our possessing the West." The popular conception of the value of the frontier was summed up in a single famous phrase: "It is sometimes said, that the abundance of vacant land operates as the safety valve of our system."

Yet the safety-valve theory was already beginning to crack at the seams. Anticipating the historians' controversy of a century later, journalists were busily engaged in pointing out how much of it was already illusion. Orestes A. Brownson was not alone in emphasing the increasing unreality of the escape. The population of a manufacturing town, the *Boston Post* noted as early as 1834, was "physically and morally indisposed for the hardy life of a western agriculturist." Few wage earners had laid enough by to get the more fertile land, few perhaps could even afford to move home and family a thousand weary miles to the West. A New England reformer put the case forcibly in 1847:—

> One hundred and sixty acres of land even may be yours in Iowa or Wisconsin, if you will settle upon it, and yet this offer may be of no advantage to you. You may not have the ability to go there, or be able to make a settlement, when arrived. Barren, unimproved acres do not present a very inviting aspect to a destitute man. Or you may not wish to go there. You may not wish to exile yourself from your early and long cherished home. You may not wish to withdraw from civilization to the wilderness. You may not wish to give up the social institutions of New England, her Sabbath and her churches, her schools and her widely diffused intelligence; the social intercourse of friends and of a comparatively dense population for the far West, where all these are wanting. . . . Besides, you are not cultivators; you are mechanics, artizans, clerks, laborers of every variety. . . . This is not a corrective of the evil; it is only a fleeing of it. And woe is left for them who cannot escape.

Whatever broad effects the frontier had on the price level, the labor supply, the incentives toward capital investment or the general economic atmosphere, it had ceased even by the time of Jackson to serve as a real alternative for the workers of the Eastern states.

In the future, moreover, hung the awful possibility of its disappearance. In time, the last free acres would be foreclosed, and the safety valve would choke up. When? No one could say. In 1840 Orestes A. Brownson guessed fifty years. Others might have named longer periods, but all agreed that the free institutions of America would in the end have to face their bitterest test. "It is the accident of our situation alone," declared R. B. Rhett in 1838, "having a continent to people, which has enabled us so long to maintain them. But the time will come,— is rapidly approaching, when the way to the West will be blocked up."

What then? "Decree that when her workpeople feel the iron hand of competition pressing too harshly, they shall not be allowed to escape to the free woods and rich lands of the Far West," said Robert Dale Owen. "And what assurance should we have that in Lowell, and Lynn, and Salem, the same scenes would not soon be re-produced that now win our sympathy for the oppressed laborer of Britain?"

The Jacksonians thus regarded the keeping open of the public domain as a democratic imperative. It was not for them a sectional question alone. The poorer people of the West demanded easy access and cheap lands for their own direct benefit. The poorer people of the East similarly required a liberal land policy, to provide for some a refuge, and to relieve the pressure on the great majority by draining off rural population which might otherwise flock to town and swell the labor surplus. All agreed in advocating every preference for the actual settler in order to prevent the seizure of large areas of fertile land by speculators.

For the Eastern conservatives the land problem assumed the same significance. Westward migration, as John Quincy Adams's Secretary of the Treasury explained in candid detail in 1827, was against the interests of manufacturing capital. It was clearly to their advantage to have a large labor supply driving wages down by competition among themselves.

The conflict of interests bred two opposing theories about the public lands. John Quincy Adams and Henry Clay wanted to sell land high, using the domain primarily as a fund to finance internal improvements and hoping to hold back colonization. In 1830 Senator Foot of Connecticut even offered a resolution inquiring into the expediency of limiting the further sale of public lands. Benton's massive attack on this proposal laid the preliminaries for the celebrated (if comparatively unimportant) debate between Webster and Hayne. As Benton charged in 1832, "It is well known that the manufacturers are opposed to any relaxation in the sale or disposition of the public lands; because they want to confine the poor people to the old States, to work in the factories."

Against this "revenue" theory of the national domain, the Jacksonians, for whom Benton was the chief spokesman on land policy, advanced the "settlement" theory, proposing to lower land prices and thus to encourge migration. Though the political revolution of the thirties compelled the Whigs to disguise their attitude under various specious theories, and eventually to support certain forms of homestead provision, the initiative toward actual settlement continued to come from the Democrats.

Jackson and Van Buren both called in their annual messages for a liberalization of the land laws. Their proposals generally recommended themselves to the West without delay; but the job of awakening the East to the land issue fell to that small group of radicals around the *Working Man's Advocate,* of which George H. Evans was the leading spirit. As early as 1834 Evans was beginning to dwell on the stake of Eastern workingmen in the national domain. During his years on his New Jersey farm he slowly built up an elaborate scheme of land reform. In 1841 he began to expound his views in a monthly called *The Radical,* urging the opening up of the land to actual settlers, the limitation of the holdings of any single person, and the exemption of the homestead from suits for debt. His program was decorated by a complex theory of natural right in land which explained all the deformities of society as the consequences of improper alienation.

Gradually his plan gripped him with a kind of fanatic intensity. No substantial improvement, he felt, was possible until the land monopoly was destroyed; then all problems were solved. In February, 1844, he returned to New York and called some of his old friends together for a meeting in John Windt's print shop. Here he set forth his scheme with persuasive eloquence, and in the next month he began a new series of the *Working Man's Advocate,* soon to be rechristened *Young America.* His enthusiasm infected many of the New York radicals. Windt, John Commerford and for a time the ebullient Mike Walsh espoused the cause.

The group organized itself into a corps of speakers, assembling in parks and on street corners, passing broadsides out to workmen as they went home at sunset, and holding vociferous evening meetings at Croton Hall, on the corner of Division Street and the Bowery. Their motto—*Vote yourself a farm*—passed quickly into circulation, and Horace Greeley, always on the lookout for safe reforms, flirted with them ardently in the columns of the *Tribune*. For five hard years Evans kept his paper going, in the expectation that one day his plan would sweep the country. In 1849, worn out and penniless, he sadly went back to New Jersey where he died seven years later. The National Reform Association, as he called his group, broke up and scattered away.

Yet his work was not in vain. The seed was planted, and the compulsions of geography would bring it to maturity. Whatever the objections of Eastern capitalists or Southern planters or Western speculators, the West had to be opened up; the common man everywhere demanded it; no one could check the course of empire. From 1846 on, a morose, ambitious and extremely able young Jacksonian from Tennessee named Andrew Johnson kept up a persistent agitation for a homestead bill. In May, 1852, he went to New York and spoke at a mass meeting arranged by friends of Evans. In the meantime Horace Greeley, serving a term in Congress, introduced another homestead bill in 1849, and after 1850 the forces of land reform were strengthened by the addition of Galusha A. Grow, a Pennsylvania Democrat, intimate friend and disciple of Benton. Their efforts finally triumphed with the passage of the Homestead Act of 1862.

Though the national domain may have been in the narrow sense a Western problem, the needs and energies which shaped the national policy toward it were by no means exclusively Western. The opening up of the public lands was nearly as vital for Eastern workingmen and farmers as for the people of the West. The importance of the land question is evidence less of the Western character of Jacksonianism than of its overmastering desire to preserve everywhere the economic democracy which alone could give political democracy meaning.

## For Further Reading

No recent biography has been written of Andrew Jackson. James Parton's *Life of Andrew Jackson* (3 vols., 1860) contains much important material on Old Hickory, and J. S. Bassett's *The Life of Andrew Jackson* (1916) is still valuable. The student will find, however, Marquis James' *The Life of Andrew Jackson* (1938) more readable. Thomas P. Abernethy, whose *From Frontier to Plantation in Tennessee* (1932) stresses Jackson's early career, portrays his subject as a frontier "aristocrat," rather than "democrat." Richard Hofstadter's perceptive essay on Jackson in *The American Political Tradition* (1948) should not be missed.

A classic statement of Jackson's period is Carl R. Fish, *The Rise of the Common Man* (1927), an account that exhibits the ambivalence of the intellectual toward the "common man." The most recent political survey of the era is Glyndon VanDeusen's *The Jacksonian Era* (1959), a work more scholarly and judicious than Claude G. Bowers' dramatic, almost lurid *The Party Battles of the Jackson Period* (1922). Three recent monographs have made major contributions to an understanding of political life of the period: Lee Benson, *The Concept of Jacksonian Democracy* (1961), a close look at New York State and a rejection of the term "Jacksonian Democracy," Walter Hugins, *Jacksonian Democracy and the Working Class* (1960), and Richard P. McCormick, *The Second American Party System* (1966), which like Benson's, minimizes Jackson's role. John William Ward's *Andrew Jackson: Symbol for an Age* (1955) and Marvin Meyer's *The Jacksonian Persuasion* (1957) are brilliant studies of imagery, rhetoric, and culture. For works on government and patronage, see Leonard White, *The Jacksonians* (1954), and Carl R. Fish, *The Civil Service and the Patronage* (1905).

The Bank War has received extensive attention, the best works being Bray Hammond, *Banks and Politics in America* (1957); R. C. H. Catterall, *The Second Bank of the United States* (1903); Walter Smith, *Economic Aspects of the Second Bank of the United States* (1953); Thomas P. Govan, *Nicholas Biddle* (1959); Robert V. Remini, *Andrew Jackson and the Bank War* (1967); Jean Alexander Wilburn, *Biddle's Bank* (1967); and Peter Temin, *The Jacksonian Economy* (1969).

# The Socialization of Christianity

## Henry Steele Commager

The drumbeat of reform stirred America in the 1830's, not to be stilled for decades. A host of leaders joined the march. From the South came Sarah and Angelina Grimké and James G. Birney; from New England came William Lloyd Garrison, Wendell Phillips, Samuel Gridley Howe, and Theodore Parker; from the Middle Atlantic region came Arthur and Lewis Tappan, Lucretia Mott, and Henry and Elizabeth Cady Stanton; and from the West came Theodore Dwight Weld and Joshua Giddings. The roster was long; the causes varied: peace, temperance, women's rights, education, penal codes, care of the deaf and dumb and insane, and abolition of slavery. These concerns were tightly related, all belonging to the broad humanitarian thrust of an optimistic age. As Americans surged westward, freed temporarily from entanglement in European politics, with both abundance and God's will on their side, it appeared possible to construct a purer society. Humanitarianism was the spiritual analogue to building canals and perfecting the political system. Equally as important, the reformers rarely confined themselves to just one cause.

*Source:* Henry Steele Commager, *Theodore Parker* (Boston: Little, Brown and Company, 1936), pp. 168–196. Reprinted by permission of the author.

In their persons they linked many reforms, refusing to compartmentalize their efforts to better the conditions of their fellow men.

Abolition of slavery, touching as it did the nation's most grievous ill, attracted the most attention. Antislavery sentiment had existed side by side with the "peculiar institution" throughout the colonial and early republic years. Quakers had long been actively preaching and petitioning against slavery. Benjamin Lundy, an itinerant Quaker publicist, had been instrumental in igniting William Lloyd Garrison's abolitionist fervor. The new firebrand's first major step came with the appearance of *The Liberator* (a successor to the *Genius for Universal Emancipation* which, in 1829–1830, Garrison had edited with Lundy). The first issue of *The Liberator* of January 1, 1831, testified to the editor's militant commitment: "I *will be* as harsh as truth, and as uncompromising as justice.... I am in earnest—I will not equivocate—I will not excuse—I will not retreat a single inch—AND I WILL BE HEARD." He was heard; yet ironically Southern proslavery apologists, in casting Garrison as the symbol of Northern extremism, probably were most responsible for his growing notoriety.

Garrison's call in *The Liberator* serves as a convenient device for dating the advent of a sustained and growing movement against slavery. But it does not stand alone. Other events and personalities helped to add force and direction to the reform movement. The dramatic Nat Turner rebellion in Virginia in 1831; the recriminations against Prudence Crandall's experiment in racially integrated schooling in Connecticut in 1832; the South's hardening proslavery position in response to external and internal criticism throughout the 1830's; the corresponding abuses of northerners of the abolitionists' civil liberties; the murder of the antislavery editor Elijah P. Lovejoy at Alton, Illinois, in 1837; the refusal of Southern leadership in the House of Representatives to receive antislavery petitions, despite the advocacy of abolition by one of the House's most esteemed members, former President John Quincy Adams; and the quiet, but effective, grass-roots propagandizing achieved by Theodore Dwight

Weld and his cohorts at Oberlin College in Ohio—all contributed significantly to the abolitionist cause.

Scholars have pointed to weaknesses in the antislavery campaign of the 1830's. Some assert that Garrison's radical statements and acts, such as the burning of the United States' Constitution at a public gathering to dramatize his assertion of a "higher law," produced as many foes as friends. Others have observed flaws in the abolitionist philosophical position. Confusion existed over terms like "gradual immediatism" or "immediate gradualism" in freeing slaves. Even Garrison, who had soon brushed aside William Channing's philosophic niceties by advocating an unequivocal immediatism had no practical program. Morality demanded freedom; how the latter could be achieved was unimportant. The reformers' sense of individualism, it has been suggested, militated against effective and cohesive organization of the movement. Antislavery societies had an unhappy tendency of splintering into warring factions, thus diffusing their impact. Finally, the abolitionists of the 1830's were so anti-institutional that by and large they avoided channeling their energies into the one institution, the political party, that could promise some practical results. Their anti-institutionalism (Man could not avoid, Thoreau said, having other men "pursue and paw him with their dirty institutions"), of course, flowed logically from their highly developed sense of individualism; but aversion to political party received added force because many of the reformers were Whigs in an age of Democratic hegemony. Hobbled as they were by philosophic abstraction, individualism, and anti-institutionalism, the abolitionists still possessed a heightened sense of personal guilt about slavery. They could not slough off responsibility onto others' shoulders. This last quality, according to some historians, explains the movement's pertinacity despite internal dissension and external harassments.

To a large extent historical inquiry into abolition has focused on the 1830's and early 1840's. This is understandable. As noted earlier, the reform movement symbolized the humanitarian character of that era, giving social historians a fertile field of research. Intellectual historians too have had much to ponder, for many abolitionists were Transcendentalists: believers in the spiritual and intellectual doctrine that man contains the immanent Truth which, acting both as ideal and as motivator, can be perceived by man's higher intellect; thus perceived, it could be acted out, transcending baser emotions, ultimately leading man into communion with the Supreme Being, or Oversoul. The process of transcendentalism differed with each man; Ralph Waldo Emerson in Concord and Theodore Parker in Boston each had their unique view. Each came to embrace abolition, although in different fashions.

Because of the volume of interest in abolition in the 1830's it seems appropriate to illuminate the full range of reform activity. Historians of course have picked up the later abolitionist story, yet often in political terms. Later selections in this volume will present that perspective. There follows here a segment of a splendid biography of a leading reformer. We have chosen a portion of Henry Steele Commager's *Theodore Parker* (1936) that relates to the interconnection of the various reform movements. Commager ranks as one of America's leading historians. A prolific writer, reviewer, and editor, he is best known for his work as an intellectual historian—perhaps chiefly for his *The American Mind* (1950), a book written to complete the work of Vernon Louis Parrington, cut short by the latter's death. *Theodore Parker*, unlike some works of intellectual historians, demonstrates the author's sure narrative touch. It is a happy blend of narration, exposition, and interpretation. The work also has current relevance for a nation that still wrestles with problems unresolved since Parker's day and before. Thoreau was not the only aspostle of civil disobedience in the face of what he considered morally unjust laws; Parker also spoke eloquently on this subject, as well as acting on his beliefs.

*P*arker threw himself into the various reform movements of the day with characteristic energy, and soon he was as immersed in the reports of state boards of charities, of prisons, and asylums as ever he had been in the transactions of the philosophical societies. "When I first came to Boston," he remembered later, "I meant to do something for the perishing and dangerous classes in our great towns—for the poor, the drunkard, the ignorant, for the prostitute, and the criminal. But, alas, I did not quite understand all the consequences of my relation to these great social forces, or how much I had offended the religion of the state, the press, the market, and the church. I soon found my very name was enough to ruin any new good enterprise. I knew there were three periods in each great movement of mankind—that of sentiment, ideas, and action; I fondly hoped the last had come; but when I found I had reckoned without the host, I turned attention to the two former and sought to arouse the sentiment of justice and mercy, and to diffuse the ideas which belonged to this five-fold reformation. Hence I took pains to state the facts of poverty, drunkenness, ignorance, prostitution, crime; to show their cause, their effect, and their mode of cure, leaving it for others to do the practical work."

Yet this was a palpable exaggeration; when did Parker ever leave it to others to do work that must be done? His genius lay in agitation, and he gave it full play, but he did what work he could. He served on committees, circulated petitions, organized charitable and social welfare societies, he lectured, he wrote, and he preached. He sought to make his home in Exeter Place a clearinghouse for the reform work of the day, and not without success.

No sooner was he settled in Boston than he issued an invitation to a "Council of Reformers" whose object was to discuss the "General Principles of Reform" and the best means of promoting them. Everyone came: Emerson and Alcott from Concord, Garrison and Phillips who lived near by, James and Lucretia Mott up from Philadelphia and Sam Jo May from Syracuse, Chevalier Howe and Charles Sumner and Edmund Quincy, James Freeman Clarke from the Church of the Disciples, E. H. Chaplin, the eloquent Universalist, and Caleb Stetson, who had delivered the charge at Parker's ordination, but had scarcely contemplated this. For six hours they discussed what Garrison called All the Holy Principles of Reform. They had a sublime faith in discussion, these men; they thought that if only you could get at the truth, the truth would make you free. And when the possibilities of private discussion were exhausted, they had recourse to Conventions.

There was, for example, the Anti-Sabbath Convention of March, 1848. Parker helped to organize it, and it met in his own Melodeon, and for two days the reformers had at each other, hammer and tongs. This question of Sabbath reform was not in itself of great importance (Garrison thought it was, Garrison who hated the enslavement of the spirit as fiercely as he hated the enslavement of the body), but it was important in its implications, in the principles that were at stake. It was not so much that they opposed the old Puritan Sunday, though that was dismal enough; what they objected to were those penal laws which an overanxious State had thrown around the day and which the Sabbath Union was now agitating with such misspent energy. The laws were innocuous enough, to be sure, rarely observed, more rarely enforced, but even the mildest of laws represented an assertion of the authority of the State over the consciences of men. In this matter of religious observance, they thought, the State had no proper concern. "Let Sunday and preaching stand on their own merits," said Parker. Better empty pews than attendance dictated by laws or by custom or even by inertia. He preached a sermon on the matter; history was gutted and philosophy exhausted to prove that the Sabbath was made for man.

Yet Parker was no extremist. "I have all along," he confessed to a clerical friend, "been a little afraid of a reaction from the sour, stiff, Jewish way of keeping Sunday into a low, coarse, material, voluptuous or mere money-making abuse of it." In the Convention he spoke for moderation (a rare thing, this), and his resolutions were conciliatory in tone: "We consider the superstitious opinions respecting the origin of the institution of Sunday as a day to be devoted to religious purposes to form the chief obstacle to a yet more profitable use of that day." "But," said another resolution, "we should lament to see the Sunday devoted to *labor* or *sport*; for though we think all days are equally holy we yet consider that the custom of devoting one day in each week mainly to spiritual culture is still of great advantage to mankind." But the extremists were not satisfied with these. They represented a compromise, and Garrison was even less accustomed to compromise than was Parker. He introduced his own resolutions, twenty of them, and supported them with argument and poesy, and in the end all of his were adopted and only four of Parker's. "I was between two fires," Parker wrote, "*cross*-fires, too."

There was the Anti-Capital Punishment Convention. "Nothing remarkable," Parker wrote in his Journal, "but as a sign of the times." And a sign of the times it assuredly was; not for half a century had men inquired so critically into the whole problem of crime and punishment or sought so earnestly to fix responsibility where it really belonged. Parker had long been familiar with this problem. When he was a student in the Divinity School he had gone out and preached to the convicts in the Charlestown prison, and he had never passed up an opportunity to acquaint himself with prison conditions and the statistics of crime. "If I were governor of Massachusetts," he wrote once to John Sargent, "I should know exactly the condition of every jail and house of correction in the state, and of all the institutions for preventing crime and ignorance." He read Plato's "Republic," and was moved to observe that "penal legislation now-a-days has all the effect of the purest injustice, in driving the half-guilty to increased crime, and in making doubly deep the hatred of the revengeful." He visited the Tombs of New York and asked: "How can it be justice to punish as a crime that which the institutions of society render unavoidable? How could anything better be expected of the poor wretches daily brought up to that court, exposed naked as they are, to all the contamination of corrupt society?"

West Roxbury offered little opportunity for a realistic study of the problem of crime, and it was not until Parker came to Boston that his suspicions became certainty and his inchoate idealism a program of action. No sooner had he announced his true idea of a Christian Church than he turned from generalization to particulars, and delivered a series of sermons on the

Dangerous and Perishing Classes of society, all of them touching closely this problem of the responsibility of society for crime, poverty, and ignorance, all of them revealing the characteristic alliance of intuition and fact. *A priori* ideas were scrupulously proved, and every moral axiom was appealed to the Census Bureau.

Philosophy and experience, theory and fact, united to point one inescapable moral: it was society, not the individual, that was at fault. Nine tenths of all prisoners, Parker found came from the "perishing" classes, and seventeen twentieths of all crimes were crimes against property. Over one half of all the persons confined in the Boston House of Correction were foreigners, newcomers gone astray in a strange, a hostile, environment. Of the 547 women on Blackwell's Island in New York, 519 had been committed for vagrancy—"women with no capital but their person, with no friend, no shelter." Equally impressive was the correlation of crime and ignorance: in Massachusetts one third of the criminals could not read or write; New York, of course, didn't do even that well: at Mount Pleasant six sevenths of the prisoners were illiterate. The statistics from abroad merely emphasized the obvious: over ninety per cent. of all the prisoners in England and Wales, in the year 1841, were illiterate, and the figures from the Continent were just as shocking.

The moral was obvious, but Parker did not forbear to point it. The statistics of crime furnished an index not of character but of opportunity, and it was inevitable that our prisoners should be recruited from among the poor and the ignorant. "The effect of property in elevating and moralizing a class of men is seldom realized," Parker concluded.

Nor would Parker leave it all to the pleasant anonymity of "society." Property was at fault, the State was at fault, the Church was at fault. Men who paid low wages and high dividends, men who collected exorbitant rentals for wretched slums or, worse still, for grog shops or houses of ill fame, men who were willing to pay taxes for war but not for schools, these were the real foes of society. Bankers who exacted usurious rates of interest, journalists who reveled in the most loathsome details of vice, lawyers who would defend, for a fee, the worse of causes, judges who thought it a crime for anyone to be poor, clergymen who argued the divine sanction of the gallows, statesmen who made war and called it honorable, these were the men who organized the sins of society.

> The nation sets the poor an example of fraud by making them pay the highest on all local taxes; of theft by levying the national income on persons, not property. Our navy and army set them the lesson of violence; and to complete their schooling, at this very moment we are robbing another nation of cities and lands, stealing, burning, and murdering, for lust of power and gold. Everybody knows that the political action of a nation is the mightiest educational influence in that nation. But such is the doctrine the State preaches to them, a constant lesson of fraud, theft, violence, and crime.

Nor did our system of punishment possess even the dubious virtue of efficiency. It neither prevented crime nor reformed criminals. Over half of the offenders haled before the Courts of Boston had already served prison sentences and, within five years, over three hundred criminals had been jailed ten times or more. It was clear that the jails made more criminals than they cured. For all the harshness of the penal code and the horrors of the prisons, the statistics of crime mounted every year. "You may punish the man," Parker said, "but it does no good. You can seldom frighten men out of a fever. Can you frighten them from crime, when all the circumstances about them impel to crime? Can you frighten a starving girl into chastity? You cannot keep men from lewdness, theft and violence, when they have no self-respect, no culture, no development of mind, heart and soul. The gaol will not take the place of the church, of the schoolhouse, of home. It will not remove the causes which are making new criminals. It does not reform the old ones. The gaol does not alter the circumstances which occasioned the crime, and until these causes are removed, a fresh crop will spring out of the festering soil." And when the Reform School at Westborough burned down, Parker wrote, "I am not sorry. It was a school for crime and must graduate villains."

The trouble was that this whole business of punishment rested upon a false philosophy, a mistaken conception of Man. It was based upon hate and revenge, not upon love and respect for the dignity of man. Did it take a transcendentalist to see this, a Bronson Alcott, an Emerson, a Parker? It was so obvious that every man of sense should see it. "How long will it be," Parker asked, with a curious emphasis, "before we apply good sense and Christianity to the prevention of crime? One day we must see that a gaol is no more likely to cure a crime than a lunacy or a fever. A gaol, as a mere house of punishment, ought to have no place in an enlightened people. It ought to be a moral hospital where the offender is kept till he is cured." And how illogical this custom of fixed sentences, as if five years of prison would cure a thief and ten years an embezzler. "It is wrong to detain a man after he is cured; wrong to send him out before he is cured." How immoral the fever of the State to remove men from society, the indifference of the State to the task of restoring men to society. "I doubt not," Parker wrote, "the angel of humanity will beat with her golden pinions, all prisons to small dust."

If jails were bad, how much worse were the gallows, and how monstrous that Christian ministers should justify them. There was the Reverend George B. Cheever, self-appointed guardian of public morals, who erected a "Defense of Capital Punishment" on the foundations of the Old Testament; Phillips tried to meet him on his own ground, and presented a lawyer's brief citing chapter and verse for a different interpretation of the Scriptures. But Parker would have none of such truckling to religious prejudices. If the Bible sanctioned capital punishment, the Bible was wrong. "It fills me with amazement," he said, "that worthy men in these days should go back to such sources for their wisdom; should walk dry-shod through the Gospels, and seek in the records of a barbarous people to justify their atrocious acts." And he had no more respect for the authority of the State than for the authority of the Church. "I know," he said, "that society claims the right of eminent domain over person and life not less than over house and land. I deny the right. Certainly it has never been shown. To me, resting on the broad ground of natural justice, capital punishment seems wholly inadmissible, homicide with the pomp and formality of law. To put a criminal to death seems to me as foolish as for the child to beat the stool it has stumbled over, and as useless too."

Easy enough to indict society for its mismanagement of this business, but what was to be done? Some of the reforms were obvious and close at hand. Society must assume responsibility for its own shortcomings; the idea of punishment must be discarded and that of cure substituted. Houses of correction must justify their name, and another Horace Mann should be found to make them institutions of education. The gallows, symbol of vengeance, must go; fixed terms of sentence, symbol of punishment, must go; even prison uniforms must go, for they were degrading. Above all, the attitude of mind that these things represented, must be abandoned.

Nor did the responsibility of the State end when it had discharged its patients. It must see to it that the cure was permanent, that society took back its own. It should maintain a public defender as well as a public prosecutor. It should establish a system of moral police to discover the causes of crime and remove them. It should follow up discharged criminals and see to it that they became useful citizens. Above all it should take care of the children of offenders, protect them from society and from a dangerous environment. This whole business of the care of children had to be changed, and above all the manner of dealing with juvenile delinquents, for here, surely, the fault of society was clear. Reform schools were better than jails, but better still the establishment of state farms where the children could be taught healthy and useful work, or the distribution of children in homes throughout the State. "I wonder," Parker wrote, "men don't see that they can never safely depart from the natural order which God has appointed. Boys are born in *families;* they grow up in *families;* a few in each household, mixed with girls and with their elders." It was a policy that worked well in France; it ought to be tried in America.

Yet these things were palliatives, not cures. "The greater portion of this work," Parker concluded, "is not special and for the criminal, but general and for society. To change the treatment of criminals, we must change everything else. The dangerous class is the unavoidable result of our present civilization, of our present ideas of man and social life. To reform and elevate the class of criminals we must reform and elevate all other classes."

More and more Parker came to understand the interrelationship between all social problems, came to see the larger issues behind particular reforms. You could not touch an open wound without irritating the entire nervous system of society; you could not treat an infection without studying social pathology. If you tried to do something about crime and punishment, you ran into the whole question of the ultimate responsibility for crime and the authority of the State; if you tried to grapple with the problem of prostitution, you came up against the Woman Question and the mistaken ideas about sex. Was it pauperism you would eliminate, you would have to face the whole problem of property and property rights. Was it war you would end, you would have to fight down the false notions of national honor and the function of the State. Temperance could not be achieved by regulatory laws, it affected property rights and human rights and demanded a higher conception of the Dignity of Man; the labor question was not merely a matter of hours and wages, but brought up the most far-reaching considerations of the nature of property and the function of labor and of capital in society. Challenge a single wrong and you would find every vested interest arrayed against you; propound a new idea and you would run up against a Chinese wall of inertia, superstition and ignorance.

Take, for example, this matter of prostitution. It would seem so glaring an evil that it would be easy enough to cope with it. No one would defend the institution, yet here were over two hundred brothels in Boston alone. There were laws, of course, but who cared about them? Exhortation was futile, threats worse than useless, and even the practical work of rescue and reform seemed of little avail. All during the Boston years Parker was busy with this practical work. He visited Charles Loring Brace in New York in order to study at first hand the methods of that pioneer welfare worker, and he found a capital friend; the conversations soon drifted away from the conditions of boys and girls in the slums to the Icelandic sagas and Mallet's work on Scandinavian Antiquities. But Parker got something out of it, despite these distractions, and he came back to Boston and tried to do there what Brace was doing in New York. With Phillips and Henry Bowditch and Edward Beecher, brother of the more famous Henry, he organized a society to rescue delinquent girls, instruct them in housework, and place them in homes throughout the State. Sargent, who had been dismissed from the Suffolk Street Chapel for permitting Parker to preach there, was made the agent of the society, and half the reformers of the city enlisted in the crusade.

But it was uphill work, and little to show for it. Parker could not but admire the success of that obscure cobbler John Augustus, who never lost faith in practical philanthropy and who made himself the guardian angel of the poor of Boston. He was a rare person, John Augustus, one of the real Christians of his age; he did not concern himself with social philosophy or theories of reform, but quietly went about his self-appointed task of saving the sinner and the publican. Every day he sat in the police courts, taking care of his own: going bail for the vagrant and the drunkard and the prostitute, for boys and girls who had run afoul of the law. For twenty years he had been a familiar figure in the streets of Boston, this odd, crotchety, wrinkled old man, hurrying around to the courts and the jails and sometimes to the churches, finding money for his wards, getting them work, placing them in homes. Parker knew him well; he had been born in Lexington (Hannah Parker had known his mother, but no one knew his father), and he had found time and money for his charities there before he moved on to Boston; and when he died Parker grieved that he was not there to point the moral of that life. "All the members of the Supreme Court might die next month," he wrote, "and the President follow suit, and half the Governors of the Union, and unitedly they would not be so great a loss as poor old John Augustus."

Yet for all his admiration of John Augustus, Parker had little confidence in this hit-or-miss philanthropy. You could not end prostitution unless you ended the poverty which drove girls into prostitution and the poverty which prevented men from marriage. Nor was the question one of economics only. You could not end prostitution until you introduced sanity into this matter of sex, broke through the conspiracy of silence and shame that surrounded the subject. And behind all these things was the Woman Question, for prostitution, after all, was merely one of the crimes against Woman, the most flagrant, but perhaps not the most radical one.

Parker handled the question of sex with a wholesome robustness that contrasted sharply with the timidity and priggishness of most of his friends, Thoreau, for example, or even Emerson. "A history of the gradual development of the sexual element in mankind," he wrote, "would be a noble theme. What a deal of prudery there is about the matter here in New England." His own attitude was a characteristic blend of the scientific and the poetic, and that, he thought, was the way to understand sex. He had read something of psychology and physiology as well as the history of monasticism, and his reading proved what his common sense affirmed: that celibacy, voluntary or enforced, was unnatural and dangerous. "If there is a damnable institution on earth," he wrote from Rome, "it is compulsory celibacy of women; if the men take the unnatural vow they can break it and, God be thanked, they commonly do; but it is different with women, they must keep the loathsome vow." And in a long correspondence with the venerable Shaker, Robert White, he elaborated this point of view. The body itself, he wrote, was an irrefutable argument for marriage, and the testimony of the instincts was more convincing by far than any of those arguments from Scripture which Mr. White so confidently advanced. And the suppression of these instincts, Parker said, led to terrible evils, to licentiousness, to hysteria and insanity, to vices of the spirit and corruption of the flesh. He was very earnest about it, and in the end even Mr. White was convinced.

But it was not the Catholic Church alone that was at fault;

even in America it was generally assumed that the sexual relation was somehow sinful. What was needed, Parker felt, was a frank acceptance of the beauty and power of sex, and the sublimation of the sexual instinct into the spiritual realm. "Those old Greeks," he wrote, apropos of Homer, "were brutes in their lust; for it was not always love. Yet there is something quite aesthetic and graceful about their love adventures. Why cannot old Greek freedom and real, unconventional, love be united with Christian morality, and woman stand in her true position."

Parker knew that it wasn't all a matter of celibacy; there was more than one way of betraying natural law. He knew well enough the psychological rocks upon which so many marriages were wrecked; the unnatural suppression of passion, he thought, was as bad as the unnatural indulgence of lust. "When a noble person marries for the noble end, and then finds it is no marriage, there is horrible suffering; and all sorts of abnormalities of conduct, internal and external, may be expected to take their places. The very eminence of morality in New England intensifies the suffering, for elsewhere the connubial *Abschweifungen* are tolerated, and the disappointed persons find some relief, at least abatement, from their long-continued affliction." Parker didn't know what was to be done about it, and that was one subject he kept clear of in his preaching. More lenient divorce laws might help, though he wasn't at all sure even of that. But "proper notions of marriage and of divorce, can only come as the result of a slow but thorough revolution in the idea of woman."

It was a phrase that he often used, but never defined, this "revolution in the idea of woman." What did he mean by it, what did they all mean by it, Margaret Fuller and Garrison and Phillips and the rest of them? It wasn't only a matter of legal disabilities or political disqualifications (those things worried Phillips), it was more than that. It was a matter of emancipation from those habits of thought that confined her sphere of influence and held her, substantially, in contempt. He wished not only to change the divorce laws, the suffrage laws, the property laws, but to change the attitude of men, and when Wendell Phillips, hot from the Woman's Rights Convention, told him that this was "the most magnificent reform that has yet been launched upon the world," he was not disposed to challenge the exaggeration.

Yet for all of his advocacy of woman's rights, his attendance upon conventions and his sermons and his lectures and his gestures of professional hospitality (the Reverend Antoinette Brown preached from his pulpit, and so did the Reverend Sheba Smith), the Woman Question remained for Parker what it had been in the beginning, a sentiment and an abstraction. He idealized woman, he regarded her as morally superior to man, and his discussions of the subject were sicklied over with romanticism. "I think man will always lead in affairs of intellect," he said, "of reason, imagination, understanding; he has the better brain. But woman will always lead in affairs of emotion—moral, affectional, religious; she has the better heart." And the function of woman, he wrote fatuously, is "to correct man's taste, mend his morals, excite his affection, inspire his religious faculties." No wonder Higginson insisted that Parker never really understood the Woman Question, no wonder Julia Ward Howe jeered at him for his intolerable air of intellectual condescension. He meant well; he knew Elizabeth Peabody and Margaret Fuller and Lydia Maria Child, he worked with Dorothea Dix and Julia Howe and Lucretia Mott and Frances Cobbe. But when he wrote on the Woman Question he was thinking of his "glorious phalanx of old maids"; when he wrote on the Woman Question he was the husband of Lydia.

Nothing took you back to fundamentals as did the labor question, nothing revealed more glaringly the immorality of the whole social order. No sentimentality here, no polite abstractions: Parker saw with dangerous clarity the barbarism and brutality of the industrial feudalism of the nineteenth century, of America, and he lashed out against it in passionate protest. This was no hothouse radicalism; he didn't need the Census Bureau to tell him of the wretchedness and misery of the great cities, he knew his way about the slums of Boston as well as did Father Taylor himself. "See the unnatural disparity in man's condition," he told his congregation, "bloated opulence and starving penury in the same street. See the pauperism, want, licentiousness, intemperance, and crime in the midst of us; see the havoc made of woman; see the poor deserted by their elder brother, while it is their sweat which enriches your ground, builds your railroads, and piles up your costly houses." Years earlier he had written of this, the shouts of the Russell children coming across the field and through his study window as he wrote, "It is common to censure some one class of men—the rich or the educated, the manufacturers, the merchants, for example, as if the sin rested solely with them, while it belongs to society at large." But he was less academic, now, or less tolerant, perhaps, and readier to fix the blame. He had not been in Boston a year before he seared the complacency of the ruling class with a flaming "Sermon on Merchants."

He was a firebrand, he was a demagogue, he was a menace to society. Not even Channing or Brownson had talked like this. You would have to go to the socialists or the Fourierites for anything like his description of the bad merchant.

> The bad merchant still lives. He cheats in his trade; sometimes against the law, commonly with it. His truth is never wholly true nor his lie wholly false. He overreaches the ignorant; makes hard bargains with them in their trouble, for he knows that a falling man will catch at red-hot iron. He takes the pound of flesh, though that bring away all the life blood with it. He loves private contracts, digging through walls in secret. No interest is illegal if he can get it. He cheats the nation with false invoices, and swears lies at the custom-house. He oppresses the men who sail his ships, forcing them to be temperate only that he may consume the value of their drink. He provides them unsuitable bread and meat. He would not engage in the African slave trade, for that might lose his ships, but he is always ready to engage in the American slave trade, and calls you a "fanatic" if you tell him it is the worse of the two. He cares not whether he sells cotton or the man who wears it, if only he gets his money: cotton or negro, it is the same to him. He would not keep a drink-hole in Ann Street, only own and rent it. He thinks it vulgar to carry rum about in a jug, respectable in a ship. He makes paupers and leaves

others to support them. Tell him not of the misery of the poor, he knows better; nor of our paltry way of dealing with public crime, he wants more gaols and a speedier gallows. You see his character in letting his houses, his houses for the poor. He is a stone in the lame man's shoe. He is the poor man's devil. The Hebrew devil that so worried Job is gone, so is the brutal devil that awed our fathers. But this devil of the nineteenth century is still extant. He has gone into trade and advertises in the papers. He makes money; the world is poorer by his wealth. He can build a Church out of his gains, to have his morality, his Christianity, preached in it, and call that the gospel. He sends rum and missionaries to the same barbarians, the one to damn, the other to save, both for his own advantage, for his patron saint is Judas, the first saint who made money out of Christ. He is not forecasting to discern effects in causes, nor skillful to create new wealth, only spry in the scramble for what others have made. In politics he wants a Government that will ensure his dividends; so asks what is good for him, but ill for the rest. He knows no right only power; no man but self; no God but his calf of gold.

Not all the merchants were bad, there were good merchants a-plenty—Francis Jackson, dearest of friends, or George Luther Stearns, or John Murray Forbes who came sometimes to the Melodeon and whom Emerson thought the best man of his generation. But Parker was talking about the merchants as a class, and of the evil that they did. They had established an aristocracy of gold, a feudalism of money. They ruled the State, enacted the laws, appointed legislators, manufactured governments, bred judges. They owned the Church, subsidizing clergymen to preach soft words, building splendid cathedrals to show their piety, hoping to buy their way into Heaven as they bought everything else. They controlled the machinery of society; industry, finance, transportation, labor, and they abused their power. Their morals were the morals of the market place, their politics the politics of peddlers, their culture vulgar and meretricious.

You could denounce their morals but you could not dispute their power. All very well, in the flush of youth, to talk of abating private property as a nuisance; Fourierism had had its day, and the present task was to direct the power of wealth along social channels. There was much that could be done, and most of it of an obvious character. There was this matter of wages: here were the Lowell mills cutting wages ten per cent. and paying extra dividends of twelve; the Massachusetts Mills declaring a dividend of twenty per cent., the manufacturers of Connecticut taking in forty per cent. each year. "When I remember," said Parker, "that all value is the result of work, and see that no man gets rich by his own work, I cannot help thinking that labour is often wickedly underpaid and capital sometimes as grossly overfed. I shall believe that capital is at the mercy of labour when the two extremes of society change places." It was labor that needed protection, not capital. The merchants kept Daniel Webster down in Washington just to see that they were safe from competition, while they brought in wagonloads of girls from the country towns and Irishmen fresh from Limerick to work at starvation wages. "There is no protection," Parker pointed out, "for the carpenter or the bricklayer. Yet if we cared for men more than for money, and were consistent with our principles of protection, why, we should exclude all foreign workmen as well as their work, and so raise the wages of native hands."

There were the hazards of industry, as great as those of war, and as inglorious, and when the jerry-built walls of the Pemberton Mills caved in, hurtling hundreds of men and women to their death, Parker found the cause of the disaster in "human ignorance and cupidity." There were other hazards, less spectacular but even more significant, and he compiled statistics of occupational mortality and was not surprised to find that machinists died at thirty-seven and laborers at forty-five, while farmers could expect to live until they were sixty-five. There was the problem of unemployment, bad enough at all times, shocking during those years of acute depression that industry seemed unable to avoid. "What we want," Parker wrote in the black year of 1857, "is work. This time of trouble will make some men consider the chaotic condition of our social system, this antagonistic competition in place of coöperative industry." Organized charity could do something, but that was no answer to the problem. Where charity was organized, beggary was too, and Parker noted that the whole of Boston paddy-land squatted in the anteroom of his own Provident Aid Society. It was downright immoral for industry to make men paupers and then debauch them with charity. What was needed were practical measures: better pay, shorter hours, decent housing (he and Bowditch were trying to get the Legislature to do something about the tenements), lower living costs —free trade was the answer there. These things could be done, by individuals, by the merchant class, by the nation. "If we begin with taking care of the rights of man, it seems easy to take care of the rights of labour and capital. To begin the other way is quite another thing. A nation making laws for the nation is a noble sight." And then that unobtrusive phrase which Parker liked so well and used insistently until it caught the eye of Herndon's friend and was metamorphosed into immortality: "The government of all, by all, and for all, is a Democracy."

There were a score of problems that clamored for attention, and all of them went to the heart of things. Parker did not want to be a professional reformer, a common scold; he had no use for that sort of thing. He did not want to dissipate his energies, to spill over every which way. But he could not help himself. There was an interlocking directorate of reformers, and he was in it, for better or for worse. There had to be give-and-take in this reform business as in everything else. He could not take his contributions down to the office of the *Liberator* but that the editor would ply him with Sabbath reform and non-resistance. He could not serve with Phillips on Vigilance Committees without being ensnared into the Movement for Woman's Rights. If he consulted with Sam Howe about some political scheme, the Chevalier would be sure to tax him with neglecting his duty toward society's wards; if he advised with Sargent on the organization of rescue work, the Temperance Question was bound to come up. When he lectured in Worcester, there was Higginson, aflame with indignation over the mistreatment of women; when he lectured in Philadelphia, there were the Motts, James and Lucretia, to ask him why he stood aloof from the Peace Movement. In Ohio, with Horace Mann, it was education that demanded his attention; in Illinois, Herndon would draw him into politics. He would assure them all (he was rather proud of it) that his name would damn any Society, ruin any cause. But that did no good: if he didn't want to work in the open, he could work in private. Every mail brought some new request for aid; every conference divulged some new plan which needed his support. And after all, why not? He was fair game, he did the same thing to the others, posting letters of advice, sending out calls for aid, rallying the reformers to some scheme for the salvation of society. Every Sunday he gathered them in his parlors in Exeter Place, reformers of every stripe, and a hundred conspiracies would be hatched. How could he excuse himself from any of them?

The point was, you couldn't separate these reform movements, or consign these reformers to any one department. There were exceptions, of course: Theodore Weld whom nothing could distract from the struggle against slavery (nothing but the attractions of obscurity), or Dorothea Dix, who espoused one cause and conquered the world. But most of them, however they began, were Universal Reformers. Only monumental arrogance or the most profound humility could account for it, and they were not all arrogant, these men. Who was more innocent than Bronson Alcott, who invited gentlemen to form a "Club for the Study and Diffusion of Ideas and Tendencies Proper to the Nineteenth Century"? Who more modest than Emerson, but he knew that "where a man comes, there comes revolution." No doubt it was amusing that poor old Robert Owen, who ought to know better, should summon a "World Convention to Emancipate the Human Race from Ignorance, Poverty, Division, Sin, and Misery"; but after all there was a truth here that all of them recognized: you could not capture the battlements of Heaven by a series of disjointed raids.

Take Howe, for instance: he had begun life with a quixotic gesture, but his gesture became as reverent as prayer and set the pattern of his life. "I do not like caution," he said, "it betokens little faith in God's arrangement," and he gave himself to making clear God's purpose with man. God intended men to be free, and Howe threw himself with abandon into the struggle for the liberation of the Greeks and of the Poles, and for the liberation of the American slave, and his opponents could bear witness to his lack of caution. God intended men to use their talents, and Howe brought sight to the blind and speech to the mute and knowledge to the ignorant and surcease to those who were in pain. No worthy cause failed to enlist his support: he was director of the Institution for the Blind and his achievements were famous in two continents; he established a school for the feeble-minded and one for the deaf-mutes; he organized the Prisoner's Aid Society and the Board of State Charities; he served on the Boston School Committee and sustained Mann in his work; he fought all through the slavery struggle and was a tower of strength to the less practical abolitionists. His versatility, his coruscating brilliance, his volcanic energy, sprang from an inner harmony: it was the same man who had the infinite patience to work a miracle with Laura Bridgman and the impetuosity to organize the Kansas Crusade. The most generous, the least fanatical, of men, it was faith, not intolerance, that drove him into so many causes. He fulfilled the logic, he justified the philosophy, of reform.

Or, if you wanted the Universal Reformer, there was Wendell Phillips. "Don't shilly-shally, Wendell," his wife would say, and from his first dramatic appearance on the platform of Faneuil Hall to his last outrageous defiance of the Boston aristocracy, as he charged them with recreancy to justice and humanity and flung in their faces the taunt of Henry IV to Crillon, his life was a demonstration of courage. He had a relentless consistency; he was trained to the bar and he followed the logic of reform as a lawyer follows precedents. He had begun, simply enough, as an abolitionist, and before he knew it, he found himself drawn in as defense attorney for every unpopular cause in Boston. Soon he was agitating the Woman Question, peace, temperance, capital punishment, and a dozen other reforms, and with him agitation took on the mantle of dignity. Soon he was execrated on the

Exchange and ostracized in the Clubs and his name was anathema in all the best houses, he who had been born on Beacon Street and who could look down his nose at half the families on the Hill. He had enlisted for the duration of the war and for him the war never ended, and it was well that Parker did not witness the tragic isolation of his later years as he stunned a generation of smug conservatives and self-righteous liberals with the revolutionary commonplaces of transcendentalism.

Even Garrison revealed the pervasive, the osmotic, force of the reform movement. How mistaken they were who thought of him as an abolitionist merely. "Our country is the world," he said, "our countrymen all mankind," and he meant it literally. Was it a coincidence that his papers were named the *Genius of Universal Emancipation* and the *Liberator?* "I feel somewhat at a loss to know what to do," he confided once to G. W. Benson, "whether to go into all the principles of holy reform and make the abolitionist cause subordinate or whether still to persevere in the one beaten track as hitherto," and John Humphrey Noyes when he visited him, learned that "his mind was heaving with the subject of Holiness and the Kingdom of Heaven and he would devote himself to them as soon as he could get anti-slavery off his hands." But he did not wait for this consummation of his hopes. He espoused as many reforms as did Noyes himself: he was a no-government man, a no-Bible man, a non-resistant; he was a Perfectionist. He had the intolerance of a fanatic and the benevolence of a philosopher. He antagonized every organization, he flouted every institution, he outraged every convention. He was as dangerous to the established order in New England as to the established order in the South, and they were right who dragged him through the streets of Boston with a halter around his neck. No doubt it was most inexpedient of him to imperil the cause of anti-slavery by mixing it up with woman's rights and non-resistance and Sabbath reform and what not; Theodore Weld and Lewis Tappan thought it was downright wicked. But it was Garrison who was consistent, after all, not they. "No man," said Channing, "should take on himself the office of a reformer whose zeal in a particular cause is not tempered by extensive sympathies and universal love." Regardless of consequences, your reformer had to be an eclectic.

Parker knew this as an axiom of philosophy, but it was not so easy to adopt it as a principle of action. Theology, philosophy, Fourierism, Perfectionism, the Dangerous Classes, the Perishing Classes, war, slavery—sometimes his head was in a whirl. There were so many reforms, there was never any end to the things that needed to be done; and he hurried so desperately, trying to keep up with it all, trudging up and down the streets of Boston (there were parish duties, there were Negroes who looked to him), speaking out at every convention, taking on lecture engagements by the score, scratching out letters in his painful scrawl, hundreds of them in a single month, working fourteen, sixteen hours a day, his beard gray, his health shattered, when he was forty-five. But sometimes it was too much for him. He felt that he was being rushed into things; he needed time to think, to get his philosophic bearings.

Here was this Temperance Movement. All of his friends were in it up to their necks: Chevalier Howe and Horace Mann, Lewis Tappan and Gerrit Smith in New York, the Motts in Philadelphia and Sam May in Syracuse. Phillips thundered from the lecture platform, Pierpont wrote poems about it—and a play too; and Garrison edited a temperance journal. Sometimes Parker was ready to believe that it was one of the vital reforms of the century, and he would speak out with a vigor that shocked even the most lethargic, commingling statistics and aphorisms to prove the dreadful consequences of drunkenness. Sometimes he felt that the whole question was befogged in emotion, that all the temperance reformers had the vapors. He distrusted an incapacity for emotion (nothing worse than the dry-rot of Unitarian intellectualism): the contemplation of social statistics never made a drunkard sober. He distrusted an excess of emotion (nothing worse than evangelical revivals): mass meetings and parades managed by Barnum and Company never kept a teetotaler to his pledge. Temperance was a moral question: Neal Dow and John Gough and lusty John Hawkins were on the right track, and Parker cheerfully signed the pledge, with a gold pen, too. Temperance was a scientific question: he read his French treatises and his German monographs and noted the harmful effects of alcohol here and the beneficial effects there. Temperance was a personal matter, a matter for each man to work out for himself, knowing his own character, answerable to his body and his conscience; all sumptuary legislation was worse than useless, coercion in the realm of morals, inviting all sorts of abuses. Temperance was a social problem, society had the right and the duty to protect itself from drunkenness as from disease or crime, and the Maine law was a good thing.

> They have a new law in Maine. It makes the whole State an asylum for the drunkard. . . . The law seems an invasion of private right. It is an invasion, but for the sake of preserving the rights of all. I think wine a good thing; so is beer, rum, brandy, and the like, when rightly used. I think teetotalers are right in their practice *for these times,* but wrong in their principles. I believe it will be found on examination that, other things being equal, men who use stimulants moderately live longer, and have a sounder old age, than teetotalers. But now I think that nine-tenths of the alcoholic stimulus that is used is abused. The evil is so monstrous, so patent, so universal, that it becomes the duty of the State to take care of its citizens; the whole of its parts.

There you had the whole of it, both sides of the question neatly put. If only the agitators wouldn't go to extremes; if only we could have drinking such as he had found in France and Italy and Germany! But the American character was one of extremes, you had to recognize that, after all. If only the reformers wouldn't make drinking a matter of personal morals; he knew perfectly well that there was nothing sinful about drinking, he who, as a boy, had taken Grandmother Parker her daily mug of flip. Yet what was to be done about it all: when he came to Boston there were a thousand grogshops; fifteen years later there was prohibition, but the number had doubled, and every year ten thousand men and women were taken up for drunkenness.

Too bad that the workingman spent his wages at the tippling-house; too bad that the innkeeper flouted the law, dispensing damnation to keep himself and his family alive. But if there were no rich men in the trade, Parker observed, there would soon be no poor ones. It was when you began to trace the infection to its source that you got into trouble. When you described the drunkard's fate your parishioners applauded you, but when you told of the distillers who made the rum and the merchants who sold it, they called you a fanatic and turned you out. Parker had not forgotten how they had treated noble John Pierpont, the cellar of his church filled with barrels of rum, nor how the Unitarians had deserted him, conniving at his dismissal. You could not always gauge the merits of these reforms by the men who advocated them, but you could generally tell something about them from the opposition they aroused. If Parker deprecated the fanaticism of the teetotalers, he was likely to find himself in embarrassing company.

No, it wasn't easy to take sides on all of the reforms, to sign up for every crusade. Here was this question of war. What had Parker to say when Phillips stormed and Garrison declaimed? Here in New England, in his own time, had been inaugurated the greatest of crusades, the crusade to end war: a sailor from Maine and a blacksmith from Connecticut had caught the splendid vision, the great and learned of the world glad to do their bidding. There were peace societies everywhere (even in the South, even in Georgia), and the Legislature of Massachusetts memorialized Congress to arbitrate all disputes, and a million people read Elihu Burritt's "Olive Leaves."

What did Parker think of it all? When Charles Sumner delivered that terrific oration on "The True Grandeur of Nations," standing there so arrogant, so handsome, as he told the representatives of the Army and the Navy, puffed up in their uniforms, that no war was honorable, no peace dishonorable, Parker could not wait to hurry off a note of congratulation. And the next year he was saying the same thing himself, our armies marching on Mexico City, our patriots panting for Darien. "War is an utter violation of Christianity," he said. "If war be right, then Christianity is wrong, false, a lie. Every man who understands Christianity knows that war is wrong." And he proceeded to prove what every man knew. There were fewer classical allusions than Sumner had displayed, but more statistics, and he was churlish indeed who failed to be convinced by this blend of philosophy and figures.

"War is treason to the people, to mankind, to God." But he didn't really mean it, any more than Sumner meant it when fifteen years later the bullets spattered on the ramparts of Fort Sumter. What he meant was that the Mexican War was an infamous war. He would prove it. Here was its genesis, here its secret history, here its shabby purpose. It was conceived in iniquity and prosecuted with brutality and greed. It was inspired by every ignoble motive, it aroused every base passion. He would prove, too, that it was an inexpedient and unprofitable war. Here is what it cost in men, here is what it cost in dollars, and here it what we might have done with the money. Here were the consequences, too—the effect on the morals of the soldiers, the morals of the nation, on domestic politics and international relations. In short, this war was discreditable and dishonorable, and it should not be sustained. When it came to this war, Parker was as ready to preach the duty of civil disobedience as ever Thoreau was, or Edmund Quincy—Thoreau who would not pay taxes to a government that fought an unjust war, Quincy who turned in his commission as Justice of the Peace rather than serve a government that resorted to force. "What shall we do," Parker asked, "in regard to this present war. We can refuse to take any part in it; we can encourage others to do the same; we can aid men, if need be, who suffer because they refuse. Men will call us traitors; what then? That hurt nobody in '76. We are a rebellious nation; our whole history is treason; our blood was attained before we were born; our creeds are infidelity to the mother church; our constitution treason to our fatherland. What of that? Though all the governors in the world bid us commit treason against man, and set the example, let us never submit. Let God only be a master to control our conscience."

All very well for the Mexican War, but what of a war inspired by some lofty motive, fought for some righteous end? What of the war for American Independence (Grandfather

Parker there on Lexington Common: "If they mean to have a war, let it begin here.")? What of a war to end slavery? He was ready enough to give money for Beecher's Bibles and for old John Brown; for ten years his letters were filled with the irrepressible conflict, and he did not deprecate it. A war for liberty was a very different thing from a war for greed. "I think," he wrote to Frances Cobbe, "we should agree about war. I hate it, I deplore it, but yet see its necessity. All the great charters of humanity have been *writ in blood,* and must continue to be for some centuries. I should let the Italians fight for their liberty till the twenty-eight million men were only fourteen million."

He was no non-resistant, not he. All very well for the Quakers to make pacifism an article of faith, the gentle Whittier wishing men

> Free, not by blood; redeemed, but not by crime,
> Each fetter broken; but in God's good time.

All very well for Garrison, to whom all government was odious. ("There is such a thing," said William Ladd, "as going beyond the Millennium.") But he was the grandson of Captain Parker, and two muskets from Lexington hung over the desk in his study; he would counsel any fugitive to sell his life dearly, and he was ready to storm the Court House any day if that would save an Anthony Burns.

Was he a spiritual Martha, distracted about much serving and troubled about many things? He had abandoned himself to good works, yet every year the state of society seemed more desperate. He had sounded a hundred blasts on the trumpet of reform and the walls of Hunkerdom still stood. What was he about, worrying institutions, exacerbating his fellow men, making a public nuisance of himself? "I am the best hated man in America," he could admit, and to what purpose? Perhaps Emerson was right: "Why so hot, my little man," he had said, and again, "There is a sublime prudence which, believing in a vast future, sure of more to come than is yet seen, postpones always the present hour to the whole life." Parker had been schooled in all the philosophies, even Stoicism, but he had never found Emerson's sublime prudence. A minister, he dwelt in eternity; a scientist, he took a million years in his stride, but he could never postpone the present hour even for the morrow. He had an invincible faith in the future, but he acted as if every moment were the last, as if salvation had to come now, or never.

He knew better. He knew that social institutions were a long and complex growth, that social improvement was gradual, not always to be seen in one generation or even in one century. He subscribed to the theory of Progress and was on familiar terms with the doctrine of Evolution. "It takes a deal of time to accomplish any great work of human progress," he wrote. "It is with men as with the geological formation of the earth." (Did he remember Lyell's book, there on his shelves?) "Enormous periods of time are found indispensable for what we once thought was done in six days. How many thousand experiments must go to one human success in the great departments of our progress. When the civilization you and I dream of is attained, men will find it is underlaid by thick strata full of the organic remains of inferior civilizations, each helpful to the higher one, which itself is no finality, but only provisional for something more grand and glorious." And again, he said to the Progressive Friends: "In the world of matter you find a Plan everywhere, things working out in order." (Did he remember those lectures by Geoffroy St. Hilaire he had thought so brilliant at the time?) "All is orderly, never a break in the line of continuity. In the fossil animals which perished a million years ago you find proximate formations which point to man; nay, yet further back in the structure of the earth, the fashion of the solar system itself, do we find finger-posts which indicate the road to humanity, distinctly pointing unto man."

Things were bound to come out all right in the end. Given time enough, Man would fulfill his destiny. "We have seen only the beginning," Parker assured his friends, "the future triumphs of the race must be vastly greater than all accomplished yet," and it was an echo of Priestley's famous boast, "Whatever was in the beginning of this world, the end will be glorious and paradisiacal beyond what our imagination can now conceive." Yet this faith in the future, this ineffable confidence in progress, did not lead to fatalism, any more than belief in predestination had led to fatalism among the Puritans. Granted that the best was yet to be, the last of life for which the first was made, was that to temper his enthusiasm or paralyze his thought? He himself was part of the evolutionary process; his work of reform in harmony with the plan of the Universe. The doctrine of evolution served merely to authenticate transcendental hope, to justify idealism. It added the experience of all mankind to the experience of the individual man; it brought the support of science to the intuitions of the soul.

So Parker went from philosophy to philanthropy and he justified himself. To his parcel of *a priori* principles and intuitive truths he added this doctrine of evolution; he balanced them all on his shoulders (easy enough, if you knew the trick) and went doughtily on his way. He lived in the wonderful afterglow of the Enlightenment, reason tinged with humanitarianism, realism with romanticism. He lived in an age of faith and hope, in a country where all things seemed possible. He was the heir of the rationalists, but their skepticism seemed irrelevant, here, in America. He was the heir of the idealists, and their abstractions seemed concrete, here in this brave new world. He was warmed by the first generous winds of science, and they brought certainty, not doubt. He knew that reason would triumph over unreason, that the righteous would be filled. He knew that Paradise Lost would be Regained. All the evils that afflicted mankind would pass away—vice and crime, poverty and ignorance, war and disease.

All evils would pass away—even the greatest of them, even slavery.

## *For Further Reading*

The most able narrative of the bewildering variety of antebellum reform movements is still Alice Felt Tyler, *Freedom's*

*Ferment* (1944). A good, brief interpretative essay is C. S. Griffin, *The Ferment for Reform* (1967). The dark side of reform—American nativism—is chronicled by Ray Allen Billington, *The Protestant Crusade, 1800–1860* (1938). Reform's multiple religious settings have been dealt with by Whitney R. Cross, *The Burned-Over District* (1950); Timothy L. Smith, *Revivalism & Social Reform* (1957); C. S. Griffin, *Their Brother's Keepers* (1960); and Octavius B. Frothingham, *Transcendentalism in New England* (1876).

For accounts of individual reform movements see, on education: Rush Welter, *Popular Education and Democratic Thought* (1962); on poverty: Robert H. Bremner, *From the Depths* (1956); on women's rights: Eleanor Flexner, *A Century of Struggle* (1959), and Robert E. Riegel, *American Feminists* (1963); on temperance: John A. Krout, *The Origins of Prohibition* (1925), and Frank L. Byrne's biography of Neal Dow, *Prophet of Prohibition* (1961); on penal reform: W. David Lewis, *From Newgate to Dannemora* (1965), and Blake McKelvey, *American Prisons* (1936); on utopianism and communitarianism: Donald Egbert and Stow Persons, eds., *Socialism and American Life* (1952), and Arthur Bestor, *Backwoods Utopias* (1950); and on pacifism: Merle Curti, *The American Peace Crusade* (1929).

Three fine syntheses on abolition, the chief antebellum reform movement, are Louis Filler, *The Crusade Against Slavery* (1960), Dwight L. Dumond, *Antislavery* (1961), and Gilbert H. Barnes, *The Antislavery Impulse* (1933). A convenient collection of perceptive essays is Martin Duberman, ed., *The Antislavery Vanguard* (1965). One of the best biographies of an abolitionist is John L. Thomas, *The Liberator* (1963), a study of William Lloyd Garrison; other useful biographies are Irving H. Bartlett, *Wendell Phillips* (1961), and Benjamin P. Thomas, *Theodore Weld* (1950).

# Slavery and Personality

## Stanley Elkins

"Slavery was the greatest misery, the greatest wrong, the greatest curse to white and black alike that America has ever known." So wrote historian Allan Nevins in 1947. Few Americans today would dispute his assessment. The bitter heritage of the South's "peculiar institution"—the long and durable economic, social, and political subservience of blacks freed by war but repressed by white racism in peace—has proved him right beyond peradventure of doubt. Cities scarred by ghettos and violence, suburbs ridden by fears of Negro neighbors, and civil-rights workers exposed to hatred and assassins' bullets are the familiar testimonies to deep divisions born in slavery.

Historians, however, have not always agreed about the impact of slavery on American life. Controversy over the moral implications of holding Afro-Americans in enforced bondage waged unceasingly from the eighteenth century on; not until the decade of the 1940's had unanimity been achieved. The long and acrimonious debate,

*Source:* Stanley M. Elkins, *Slavery: A Problem in American Institutional & Intellectual Life* (Chicago: University of Chicago Press, 1959), pp. 81–89, 98–133. Copyright © 1959 by the University of Chicago. Reprinted by permission of the author and publisher.

joined early by Southern apologists and Northern critics, rapidly took on a sectional cast. From the 1820's through the 1850's publicists like William Harper, James H. Hammond, W. Gilmore Simms, Thomas R. Dew, George Fitzhugh, and John C. Calhoun proposed that their peculiar institution was divinely ordained, naturally ordered, and benevolently disposed. Fitzhugh, for example, observed that "the negro slaves of the South are the happiest, and, in some sense, the freest people in the world.... They enjoy liberty, because they are oppressed neither by care nor labor." Northern abolitionists challenged these views. Richard Hildreth, Frederick Law Olmstead, William Lloyd Garrison, and other Northern abolitionists heaped scorn on the Southerners' defense. Garrison assailed the "divinely ordained" argument by citing the Declaration of Independence's "self-evident" truths that all men are created equal. As for the "natural order" defense, Hildreth observed that "the relation of master and slave, like most other kinds of despotism, has its origins in war. By the confession of its warrant defenders, slavery is at best, but a substitute for homicide. ... The relation of master and slave ... is a relation purely of force and terror."

The Civil War freed the slaves but it did not still the argument. By the early decades of the twentieth century Southern historians had renewed, embellished, and confirmed the general position of their antebellum forerunners. The chief architect of the postbellum defense of slavery was Ulrich Bonnell Phillips. Phillips, born in Georgia in 1877, devoted his energies to an analysis of the antebellum South. His two major works, *American Negro Slavery* (1918) and *Life and Labor in the Old South* (1930), were based mainly on original manuscript sources of the large plantations. Phillips viewed slavery fundamentally as an institution of racial accommodation. Two races of unequal capacities, he asserted, could not live in harmony side by side without the superior one exerting paternal guidance on the inferior: "On the whole the plantations were the best schools yet invented for the mass training of that sort of inert and backward people which the bulk of American negroes represented. . . . The slave plantation regime, after having wrought the initial and irreparable misfortune of causing the negroes to be imported, did at least as much as any system possible in the period could have done toward adapting the bulk of them to life in a civilized community." Slaves, on the whole, were happy under the benevolent tutelage of white masters. Phillips concluded that "it is impossible to agree that [slavery's] basis and its operations were wholly evil, the law and the prophets to the contrary notwithstanding."

Phillips' influence was pervasive; by the time of his death in 1934 the academic community generally had been impressed with his thorough, mellow, and insightful view of the peculiar institution. But even at the height of his acceptance, demurrers had been entered against his racism and his research methods. In 1944 Gunnar Myrdal, a Swedish scholar, produced *The American Dilemma,* a work that clinically exposed the inherent racial tensions in American society. White Americans, ideologically committed to human equality and freedom, practiced both blatant and covert repression of their black fellow citizens. More fundamentally, Myrdal's work—along with a generation of anthropological studies—undercut the prevailing notions about the alleged Negro racial inferiority. Ten years later, the historical synthesis on slavery had come full circle. Kenneth Stampp, in his book *The Peculiar Institution,* using many of Phillips' sources, answered the Georgian's benevolent view of slavery. Stampp proceeded from the assumption that Negroes were white men with black skins. Slavery was not a training institution to civilize Negroes; it was merely a school to make better slaves. By nature the peculiar institution was cruel and harsh; by nature slaves rebelled against repression either by insurrections or, more often, by "shirking their duties, injuring the crops, feigning illness, and disrupting the routine." Stampp's work culminated the historical controversy on the ethical question of slavery; it stands as the logical sequel to the Northern antebellum critics of slavery, the Radical Republicans, and the notes of protest against the Phillips' view sounded by Negro historians (like Carter Woodson and William Du Bois) during the first half of the twentieth century, and by the Marxist historian of Negro slave revolts, Herbert Aptheker.

With the main ethical question laid to rest after more than a century of discussion, historical accounts of slavery have taken new directions. Among others, the question of slavery's profitability has received additional attention. Whether slavery paid a profit to masters, of course, does have moral overtones; if not, for example, then a war to eliminate the institution was perhaps unnecessary. Nonetheless scholars have attempted to divest their inquiry of such themes and concentrate on technical research, although the results to date are inconclusive. Some students, moreover, viewing slavery as an undergirding of an entire cultural way of life, point out that profitable or not the institution could not have been overturned without conflict.

Another approach to slavery has proved to be most exciting—and controversial. In 1959, Stanley Elkins published a slim volume with the unpretentious title *Slavery*. His essay surveyed slavery as a historiographical problem, as an institution in a time of institutional instability, as a force in affecting the slave's personality, and as a challenge to contemporary Northern and Southern intellectuals. In the selection that follows, extracted from the most controversial portion of his work, the reader can see Elkins' innovative techniques. He relies heavily on works by scholars in the behavioral sciences of psychology and sociology. This cross-disciplinary approach to historical inquiry, not often attempted by historians, gives Elkins vantage points from which new insights can be achieved. The use of the Nazi concentration camp analogy, for instance, is a brilliant comparative method to illuminate the nature of the slave's personality.

Elkins' work marks a turning point in the study of antebellum slavery. Already, to be sure, he has been attacked sharply. Traditionalists are disturbed by his failure to utilize original sources of Southern plantation slavery, radicals dislike his alleged conservatism, and blacks have denied the existence of any large numbers of fawning subservient "Sambo" types among the slaves. Others have criticized in particular the concentration camp analogy.

The overly dramatic quality of the analogy may, they suggest, actually obscure the point he attempts to make; moreover, he may have overstressed the extent of infantilization that actually occurred at Belsen and Buchenwald. Still others contest Elkins' observations about the differences between Latin American and Southern slavery; the two systems were more similar, they argue, than different.

Despite the varied criticism of the work, Elkins has opened new fields for inquiry. It will be difficult for future historians of antebellum slavery to ignore his contribution.

An examination of American slavery, checked at certain critical points against a very different slave system, that of Latin America, reveals that a major key to many of the contrasts between them was an institutional key: The presence or absence of other powerful institutions in society made an immense difference in the character of slavery itself. In Latin America, the very tension and balance among three kinds of organizational concerns—church, crown, and plantation agriculture—prevented slavery from being carried by the planting class to its ultimate logic. For the slave, in terms of the space thus allowed for the development of men and women as moral beings, the result was an "open system": a system of contacts with free society through which ultimate absorption into that society could and did occur with great frequency. The rights of personality implicit in the ancient traditions of slavery and in the church's most venerable assumptions on the nature of the human soul were thus in a vital sense conserved, whereas to a staggering extent the very opposite was true in North American slavery. The latter system had developed virtually unchecked by institutions having anything like the power of their Latin counterparts; the legal structure which supported it, shaped only by the demands of a staple-raising capitalism, had defined with such nicety the slave's character as chattel that his character as a moral individual was left in the vaguest of legal obscurity. In this sense American slavery operated as a "closed" system—one in which, for the generality of slaves in their nature as men and women, *sub specie aeternitatis,* contacts with free society could occur only on the most narrowly circumscribed of terms. The next question is whether living within such a "closed system" might not have produced noticeable effects upon the slave's very personality.

The name "Sambo" has come to be synonymous with "race stereotype." Here is an automatic danger signal, warning that the analytical difficulties of asking questions about slave personality may not be nearly so great as the moral difficulties. The one inhibits the other; the morality of the matter has had a clogging effect on its theoretical development that may not be to the best interests of either. And yet theory on group personality is still in a stage rudimentary enough that this particular body of material—potentially illuminating—ought not to remain morally impounded any longer.

Is it possible to deal with "Sambo" as a type? The characteristics that have been claimed for the type come principally from Southern lore. Sambo, the typical plantation slave, was docile but irresponsible, loyal but lazy, humble but chronically given to lying and stealing; his behavior was full of infantile silliness and his talk inflated with childish exaggeration. His relationship with his master was one of utter dependence and childlike attachment: it was indeed this childike quality that was the very key to his being. Although the merest hint of Sambo's "manhood" might fill the Southern breast with scorn, the child, "in his place," could be both exasperating and lovable.

We he real or unreal? What order of existence, what rank of legitimacy, should be accorded him? Is there a "scientific" way to talk about this problem? For most Southerners in 1860 it went without saying not only that Sambo was real—that he was a dominant plantation type—but also that his characteristics were the clear product of racial inheritance. That was one way to deal with Sambo, a way that persisted a good many years after 1860. But in recent times, the discrediting, as unscientific, of racial explanations for any feature of plantation slavery has tended in the case of Sambo to discredit not simply the explanation itself but also the thing it was supposed to explain. Sambo is a mere stereotype—"stereotype" is itself a bad word, insinuating racial inferiority and invidious discrimination. This modern approach to Sambo had a strong counterpart in the way Northern reformers thought about slavery in antebellum times: they thought that nothing could actually be said about the Negro's "true" nature because that nature was veiled by the institution of slavery. It could only be revealed by tearing away the veil. In short, no order of reality could be given to assertions about slave character, because those assertions were illegitimately grounded on race, whereas their only basis was a corrupt and "unreal" institution. "To be sure," a recent writer concedes, "there were plenty of opportunists among the Negroes who played the role assigned to them, acted the clown, and curried the favor of their masters in order to win the maximum rewards within the system. . . ." To impeach Sambo's legitimacy in this way is the next thing to talking him out of existence.

There ought, however, to be still a third way of dealing with the Sambo picture, some formula for taking it seriously. The picture has far too many circumstantial details, its hues have been stroked in by too many different brushes, for it to be denounced as counterfeit. Too much folk-knowledge, too much plantation literature, too much of the Negro's own lore, have gone into its making to entitle one in good conscience to condemn it as "conspiracy." One searches in vain through the literature of the Latin-American slave systems for the "Sambo" of our tradition—the perpetual child incapable of maturity. How is this to be explained? If Sambo is not a product of race (that "explanation" can be consigned to oblivion) and not simply a product of "slavery" in the abstract (other societies have had slavery), then he must be related to our own peculiar variety of it. And if Sambo is uniquely an American product, then his existence, and the reasons for his character, must be recognized in order to appreciate the very scope of our slave problem and its aftermath. The absoluteness with which such a personality ("real" or "unreal") had been stamped upon the plantation slave does much to make plausible the ante-bellum Southerner's difficulty in imagining that blacks anywhere could be anything but a degraded race—and its goes far to explain his failure to see any sense at all in abolitionism. It even casts light on the peculiar quality of abolitionism itself; it was so all-enveloping a problem in human personality that our abolitionists could literally not afford to recognize it. Virtually without exception, they met this dilemma either by sidetracking it altogether (they explicitly refused to advance plans for solving it, arguing that this would rob their message of its moral force) or by countering it with theories of infinite human perfectibility. The question of personality, therefore, becomes a crucial phase of the entire problem of slavery in the United States, having conceivably something to do with the difference—already alluded to—between an "open" and a "closed" system of slavery.

If it were taken for granted that a special type existed in significant numbers on American plantations, closer connections might be made with a growing literature on personality and character types, the investigation of which has become a widespread, respectable, and productive enterprise among our psychologists and social scientists. Realizing that, it might then seem not quite so dangerous to add that the type corresponded in its major outlines to "Sambo."

Let the above, then, be a preface to the argument of the present essay. It will be assumed that there were elements in the very structure of the plantation system—its "closed" character—that could sustain infantilism as a normal feature of behavior. These elements, having less to do with "cruelty" per se than simply with the sanctions of authority, were effective and pervasive enough to require that such infantilism be characterized as something much more basic than mere "accommodation." It will be assumed that the sanctions of the system were in themselves sufficient to produce a recognizable personality type.

It should be understood that to identify a social type in this sense is still to generalize on a fairly crude level—and to insist for a limited purpose on the legitimacy of such generalizing is by no means to deny that, on more refined levels, a great profusion of individual types might have been observed in slave society. Nor need it be claimed that the "Sambo" type, even in the relatively crude sense employed here, was a universal type. It was, however, a plantation type, and a plantation existence embraced well over half the slave population. Two kinds of material will be used in the effort to picture the mechanisms whereby this adjustment to absolute power—an adjustment whose end product included infantile features of behavior—may have been effected. One is drawn from the theoretical knowledge presently available in social psychology, and the other, in the form of an analogy, is derived from some of the data that have come out of the German concentration camps. It is recognized in most theory that social behavior is regulated in some general way by adjustment to symbols of authority—however diversely "authority" may be defined either in theory or in culture itself—and that such adjustment is closely related to the very formation of personality. A corollary would be, of course, that the more diverse those symbols of authority may be, the greater is the permissible variety of adjustment to them —and the wider the margin of individuality, consequently, in the development of the self. The question here has to do with the wideness or narrowness of that margin on the ante-bellum plantation.

The other body of material, involving an experience undergone by several million men and women in the concentration camps of our own time, contains certain items of relevance to the problem here being considered. The experience was analogous to that of slavery and was one in which wide-scale instances of infantilization were observed. The material is sufficiently detailed, and sufficiently documented by men who not only took part in the experience itself but who were versed in the use of psychological theory for analyzing it, that the advantages of drawing upon such data for purposes of analogy seem to outweigh the possible risks.

The introduction of this second body of material must to a certain extent govern the theoretical strategy itself. It has been recognized both implicitly and explicitly that the psychic impact and effects of the concentration-camp experience were not anticipated in existing theory and that consequently such theory would require some major supplementation. It might be added, parenthetically, that almost any published discussion of this modern Inferno, no matter how learned, demonstrates how "theory," operating at such a level of shared human experience, tends to shed much of its technical trappings and to take on an almost literary quality. The experience showed, in any event, that infantile personality features could be induced in a relatively short time among large numbers of adult human beings coming from very diverse backgrounds. The particular strain which was thus placed upon prior theory consisted in the need to make room not only for the cultural and environmental sanctions that sustain personality (which in a sense Freudian theory already had) but also for a virtually unanticipated problem: actual change in the personality of masses of adults. It forced a reappraisal and new appreciation of how completely and effectively prior cultural sanctions for behavior and personality could be detached to make way for new and different sanctions, and of how adjustments could be made by individuals to a species of authority vastly different from any previously known. The revelation for theory was the process of detachment.

These cues, accordingly, will guide the argument on Negro slavery. Several million people were detached with a peculiar effectiveness from a great variety of cultural backgrounds in Africa—a detachment operating with infinitely more effectiveness upon those brought to North America than upon those who came to Latin America. It was achieved partly by the shock experience inherent in the very mode of procurement but more specifically by the type of authority-system to which they were introduced and to which they had to adjust for physical and psychic survival. The new adjustment, to absolute power in a closed system, involved infantilization, and the detachment was so complete that little trace of prior (and thus alternative) cultural sanctions for behavior and personality remained for the descendants of the first generation. For them, adjustment to clear and omnipresent authority could be more or less automatic—as much so, or as little, as it is for anyone whose adjustment to a social system begins at birth and to whom that system represents normality. We do not know how generally a full adjustment was made by the first generation of fresh slaves from Africa. But we do know—from a modern experience—that such an adjustment is possible, not only within the same generation but within two or three years. This proved possible for people in a full state of complex civilization, for men and women who were not black and not savages.

* * * * *

We may suppose that every African who became a slave underwent an experience whose crude psychic impact must have been staggering and whose consequences superseded anything that had ever previously happened to him. Some effort should therefore be made to picture the series of shocks which must have accompanied the principal events of that enslavement.

The majority of slaves appear to have been taken in native wars, which meant that no one—neither persons of high rank nor warriors of prowess—was guaranteed against capture and enslavement. Great numbers were caught in surprise attacks upon their villages, and since the tribes acting as middlemen for the trade had come to depend on regular supplies of captives in order to maintain that function, the distinction between wars and raiding expeditions tended to be very dim. The first shock, in an experience destined to endure many months and to leave its survivors irrevocably changed, was thus the shock of capture. It is an effort to remember that while enslavement occurred in Africa every day, to the individual it occurred just once.

The second shock—the long march to the sea—drew out the nightmare for many weeks. Under the glaring sun, through the steaming jungle, they were driven along like beasts tied together by their necks; day after day, eight or more hours at a time, they would stagger barefoot over thorny underbrush, dried reeds, and stones. Hardship, thirst, brutalities, and near starvation penetrated the experience of each exhausted man and woman who reached the coast. One traveler tells of seeing hundreds of bleaching skeltons strewn along one of the slave caravan routes. But then the man who must interest us is the man who survived—he who underwent the entire experience, of which this was only the beginning.

The next shock, aside from the fresh physical torments which accompanied it, was the sale to the European slavers. After being crowded into pens near the trading stations and kept there overnight, sometimes for days, the slaves were brought out for examination. Those rejected would be abandoned to starvation; the remaining ones—those who had been bought—were branded, given numbers inscribed on leaden tags, and herded on shipboard.

The episode that followed—almost too protracted and stupefying to be called a mere "shock"—was the dread Middle Passage, brutalizing to any man, black or white, ever to be involved with it. The holds, packed with squirming and suffocating humanity, became stinking infernos of filth and pestilence. Stories of disease, death, and cruelty on the terrible two-month voyage abound in the testimony which did much toward ending the British slave trade forever.

The final shock in the process of enslavement came with the Negro's introduction to the West Indies. Bryan Edwards, describing the arrival of a slave ship, writes of how in times of labor scarcity crowds of people would come scrambling aboard, manhandling the slaves and throwing them into panic. The Jamaica legislature eventually "corrected the enormity" by enacting that the sales be held on shore. Edwards felt a certain mortification at seeing the Negroes exposed naked in public, similar to that felt by the trader Degrandpré at seeing them examined back at the African factories. Yet here they did not seem to care. "They display . . . very few signs of lamentation for their past or of apprehension for their future condition; but . . . commonly express great eagerness to be sold." The "seasoning" process which followed completed the series of steps whereby the African Negro became a slave.

The mortality had been very high. One-third of the numbers

first taken, out of a total of perhaps fifteen million, had died on the march and at the trading stations; another third died during the Middle Passage and the seasoning. Since a majority of the African-born slaves who came to the North American plantations did not come directly but were imported through the British West Indies, one may assume that the typical slave underwent an experience something like that just outlined. This was the man—one in three—who had come through it all and lived and was about to enter our "closed system." What would he be like if he survived and adjusted to that?

Actually, a great deal had happened to him already. Much of his past had been annihilated; nearly every prior connection had been severed. Not that he had really "forgotten" all these things—his family and kinship arrangements, his language, the tribal religion, the taboos, the name he had once borne, and so on—but none of it any longer carried much meaning. The old values, the sanctions, the standards, already unreal, could no longer furnish him guides for conduct, for adjusting to the expectations of a complete new life. Where then was he to look for new standards, new cues—who would furnish them now? He could now look to none but his master, the one man to whom the system had committed his entire being: the man upon whose will depended his food, his shelter, his sexual connections, whatever moral instruction he might be offered, whatever "success" was possible within the system, his very security—in short, everything.

The thoroughness with which African Negroes coming to America were detached from prior cultural sanctions should thus be partly explainable by the very shock sequence inherent in the technique of procurement. But it took something more than this to produce "Sambo," and it is possible to overrate—or at least to overgeneralize—this shock sequence in the effort to explain what followed. A comparable experience was also undergone by slaves coming into Latin America, where very little that resembled our "Sambo" tradition would ever develop. We should also remember that, in either case, it was only the first generation that actually experienced these shocks.

It could even be argued that the shock sequence is not an absolute necessity for explaining "Sambo" at all.

So whereas the Middle Passage and all that went with it must have been psychologically numbing, and should probably be regarded as a long thrust, at least, toward the end product, it has little meaning considered apart from what came later. It may be assumed that the process of detachment was completed—and, as it were, guaranteed—by the kind of "closed" authority-system into which the slave was introduced and to which he would have to adjust. At any rate, a test of this detachment and its thoroughness is virtually ready-made. Everyone who has looked into the problem of African cultural features surviving among New World Negroes agrees that the contrast between North America and Latin America is immense. In Brazil, survivals from African religion are not only to be encountered everywhere, but such carry-overs are so distinct that they may even be identified with particular tribal groups. "The Negro religions and cults," Arthur Ramos adds, "were not the only form of cultural expression which survived in Brazil. The number of folklore survivals is extremely large, the prolongation of social institutions, habits, practices and events from Africa." Fernando Ortiz, writing of Cuba in 1905, saw the African witchcraft cults flourishing on the island as a formidable social problem. One of our own anthropologists, on the other hand, despite much dedicated field work, has been put to great effort to prove that in North American Negro society any African cultural vestiges have survived at all.

A certain amount of the mellowness in Ulrich Phillips' picture of ante-bellum plantation life has of necessity been discredited by recent efforts not only to refocus attention upon the brutalities of the slave system but also to dispose once and for all of Phillips' assumptions about the slave as a racially inferior being. And yet it is important—particularly in view of the analogy about to be presented—to keep in mind that for all the system's cruelties there were still clear standards of patriarchal benevolence inherent in its human side, and that such standards were recognized as those of the best Southern families. This aspect, despite the most drastic changes of emphasis, should continue to guarantee for Phillips' view more than just a modicum of legitimacy; the patriarchal quality, whatever measure of benevolence or lack of it one wants to impute to the regime, still holds a major key to its nature as a social system.

Introducing, therefore, certain elements of the German concentration-camp experience involves the risky business of trying to balance two necessities—emphasizing both the vast dissimilarities of the two regimes and the essentially limited purpose for which they are being brought together, and at the same time justifying the use of the analogy in the first place. The point is perhaps best made by insisting on an order of classification. The American plantation was not even in the metaphorical sense a "concentration camp"; nor was it even "like" a concentration camp, to the extent that any standards comparable to those governing the camps might be imputed to any sector of American society, at any time; but it should at least be permissible to turn the thing around—to speak of the concentration camp as a special and highly perverted instance of human slavery. Doing so, moreover, should actually be of some assistance in the strategy, now universally sanctioned, of demonstrating how little the products and consequences of slavery ever had to do with race. The only mass experience that Western people have had within recorded history comparable in any way with Negro slavery was undergone in the nether world of Nazism. The concentration camp was not only a perverted slave system; it was also—what is less obvious but even more to the point—a perverted patriarchy.

The system of the concentration camps was expressly devised in the 1930's by high officials of the German government to function as an instrument of terror. The first groups detained in the camps consisted of prominent enemies of the Nazi regime; later, when these had mostly been eliminated, it was still felt necessary that the system be institutionalized and made into a standing weapon of intimidation—which required a continuing flow of incoming prisoners. The categories of eligible persons were greatly widened to include all real, fancied, or "potential" opposition to the state. They were often selected on capricious and random grounds, and together they formed a cross-section of society which was virtually complete: criminals, workers, businessmen, professional people, middle-class Jews, even members of the aristocracy. The teeming camps thus held all kinds—not only the scum of the underworld but also countless men and women of culture and refinement. During the war a specialized objective was added, that of exterminating the Jewish populations of subject countries, which required special mass-production methods of which the gas chambers and crematories of Auschwitz-Birkenau were outstanding examples. Yet the basic technique was everywhere and at all times the same: the deliberate infliction of various forms of torture upon the incoming prisoners in such a way as to break their resistance and make way for their degradation as individuals. These brutalities were not merely "permitted" or "encouraged"; they were prescribed. Duty in the camps was a mandatory phase in the training of SS guards, and it was here that particular efforts were made to overcome their scruples and to develop in them a capacity for relishing spectacles of pain and anguish.

The concentration camps and everything that took place in them were veiled in the utmost isolation and secrecy. Of course complete secrecy was impossible, and a continuing stream of rumors circulated among the population. At the same time so repellent was the nature of these stories that in their enormity they transcended the experience of nearly everyone who heard them; in self-protection it was somehow necessary to persuade oneself that they could not really be true. The results, therefore, contained elements of the diabolical. The undenied existence of the camps cast a shadow of nameless dread over the entire population; on the other hand the *individual* who actually became a prisoner in one of them was in most cases devastated with fright and utterly demoralized to discover that what was happening to *him* was not less, but rather far more terrible than anything he had imagined. The shock sequence of "procurement," therefore, together with the initial phases of the prisoner's introduction to camp life, is not without significance in assessing some of the psychic effects upon those who survived as long-term inmates.

The arrest was typically made at night, preferably late; this was standing Gestapo policy, designed to heighten the element of shock, terror, and unreality surrounding the arrest. After a day or so in the police jail came the next major shock, that of being transported to the camp itself. "This transportation into the camp, and the 'initiation' into it," writes Bruno Bettelheim (an ex-inmate of Dachau and Buchenwald), "is often the first torture which the prisoner has ever experienced and is, as a rule, physically and psychologically the worst torture to which he will ever be exposed." It involved a planned series of brutalities inflicted by guards making repeated rounds through the train over a twelve- to thirty-six-hour period during which the prisoner was prevented from resting. If transported in cattle cars instead of passenger cars, the prisoners were sealed in, under conditions not dissimilar to those of the Middle Passage. Upon their arrival—if the camp was one in which mass exterminations were carried out—there might be sham ceremonies designed to reassure temporarily the exhausted prisoners, which meant that the fresh terrors in the offing would then strike them with redoubled impact. An SS officer might deliver an address, or a band might be playing popular tunes, and it would be in such a setting that the initial "selection" was made. The newcomers would file past an SS doctor who indicated, with a motion of the forefinger, whether they were to go to the left or to the right. To one side went those considered capable of heavy labor; to the other would go wide categories of "undesirables"; those in the latter group were being condemned to the gas chambers. Those who remained would undergo the formalities of "registration," full of indignities, which culminated in the marking of each prisoner with a number.

There were certain physical and psychological strains of camp life, especially debilitating in the early stages, which should be classed with the introductory shock sequence. There was a state of chronic hunger whose pressures were unusually effective in detaching prior scruples of all kinds; even the sexual instincts no longer functioned in the face of the drive for food. The man who at his pleasure could bestow or withhold food thus wielded, for that reason alone, abnormal power. Another strain at first was the demand for absolute obedience, the slightest deviation from which brought savage punishments. The prisoner had to ask permission—by no means granted as a matter of course—even to defecate. The power of the SS guard, as the prisoner was hourly reminded, was that of life and death over his body. A more exquisite form of pressure lay in the fact that the prisoner had never a moment of solitude: he no longer had a private existence; it was no longer possible, in any imaginable sense, for him to be an "individual."

Another factor having deep disintegrative effects upon the prisoner was the prospect of a limitless future in the camp. In the immediate sense this meant that he could no longer make plans for the future. But there would eventually be a subtler meaning: it made the break with the outside world a *real* break; in time the "real" life would become the life of the camp, the outside world an abstraction. Had it been a limited detention, whose end could be calculated, one's outside relationships—one's roles, one's very "personality"—might temporarily have been laid aside, to be reclaimed more or less intact at the end of the term. Here, however, the prisoner was faced with the apparent impossibility of his old roles or even his old personality ever having any future at all; it became more and more difficult to imagine himself resuming them. It was this that underlay the "egalitarianism" of the camps; old statuses had lost their meaning. A final strain, which must have been particularly acute for the newcomer, was the omnipresent threat of death and the very unpredictable suddenness with which death might strike. Quite aside from the periodic gas-chamber selections, the guards in their sports and caprices were at liberty to kill any prisoner any time.

In the face of all this, one might suppose that the very notion of an "adjustment" would be grotesque. The majority of those who entered the camps never came out again, but our concern here has to be with those who survived—an estimated

700,000 out of nearly eight million. For them, the regime must be considered not as a system of death but as a way of life. These survivors did make an adjustment of some sort to the system; it is they themselves who report it. After the initial shocks, what was the nature of the "normality" that emerged?

A dramatic species of psychic displacement seems to have occurred at the very outset. This experience, described as a kind of "splitting of personality," has been noted by most of the inmates who later wrote of their imprisonment. The very extremity of the initial tortures produced in the prisoner what actually amounted to a sense of detachment; these brutalities went so beyond his own experience that they became somehow incredible—they seemed to be happening no longer to him but almost to someone else. "[The author] has no doubt," writes Bruno Bettelheim, "that he was able to endure the transportation, and all that followed, because right from the beginning he became convinced that these horrible and degrading experiences somehow did not happen to 'him' as a subject, but only to 'him' as an object." This subject-object "split" appears to have served a double function: not only was it an immediate psychic defense mechanism against shock, but it also acted as the first thrust toward a new adjustment. This splitting-off of a special "self"—a self which endured the tortures but which was not the "real" self—also provided the first glimpse of a new personality which, being not "real," would not need to feel bound by the values which guided the individual in his former life. "The prisoners' feelings," according to Mr. Bettelheim, "could be summed up by the following sentence: 'What I am doing here, or what is happening to me, does not count at all; here everything is permissible as long and insofar as it contributes to helping me survive in the camp'."

One part of the prisoner's being was thus, under sharp stress, brought to the crude realization that he must thenceforth be governed by an entire new set of standards in order to live. Mrs. Lingens-Reiner puts it bluntly: "Will you survive, or shall I? As soon as one sensed that this was at stake everyone turned egotist." ". . . I think it of primary importance," writes Dr. Cohen, "to take into account that the superego acquired new values in a concentration camp, so much at variance with those which the prisoner bore with him into camp that the latter faded." But then this acquisition of "new values" did not all take place immediately; it was not until some time after the most acute period of stress was over that the new, "unreal" self would become at last the "real" one.

"If you survive the first three months you will survive the next three years." Such was the formula transmitted from the old prisoners to the new ones, and its meaning lay in the fact that the first three months would generally determine a prisoner's capacity for survival and adaptation. "Be inconspicuous": this was the golden rule. The prisoner who called attention to himself, even in such trivial matters as the wearing of glasses, risked doom. Any show of bravado, any heroics, any kind of resistance condemned a man instantly. There were no rewards for martyrdom: not only did the martyr himself suffer, but mass punishments were wreaked upon his fellow inmates. To "be inconspicuous" required a special kind of alertness—almost an animal instinct—against the apathy which tended to follow the initial shocks. To give up the struggle for survival was to commit "passive suicide"; a careless mistake meant death. There were those, however, who did come through this phase and who manged an adjustment to the life of the camp. It was the striking contrasts between this group of two- and three-year veterans and the perpetual stream of newcomers which made it possible for men like Bettelheim and Cohen to speak of the "old prisoner" as a specific type.

The most immediate aspect of the old inmates' behavior which struck these observers was its *childlike quality*. "The prisoners developed types of behavior which are characteristic of infancy or early youth. Some of these behaviors developed slowly, others were immediately imposed on the prisoners and developed only in intensity as time went on." Such infantile behavior took innumerable forms. The inmates' sexual impotence brought about a disappearance of sexuality in their talk; instead, excretory functions occupied them endlessly. They lost many of the customary inhibitions as to soiling their beds and their persons. Their humor was shot with silliness and they giggled like children when one of them would expel wind. Their relationships were highly unstable. "Prisoners would, like early adolescents, fight one another tooth and nail . . . only to become close friends within a few minutes." Dishonesty became chronic. "Now they suddenly appeared to be pathological liars, to be unable to restrain themselves, to be unable to make objective evaluation, etc." "In hundreds of ways," writes Colaço Belmonte, "the soldier, and to an even greater extent the prisoner of war, is given to understand that he is a child. . . . Then dishonesty, mendacity, egotistic actions in order to obtain more food or to get out of scrapes reach full development, and theft becomes a veritable affliction of camp life." This was all true, according to Elie Cohen, in the concentration camp as well. Benedikt Kautsky observed such things in his own behavior: "I myself can declare that often I saw myself as I used to be in my school days, when by sly dodges and clever pretexts we avoided being found out, or could 'organize' something." Bruno Bettelheim remarks on the extravagance of the stories told by the prisoners to one another. "They were boastful, telling tales about what they had accomplished in their former lives, or how they succeeded in cheating foremen or guards, and how they sabotaged the work. Like children they felt not at all set back or ashamed when it became known that they had lied about their prowess."

This development of childlike behavior in the old inmates was the counterpart of something even more striking that was happening to them: *Only very few of the prisoners escaped a more or less intensive identification with the SS.* As Mr. Bettelheim puts it: "A prisoner had reached the final stage of adjustment to the camp situation when he had changed his personality so as to accept as his own the values of the Gestapo." The Bettelheim study furnishes a catalogue of examples. The old prisoners came to share the attitude of the SS toward the "unfit" prisoners; newcomers who behaved badly in the labor groups or who could not withstand the strain became a liability for the others, who were often instrumental in getting rid of them. Many old prisoners actually imitated the SS; they would sew and mend their uniforms in such a way as to make them look more like those of the SS—even though they risked punishment for it. "When asked why they did it, they admitted that they loved to look like . . . the guards." Some took great enjoyment in the fact that during roll call "they really had stood well at attention." There were cases of nonsensical rules, made by the guards, which the older prisoners would continue to observe and try to force on the others long after the SS had forgotten them. Even the most abstract ideals of the SS, such as their intense German nationalism and anti-Semitism, were often absorbed by the old inmates—a phenomenon observed among the politically well-educated and even among the Jews themselves. The final quintessence of all this was seen in the "Kapo"—the prisoner who had been placed in a supervisory position over his fellow inmates. These creatures, many of them professional criminals, not only behaved with slavish servility to the SS, but the way in which they often outdid the SS in sheer brutality became one of the most durable features of the concentration-camp legend.

To all these men, reduced to complete and childish dependence upon their masters, the SS had actually become a father-symbol. "The SS man was all-powerful in the camp, he was the lord and master of the prisoner's life. As a cruel father he could, without fear of punishment, even kill the prisoner and as a gentle father he could scatter largesse and afford the prisoner his protection." The result, admits Dr. Cohen, was that "for all of us the SS was a father image. . . ." The closed system, in short, had become a kind of grotesque patriarchy.

The literature provides us with three remarkable tests of the profundity of the experience which these prisoners had undergone and the thoroughness of the changes which had been brought about in them. One is the fact that few cases of real resistance were ever recorded, even among prisoners going to their death.

> With a few altogether insignificant exceptions, the prisoners, no matter in what form they were led to execution, whether singly, in groups, or in masses, never fought back! . . . there were thousands who had by no means relapsed into fatal apathy. Nevertheless, in mass liquidations they went to their

death with open eyes, without assaulting the enemy in a final paroxysm, without a sign of fight. Is this not in conflict with human nature, as we know it?

Even upon liberation, when revenge against their tormentors at last became possible, mass uprisings very rarely occurred. "Even when the whole system was overthrown by the Allies," says David Rousset writing of Buchenwald, "nothing happened.... The American officer appointed to command of the camp was never called upon to cope with any inclination toward a popular movement. No such disposition existed."

A second test of the system's effectiveness was the relative scarcity of suicides in the camps. Though there were suicides, they tended to occur during the first days of internment, and only one mass suicide is known; it took place among a group of Jews at Mauthausen who leaped into a rock pit three days after their arrival. For the majority of prisoners the simplicity of the urge to survive made suicide, a complex matter of personal initiative and decision, out of the question. Yet they could, when commanded by their masters, go to their death without resistance.

The third test lies in the very absence, among the prisoners, of hatred toward the SS. This is probably the hardest of all to understand. Yet the burning spirit of rebellion which many of their liberators expected to find would have had to be supported by fierce and smoldering emotions; such emotions were not there. "It is remarkable," one observer notes, "how little hatred of their wardens is revealed in their stories."

The immense revelation for psychology in the concentration-camp literature has been the discovery of how elements of dramatic personality change could be brought about in masses of individuals. And yet it is not proper that the crude fact of "change" alone should dominate the conceptual image with which one emerges from this problem. "Change" per se, change that does not go beyond itself, is productive of nothing; it leaves only destruction, shock, and howling bedlam behind it unless some future basis of stability and order lies waiting to guarantee it and give it reality. So it is with the human psyche, which is apparently capable of making terms with a state other than liberty as we know it. The very dramatic features of the process just described may upset the nicety of this point. There is the related danger, moreover, of duly stressing the individual psychology of the problem at the expense of its social psychology.

These hazards might be minimized by maintaining a conceptual distinction between two phases of the group experience. The process of detachment from prior standards of behavior and value is one of them, and is doubtless the more striking, but there must be another one. That such detachment can, by extension, involve the whole scope of an individual's culture is an implication for which the vocabulary of individual psychology was caught somewhat unawares. Fluctuations in the state of the individual psyche could formerly be dealt with, or so it seemed, while taking for granted the more or less static nature of social organization, and with a minimum of reference to its features. That such organization might itself become an important variable was therefore a possibility not highly developed in theory, focused as theory was upon individual case histories to the invariable minimization of social and cultural setting. The other phase of the experience should be considered as the "stability" side of the problem, that phase which stabilized what the "shock" phase only opened the way for. This was essentially a process of adjustment to a standard of social normality, though in this case a drastic *re*adjustment and compressed within a very short time—a process which under typical conditions of individual and group existence is supposed to begin at birth and last a lifetime and be transmitted in many and diffuse ways from generation to generation. The adjustment is assumed to be slow and organic, and it normally is. Its numerous aspects extend much beyond psychology; those aspects have in the past been treated at great leisure within the rich provinces not only of psychology but of history, sociology, and literature as well. What rearrangement and compression of those provinces may be needed to accommodate a mass experience that not only involved profound individual shock but also required rapid assimilation to a drastically different form of social organization, can hardly be known. But perhaps the most conservative beginning may be made with existing psychological theory.

The theoretical system whose terminology was orthodox for most of the Europeans who have written about the camps was that of Freud. It was necessary for them to do a certain amount of improvising, since the scheme's existing framework provided only the narrowest leeway for dealing with such radical concepts as out-and-out change in personality. This was due to two kinds of limitations which the Freudian vocabulary places upon the notion of the "self." One is that the superego—that part of the self involved in social relationships, social values, expectations of others, and so on—is conceived as only a small and highly refined part of the "total" self. The other is the assumption that the content and character of the superego is laid down in childhood and undergoes relatively little basic alteration thereafter. Yet a Freudian diagnosis of the concentration-camp inmate—whose social self, or superego, did appear to change and who seemed basically changed thereby—is, given these limitations, still possible. Elie Cohen, whose analysis is the most thorough of these, specifically states that "the superego acquired new values in a concentration camp." The old values, according to Dr. Cohen, were first silenced by the shocks which produced "acute depersonalization" (the subject-object split: "It is not the real 'me' who is undergoing this"), and by the powerful drives of hunger and survival. Old values, thus set aside, could be replaced by new ones. It was a process made possible by "infantile regression"—regression to a previous condition of childlike dependency in which parental prohibitions once more became all-powerful and in which parental judgments might once more be internalized. In this way a new "father-image," personified in the SS guard, came into being. That the prisoner's identification with the SS could be so positive is explained by still another mechanism: the principle of "identification with the aggressor." "A child," as Anna Freud writes, "interjects some characteristic of an anxiety-object and so assimilates an anxiety-experience which he has just undergone. . . . By impersonating the aggressor, assuming his attributes or imitating his aggression, the child transforms himself from the person threatened into the person who makes the threat." In short, the child's only "defense" in the presence of a cruel, all-powerful father is the psychic defense of identification.

Now one could, still retaining the Freudian language, represent all this in somewhat less cumbersome terms by a slight modification of the metaphor. It could simply be said that under great stress the superego, like a bucket, is violently emptied of content and acquires, in a radically changed setting, new content. It would thus not be necessary to postulate a literal "regression" to childhood in order for this to occur. Something of the sort is suggested by Leo Alexander. "The psychiatrist stands in amazement," he writes, "before the thoroughness and completeness with which this perversion of essential superego values was accomplished in adults . . . [and] it may be that the decisive importance of childhood and youth in the formation of [these] values may have been overrated by psychiatrists in a society in which allegiance to these values in normal adult life was taken too much for granted because of the 19th Century and early 20th Century society."

A second theoretical scheme is better prepared for crisis and more closely geared to social environment than the Freudian adaptation indicated above, and it may consequently be more suitable for accommodating not only the concentration-camp experience but also the more general problem of plantation slave personality. This is the "interpersonal theory" developed by the late Harry Stack Sullivan. One may view this body of work as the response to a peculiarly American set of needs. The system of Freud, so aptly designed for a European society the stability of whose institutional and status relationships could always to a large extent be taken for granted, turns out to be less clearly adapted to the culture of the United States. The American psychiatrist has had to deal with individuals in a culture where the diffuse, shifting, and often uncertain quality of such relationships has always been more pronounced than in Europe. He has come to appreciate the extent to which these relationships actually support the individual's psychic balance—the full extent, that is, to which the self is "social" in its nature. Thus a psychology whose terms are flexible enough to permit altering social relationships to make actual differences in character structure would be a psychology especially promising for dealing with the present problem.

Sullivan's great contribution was to offer a concept whereby the really critical determinants of personality might be isolated for purposes of observation. Out of the hopelessly immense totality of "influences" which in one way or another go to make up the personality, or "self," Sullivan designated one—the estimations and expectations of others—as the one promising to unlock the most secrets. He then made a second elimination: the *majority* of "others" in one's existence may for theoretical purposes be neglected; what counts is who the *significant* others are. Here, "significant others" may be understood very crudely to mean those individuals who hold, or seem to hold, the keys to security in one's own personal situation, whatever its nature. Now as to the psychic processes whereby these "significant others" become an actual part of the personality, it may be said that the very sense of "self" first emerges in connection with anxiety about the attitudes of the most important persons in one's life (initially, the mother, father, and their surrogates—persons of more or less absolute authority), and automatic attempts are set in motion to adjust to these attitudes. In this way their approval, their disapproval, their estimates and appraisals, and indeed a whole range of their expectations become as it were internalized, and are reflected in one's very character. Of course as one "grows up," one acquires more and more significant others whose attitudes are diffuse and may indeed compete, and thus "significance," in Sullivan's sense, becomes subtler and less easy to define. The personality exfoliates; it takes on traits of distinction and, as we say, "individuality." The impact of particular significant others is less dramatic than in early life. But the pattern is a continuing one; new significant others do still appear, and theoretically it is conceivable that even in mature life the personality might be visibly affected by the arrival of such a one—

supposing that this new significant other were vested with sufficient authority and power. In any event there are possibilities for fluidity and actual change inherent in this concept which earlier schemes have lacked.

The purest form of the process is to be observed in the development of children, not so much because of their "immaturity" as such (though their plasticity is great and the imprint of early experience goes deep), but rather because for them there are fewer significant others. For this reason—because the pattern is simpler and more easily controlled—much of Sullivan's attention was devoted to what happens in childhood. In any case let us say that unlike the adult, the child, being drastically limited in the selection of significant others, must operate in a "closed system."

Such are the elements which make for order and balance in the normal self: "significant others" plus "anxiety" in a special sense—conceived with not simply disruptive but also guiding, warning functions. The structure of "interpersonal" theory thus has considerable room in it for conceptions of guided change—change for either beneficent or malevolent ends. One technique for managing such change would of course be the orthodox one of psychoanalysis; another, the actual changing of significant others. Patrick Mullahy, a leading exponent of Sullivan, believes that in group therapy much is possible along these lines. A demonic test of the whole hypothesis is available in the concentration camp.

Consider the camp prisoner—not the one who fell by the wayside but the one who was eventually to survive; consider the ways in which he was forced to adjust to the one significant other which he now had—the SS guard, who held absolute dominion over every aspect of his life. The very shock of his introduction was perfectly designed to dramatize this fact; he was brutally maltreated ("as by a cruel father"); the shadow of resistance would bring instant death. Daily life in the camp, with its fear and tensions, taught over and over the lesson of absolute power. It prepared the personality for a drastic shift in standards. It crushed whatever anxieties might have been drawn from prior standards; such standards had become meaningless. It focused the prisoner's attention constantly on the moods, attitudes, and standards of the only man who mattered. A truly childlike situation was thus created: utter and abject dependency on one, or on a rigidly limited few, significant others. All the conditions which in normal life would give the individual leeway—which allowed him to defend himself against a new and hostile significant other, no matter how powerful—were absent in the camp. No competition of significant others was possible; the prisoner's comrades for practical purposes were helpless to assist him. He had no degree of independence, no lines to the outside, in any matter. Everything, every vital concern, focused on the SS: food, warmth, security, freedom from pain, all depended on the omnipotent significant other, all had to be worked out within the closed system. Nowhere was there a shred of privacy; everything one did was subject to SS supervision. The pressure was never absent. It is thus no wonder that the prisoners should become "as children." It is no wonder that their obedience became unquestioning, that they did not revolt, that they could not "hate" their masters. Their masters' attitudes had become *internalized* as a part of their very selves; those attitudes and standards now dominated all others that they had. They had, indeed, been "changed."

There exists still a third conceptual framework within which these phenomena may be considered. It is to be found in the growing field of "role psychology." This psychology is not at all incompatible with interpersonal theory; the two might easily be fitted into the same system. But it might be strategically desirable, for several reasons, to segregate them for purposes of discussion. One such reason is the extraordinary degree to which role psychology shifts the focus of attention upon the individual's cultural and institutional environment rather than upon his "self." At the same time it gives us a manageable concept—that of "role"—for mediating between the two. As a mechanism, the role enables us to isolate the unique contribution of culture and institutions toward maintaining the psychic balance of the individual. In it, we see formalized for the individual a range of choices in models of behavior and expression, each with its particular style, quality, and attributes. The relationship between the "role" and the "self," though not yet clear, is intimate; it is at least possible at certain levels of inquiry to look upon the individual as the variable and upon the roles extended him as the stable factor. We thus have a potentially durable link between individual psychology and the study of culture. It might even be said, inasmuch as its key term is directly borrowed from the theater, that role psychology offers in workable form the long-awaited connection—apparently missed by Ernest Jones in his *Hamlet* study—between the insights of the classical dramatists and those of the contemporary social theorist. But be that as it may, for our present problem, the concentration camp, it suggests the most flexible account of how the ex-prisoners may have succeeded in resuming their places in normal life.

Let us note certain of the leading terms. A "social role" is definable in its simplest sense as the behavior expected of persons specifically located in specific social groups. A distinction is kept between "expectations" and "behavior"; the expectations of a role (embodied in the "script") theoretically exist in advance and are defined by the organization, the institution, or by society at large. Behavior (the "performance") refers to the manner in which the role is played. Another distinction involves roles which are "pervasive" and those which are "limited." A pervasive role is extensive in scope ("female citizen") and not only influences but also sets bounds upon the other sorts of roles available to the individual ("mother," "nurse," but not "husband," "soldier"); a limited role ("purchaser," "patient") is transitory and intermittent. A further concept is that of "role clarity." Some roles are more specifically defined than others; their impact upon performance (and, indeed, upon the personality of the performer) depends on the clarity of their definition. Finally, it is asserted that those roles which carry with them the clearest and most automatic rewards and punishments are those which will be (as it were) most "artistically" played.

What sorts of things might this explain? It might illuminate the process whereby the child develops his personality in terms not only of the roles which his parents offer him but of those which he "picks up" elsewhere and tries on. It could show how society, in its coercive character, lays down patterns of behavior with which it expects the individual to comply. It suggests the way in which society, now turning its benevolent face to the individual, tenders him alternatives and defines for him the style appropriate to their fulfilment. It provides us with a further term for the definition of personality itself: there appears an extent to which we can say that personality is actually made up of the roles which the individual plays. And here, once more assuming "change" to be possible, we have in certain ways the least cumbersome terms for plotting its course.

The application of the model to the concentration camp should be simple and obvious. What was expected of the man entering the role of camp prisoner was laid down for him upon arrival:

> "Here you are not in a penitentiary or prison but in a place of instruction. Order and discipline are here the highest law. If you ever want to see freedom again, you must submit to a severe training. . . . But woe to those who do not obey our iron discipline. Our methods are thorough! Here there is no compromise and no mercy. The slightest resistance will be ruthlessly suppressed. Here we sweep with an iron broom!"

Expectation and performance must coincide exactly; the lines were to be read literally; the missing of a single cue meant extinction. The role was pervasive; it vetoed any other role and smashed all prior ones. "Role clarity"—the clarity here was blinding; its definition was burned into the prisoner by every detail of his existence:

> In normal life the adult enjoys a certain measure of independence; within the limits set by society he has a considerable measure of liberty. Nobody orders him when and what to eat, where to take up his residence or what to wear, neither to take his rest on Sunday nor when to have his bath, nor when to go to bed. He is not beaten during his work, he need not ask

> permission to go to the W.C., he is not continually kept on the run, he does not feel that the work he is doing is silly or childish, he is not confined behind barbed wire, he is not counted twice a day or more, he is not left unprotected against the actions of his fellow citizens, he looks after his family and the education of his children.
>
> How altogether different was the life of the concentration-camp prisoner! What to do during each part of the day was arranged for him, and decisions were made about him from which there was no appeal. He was impotent and suffered from bedwetting, and because of his chronic diarrhea he soiled his underwear. . . . The dependence of the prisoner on the SS . . . may be compared to the dependence of children on their parents. . . .

The impact of this role, coinciding as it does in a hundred ways with that of the child, has already been observed. Its rewards were brutally simple—life rather than death; its punishments were automatic. By the survivors it was—it had to be—a role *well played*.

Nor was it simple, upon liberation, to shed the role. Many of the inmates, to be sure, did have prior roles which they could resume, former significant others to whom they might reorient themselves, a repressed superego which might once more be resurrected. To this extent they were not "lost souls." But to the extent that their entire personalities, their total selves, had been involved in this experience, to the extent that old arrangements had been disrupted, that society itself had been overturned while they had been away, a "return" was fraught with innumerable obstacles.

It is hoped that the very hideousness of a special example of slavery has not disqualified it as a test for certain features of a far milder and more benevolent form of slavery. But it should still be possible to say, with regard to the individuals who lived as slaves within the respective systems, that just as on one level there is every difference between a wretched childhood and a carefree one, there are, for other purposes, limited features which the one may be said to have shared with the other.

Both were closed systems from which all standards based on prior connections had been effectively detached. A working adjustment to either system required a childlike conformity, a limited choice of "significant others." Cruelty per se cannot be considered the primary key to this; of far greater importance was the simple "closedness" of the system, in which all lines of authority descended from the master and in which alternative social bases that might have supported alternative standards were systematically suppressed. The individual, consequently, for his very psychic security, had to picture his master in some way as the "good father," even when, as in the concentration camp, it made no sense at all. But why should it not have made sense for many a simple plantation Negro whose master did exhibit, in all the ways that could be expected, the features of the good father who was really "good"? If the concentration camp could produce in two or three years the results that it did, one wonders how much more pervasive must have been those attitudes, expectations, and values which had, certainly, their benevolent side and which were accepted and transmitted over generations.

For the Negro child, in particular, the plantation offered no really satisfactory father-image other than the master. The "real" father was virtually without authority over his child, since discipline, parental responsibility, and control of rewards and punishments all rested in other hands; the slave father could not even protect the mother of his children except by appealing directly to the master. Indeed, the mother's own role loomed far larger for the slave child than did that of the father. She controlled those few activities—household care, preparation of food, and rearing of children—that were left to the slave family. For that matter, the very etiquette of plantation life removed even the honorific attributes of fatherhood from the Negro male, who was addressed as "boy"— until, when the vigorous years of his prime were past, he was allowed to assume the title of "uncle."

From the master's viewpoint, slaves had been defined in law as property, and the master's power over his property must be absolute. But then this property was still human property.

These slaves might never be quite as human as *he* was, but still there were certain standards that could be laid down for their behavior: obedience, fidelity, humility, docility, cheerfulness, and so on. Industry and diligence would of course be demanded, but a final element in the master's situation would undoubtedly qualify that expectation. Absolute power for him meant absolute dependency for the slave—the dependency not of the developing child but of the perpetual child. For the master, the role most aptly fitting such a relationship would naturally be that of the father. As a father he could be either harsh or kind, as he chose, but as a *wise* father he would have, we may suspect, a sense of the limits of his situation. He must be ready to cope with *all* the qualities of the child, exasperating as well as ingratiating. He might conceivably have to expect in this child—besides his loyalty, docility, humility, cheerfulness, and (under supervision) his diligence— such additional qualities as irresponsibility, playfulness, silliness, laziness, and (quite possibly) tendencies to lying and stealing. Should the entire prediction prove accurate, the result would be something resembling "Sambo."

The social and psychological sanctions of role-playing may in the last analysis prove to be the most satisfactory of the several approaches to Sambo, for, without doubt, of all the roles in American life that of Sambo was by far the most pervasive. The outlines of the role might be sketched in by crude necessity, but what of the finer shades? The sanctions against overstepping it were bleak enough, but the rewards—the sweet applause, as it were, for performing it with sincerity and feeling—were something to be appreciated on quite another level. The law, untuned to the deeper harmonies, could command the player to be present for the occasion, and the whip might even warn against his missing the grosser cues, but could those things really insure the performance that melted all hearts? Yet there was many and many a performance, and the audiences (whose standards were high) appear to have been for the most part well pleased. They were actually viewing their own masterpiece. Much labor had been lavished upon this chef d'oeuvre, the most genial resources of Southern society had been available for the work; touch after touch had been applied throughout the years, and the result—embodied not in the unfeeling law but in the richest layers of Southern lore—had been the product of an exquisitely rounded collective creativity. And indeed, in a sense that somehow transcended the merely ironic, it was a labor of love. "I love the simple and unadulterated slave, with his geniality, his mirth, his swagger, and his nonsense," wrote Edward Pollard. "I love to look upon his countenance shining with content and grease; I love to study his affectionate heart; I love to mark that peculiarity in him, which beneath all his buffoonery exhibits him as a creature of the tenderest sensibilities, mingling his joys and his sorrows with those of his master's home." Love, even on those terms, was surely no inconsequential reward.

But what were the terms? The Negro was to be a child forever. "The Negro . . . in his true nature, is always a boy, let him be ever so old. . . ." "He is . . . a dependent upon the white race; dependent for guidance and direction even to the procurement of his most indispensable necessaries. Apart from this protection he has the helplessness of a child—without foresight, without faculty of contrivance, without thrift of any kind." Not only was he a child; he was a happy child. Few Southern writers failed to describe with obvious fondness the bubbling gaiety of a plantation holiday or the perpetual good humor that seemed to mark the Negro character, the good humor of an everlasting childhood.

The role, of course, must have been rather harder for the earliest generations of slaves to learn. "Accommodation," according to John Dollard, "involves the renunciation of protest or aggression against undesirable conditions of life and the organization of the character so that protest does not appear, but acceptance does. It may come to pass in the end that the unwelcome force is idealized, that one identifies with it and takes it into the personality; it sometimes even happens that what is at first resented and feared is finally loved."

Might the process, on the other hand, be reversed? It is hard to imagine its being reversed overnight. The same role might still be played in the years after slavery—we are told that it was—and yet it was played to more vulgar audiences with cruder standards, who paid much less for what they saw. The lines might be repeated more and more mechanically, with less and less conviction; the incentives to perfection could become hazy and blurred, and the excellent old piece could degenerate over time into low farce. There could come a point, conceivably, with the old zest gone, that it was no longer worth the candle. The day might come at last when it dawned on a man's full waking consciousness that he had really grown up, that he was, after all, only playing a part.

## For Further Reading

The reader seeking to fit the institution of slavery into the large perspective of western European cultural history should begin with David Brion Davis, *The Problem of Slavery in Western Culture* (1966). For a suggestive, brief comparison of slavery within the cultures of the Western Hemisphere, see Frank Tannenbaum, *Slave and Citizen* (1946), and for a more recent detailed study, see Herbert S. Klein, *Slavery in the Americas* (1967).

Among the many general works on North American slavery, four stand out: Ulrich B. Phillips, *American Negro Slavery* (1918) and *Life and Labor in the Old South* (1929), Kenneth M. Stampp, *The Peculiar Institution* (1956), and Eugene D. Genovese, *The Political Economy of Slavery* (1965). Richard C. Wade's *Slavery in the Cities* (1964) surveys the Southern urban scene. Accounts of slavery in individual Southern states are: James B. Sellers, *Slavery in Alabama* (1950); Orville W. Taylor, *Negro Slavery in Arkansas* (1958); J. Winston Coleman, Jr., *Slavery Times in Kentucky* (1940); Roger Shugg, *Origins of Class Struggle in Louisiana* (1939); Charles S. Sydnor, *Slavery in Mississippi* (1933); Guion G. Johnson, *Ante-Bellum North Carolina* (1937); Charles C. Mooney, *Slavery in Tennessee* (1957); and Robert McColley, *Slavery and Jeffersonian Virginia* (1964).

Two fine texts on Negro history are John Hope Franklin, *From Slavery to Freedom* (1963), and E. Franklin Frazier, *The Negro in the United States* (1957). For provocative historical studies on racial attitudes, see Winthrop D. Jordan, *White Over Black* (1968); Oscar Handlin, *Race and Nationality in American Life* (1957); Leon Litwack, *North of Slavery* (1961); and Melville J. Herskovits, *The Myth of the Negro Past* (1941). A scholarly account of slave insurrections is Herbert Aptheker's *American Negro Slave Revolts* (1943). But see also the more recent studies: F. Roy Johnson, *The Nat Turner Slave Insurrection* (1966), John Lofton, *Insurrection in South Carolina* (1964), and Nicholas Halasz, *The Rattling Chains* (1966).

# The Dred Scott Decision

## Allan Nevins

Civil War issues, one historian has remarked, continue to "draw fire from the hearts and minds of Americans." No other American historical phenomenon has attracted so many scholars—or produced so many conflicting interpretations about its origins and significance. For Americans living in the Atomic Era, the Civil War has particular fascination. Issues of the present seem to be mirrored in those of the 1850's and early 1860's: problems of racial adjustment, of majority will and minority rights, and of peaceful settlement of intersectional and international disputes. The parallels are so striking and urgent that one is pulled irresistibly to studies of the pre-Civil War era.

Historians have long grappled with the weighty question: what were the causes that led fellow Americans to hurl themselves before each other's grape and canister at Manassas Junction, Antietam, Gettysburg, and in the Wilderness? In the years 1861–1880—while emotions still ran high—historians, journalists, and politicians attempted to pin the blame for the war on the enemy, thus exonerating themselves. Often these analysts (who have

Source: Allan Nevins, *The Emergence of Lincoln,* 2 vols. (New York: Charles Scribner's Sons, 1950), Vol. II, pp. 90–118. Copyright 1950 by Charles Scribner's Sons. Reprinted by permission of the publisher.

been aptly dubbed "primitives") tended to rely on monistic explanations, that is, one person, like Abraham Lincoln or Jefferson Davis; one group, like Southern firebrands or Northern abolitionists; or one interest, like the Southern planter oligarchy or Northeastern textile industrialists, was responsible for the coming of war. These "primitives" may be divided into three groups. First, Northern historians Hermann Eduard Von Holst and Henry Wilson and politicians James G. Blaine and John A. Logan portrayed the Civil War as the "War of Rebellion": the South bore full responsibility in perpetrating the conflict, a rebellion born in the irreconcilable argument between the sections over slavery. Second, Southern writers and politicians—Edward A. Pollard, Robert Barnwell Rhett, and Jefferson Davis—viewed the conflict as "The War Between the States": the North was to blame; secession had been justified by the Northern states' violation of Southern constitutional rights and by the increasing hegemony of the North's commercial and industrial interests with a consequent subversion of Southern values; slavery, they claimed, had been a bogus issue. Third, individuals, like the discredited former President, James A. Buchanan, saw the contest as a "Needless War": the extremists on both sides, whose agitation about slavery, rather than the institution itself, had caused the war; and the conflict could have been averted by Southern forebearance during the crisis of 1860–1861 and by Northern willingness to guarantee slavery's expansion into federal territories.

Beginning in the 1880's a new generation began to comment on the Civil War. Time had altered perspectives. The immediacy of the conflict had passed; passions had subsided with the removal of federal troops from the South in 1877; new issues relating to industrialism, reform, and expansion had emerged; and historians, reflecting the impact of scientific history and thorough, advanced professional training, began to develop more sophisticated and detached approaches to their discipline.

Chief among the new interpreters of the war was James Ford Rhodes, a successful Ohio businessman before following Clio's call in 1885. Rhodes in 1893 published the first volumes of his *History of the United States from the Compromise of 1850*. His rejection of the terms "War of Rebellion" or "War Between the States" in favor of "Civil War" emphasizes the new generation's concept of the conflict as "history" rather than as a personally memorable event. Rhodes presented a moderate, balanced account of the war—"all the right is never on one side and all the wrong on the other." The primary cause of war was slavery. Yet, unlike his predecessors among the "primitives," Rhodes blamed slavery, not slave-owners; cotton and the cotton gin, not depraved masters. Secessionists, he asserted, represented a majority of Southerners—they were not a handful of traitorous leaders. The division between a hostile North and South had arisen over the morality of human slavery; the South had been wrong in defending an "unrighteous" cause. This division had been "irrepressible," given the opposing moral stances of the two sections. Rhodes—like his contemporary Frederick Jackson Turner—preferred to stress the inanimate forces that led North and South to battle. Assignment of personal guilt was shunned; often, in fact, the new generation of scholars saw nobility and rectitude on both sides, a mark of magnanimity largely absent from earlier interpretations. Lastly, these scholars saw the war as desirable in that it settled two questions, the supremacy of the nation and the elimination of slavery.

The first four decades of the twentieth century spawned two new and major interpretations of the coming of the war. The first interpretation, "The Second American Revolution" thesis, grew out of the social-reform ferment of the Populist-Progressive era. The second interpretation, the "Blundering Generation" approach, stemmed from the American reaction to international crises in the 1930's and 1940's. Both took issue with the dominant view espoused by Rhodes and his followers. Both represented new directions in historical scholarship and writing.

The main outlines of the Second American Revolution thesis was advanced in 1927 by Charles Austin Beard and his wife, Mary, in their two-volume *The Rise of American Civilization*. The Beards heightened the role of economics in their interpretation. The actual fighting, noble and stirring as it was, should not obscure the central fact of the Civil War: it was a "social cataclysm in which the capitalists, laborers, and farmers of the North and West drove from power in the national government the planting aristocracy of the South." The war was indeed irrepressible. But fundamentally different economic structures, not differing moral stances, lay at the roots of the conflict. Southern aristocratic planters, fighting vainly against the unfavorable census returns and mounting statistics of industrial might in the North, sought to sever the ties of Union in order to preserve their agrarian culture. Northern financiers and industrialists, impatient under the economically restrictive policies of a Southern-dominated national government, looked for a means to eliminate those restrictions and crush Southern anti-industrialist power. Proof of the thesis lay in the planters' studied exclusion of protective tariffs from the powers of the newly formed Confederate States of America and in the industrialists' corresponding success in pushing through Congress high tariffs, a strengthened banking system, and transcontinental railroad legislation. The Beards' thesis coincided with the growth of economic interpretation in historical studies; embattled in the cause of social and economic reform, the Beards saw in history prefigurations of the issues of their day. Not least important, the Beards concluded that the war had firmly established the industrial capitalist system as the controlling element in American life. They remained less impressed with the settlement of the political question of Nation versus Section than with the economic one of Industrialist versus Agrarian.

During the 1930's another perspective on the Civil War was explored by historians. Leaders in this new interpretation—the "Revisionist" or "Blundering Generation" or "Repressible Conflict" as it is variously called—were James G. Randall and Avery Craven. They and other scholars objected to the prevailing assumptions of those who held that war in 1861 could not have been avoided. Themselves disillusioned by war (here mirroring the attitudes of many Americans of the post-World War I period), Randall and Craven in their numerous books and articles condemned the political leaders and extremists of 1850–1861 for their lack of statesmanship and wisdom. Although differences did exist between antebellum North and South, similarities were greater and more important. Slavery was not a real issue; the institution was moribund and the number of slaves that could be brought into the Western territories was infinitesimal. Thus, "artificial" and "unreal" differences had been magnified and propagandized out of proportion to their real importance. The resulting heightened emotions—stimulated by unscrupulous and unwise extremists—had led to war. The war, in brief, was unnecessary. Who should Americans have heeded if not Northern Republicans and firebrand secessionists? Stephen A. Douglas and James Buchannan, the historians answer. These two men had seen what the real issues were; they had not been misled by the fraudulent moral question of slavery. Yet their appeals to reason and compromise had been ignored. Applications of this thesis to America of the late 1930's and early 1940's were evident; as with virtually all historians, the Revisionists peered into the past through the lenses of current perceptions and predilections.

The Revisionist view had won many adherents within the historical community, but with the advent of World War II and the subsequent cold war, that interpretation began to lose ground. The Revisionists found themselves under attack from at least two quarters. Individuals, impressed with the durability of the irrational behavior of man, expressed skepticism about the possibility of settling disputes in the optimistic manner implied by the Revisionist approach. They charged that "Blundering Generation" scholars denied the realities of the emotional bases of human action. Most important, in an age when a civil-rights movement preached against the immorality of whites' suppression of blacks, the significance of the moral crusade against slavery became more evident.

The swing away from the Revisionist and back toward the "Rhodesian" view is typified by the writings of Allan Nevins. Born in Illinois in 1890, schooled at the state university, and employed for eighteen years as a journalist and part-time teacher, Nevins turned to a professional historical career in 1931 on joining the history faculty at Columbia University, a post he retained until 1958. A prolific writer and industrious researcher, Nevins has enriched the literature of American history with numerous volumes, often biographical, on American business and political figures.

Perhaps Nevins' major contribution has come with his ambitious multi-volumed study of America during the period 1850–1877. Yet uncompleted, the series is designed to replace that of Rhodes. The first two sections of the work, *Ordeal of the Union* (1947) and *The Emergence of Lincoln* (1950), comprise four volumes and carry the story from 1850 to 1861. Nevins, like Rhodes, agrees that slavery was the prime cause of the Civil War. Yet it was not slavery alone, but the entire question of racial adjustment that figured so prominently. At times Nevins seems to endorse the "irrepressible conflict" notion, at others he, like the Revisionists, suggests that political leadership could have faced basic issues more squarely— thus possibly averting the recourse to bullets instead of ballots. Nevins rejects the Beardian analysis as resting on flimsy evidence; "the war was caused by social, moral, and political, not economic forces." In tone and temper Nevins' work is close to Rhodes'—but it is an improvement on the earlier work because of the incorporation of the findings of later historians.

*F*ortunately for the country, few administrations open with a thunderclap. Usually the new President and Cabinet find a few quiet months in which to settle routine affairs, and to take their bearings, before they have to deal with controversial problems. Buchanan was unfortunate when his long courtship of political quiet ended only two days after his inauguration, and the Dred Scott decision broke upon the nation with a confusing crash. His friends assured the country that the Supreme Court bolt had scattered his enemies and cleared his path for a successful term of office. It was quickly evident, however, that the thunder had brought not victory and peace, but a furious political storm.

The full implications of Dred Scott can be grasped only if we remember to what a savage pitch Pierce's recent castigation of Republican doctrines had raised the dispute upon the constitutional position of slavery in the Territories, and with what fierceness the defenders of the three main views had sprung to arms. During December and January, Congress had quivered with the debate. Senator Cass expounded his and Douglas's view that the settlers of a Territory alone had definitive power over slavery. Lyman Trumbull and John P. Hale argued that Congress possessed full power to regulate it, like other domestic institutions, throughout the public domain. Alexander H. Stephens and Senator Mason of Virginia declared that neither Congress nor the territorial legislatures had any authority to limit slavery, and that the late election had sustained the principle that the institution could not be prohibited in lands belonging to the whole nation. Perhaps the ablest speech was by Collamer of Vermont, reviewing the many historical instances in which Congress *had* acted to interdict or restrict slavery in certain Territories; but it made no Southern converts.

Everybody knew that this issue of the Negro in the Territories was the central question before the country; and the Congressional debates, running concurrently with the courtroom arguments on Dred Scott, were caught up by the press. Justice McLean's essay, arguing that Congress certainly had no power to institute slavery in a Territory where it did not exist, had lately been reprinted. Many people remembered Attorney-General Cushing's extended opinion of November, 1855, on the subject, written at Pierce's request. He had held that the United States never possessed any "municipal sovereignty" in the common territory, and that the Missouri Compromise of 1820 must have been declared by any court to be null and void because it gave certain new States a position unequal with the old States; that is, it deprived the States north of 36° 30' of the right to decide on slavery for themselves. Editors now worried the topic as dogs chew a juiceless bone. Yet for all the debate, the Court decision, far more sweeping than had been anticipated, took the country aback.

March 6, 1857: Another bright, clear day. The sunlight filtered through even into the cool, dim apartment of the Capitol basement which, beneath the throbbing discussions of Senate and House, was reserved for the Supreme Court. At eleven exactly, the procession of black-garbed judges moved from their robing room to the chamber, the younger members, as they kicked up the long gowns with their heels, adjusting their gait to that of the tremulous chief, Roger B. Taney. They found the tiny courtroom jammed. Indeed, it had been packed the previous day in expectation of the great decision, which was deferred. By this time the crowd of distinguished public men, the reporters with pad and pencil, were not disappointed. The judges bowed to the lawyers, the lawyers bowed to the judges; the crier opened the session with the immemorial "Oyez! Oyez!" that had echoed through English-speaking courts since Plantagenet days; and the Chief Justice, gathering his papers before him, began reading in a high, thin voice. He continued, with signs of ebbing strength, until half-past one, though his words became almost inaudible long before he had finished.

The general tenor of the decision was no surprise, for word of it had confidentially passed around Washington. The correspondent of the New York *Commercial Advertiser* had explicitly stated on March 5 that the Court would give judgment seven to two against the Missouri Compromise. James S. Pike had simultaneously written the *Tribune* that the judges would declare slavery coextensive with the nation outside of the free States, and would rule that its expansion must keep pace with every gain of territory. As Taney pronounced the Compromise restriction on slavery invalid, disappointment gathered on the face of John J. Crittenden of Kentucky, Clay's disciple, and indignation on the brow of Henry Wilson of Massachusetts, Webster's successor. Reporters caught a gleam of exultation on Caleb Cushing's visage, and watched anger deepen in Lewis Cass's eyes. As Justices Nelson and Catron followed Taney, the audience melted away. By midafternoon the wires were humming with the news which fell upon Northern readers next morning like a bludgeon-stroke: "Slavery Alone National—The Missouri Compromise Unconstitutional—Negroes Cannot Be Citizens—The Triumph of Slavery Complete."

The questions caught up in Dred Scott's suit for freedom were now familiar to all well-informed citizens. One issue in the case was whether any man of Dred's color, descent, and status could be a citizen of a State and hence entitled to sue in the Federal courts. Another issue was whether Dred's residence at Rock Island and Fort Snelling, on free soil, had given him a title to liberty which continued to hold good when he returned to Missouri. Bound up with this, obviously, was the third issue: the question whether the Missouri Compromise restriction, which made slavery illegal in the Territory embracing Fort Snelling, was constitutional. To everyone but Dred the third issue overshadowed all the other considerations. With some bitterness, freesoilers pointed out that the Supreme Court had once included two justices who, when members of Congress, had voted for the Compromise: Philip P. Barbour of Virginia, and Henry Baldwin of Pennsylvania. What would these men have said of the constitutionality of the law they had helped to pass?

On the question whether Dred, or any other Negro of slave ancestry, could be a citizen (the question of jurisdiction), only three judges pronounced a broad and explicit negative. They were Judges Taney, Wayne, and Daniel, who found grounds for stating that citizenship was impossible to any such person. Not one of the three cited any apposite precedent, for, while Taney mentioned that the issue of citizenship had been raised in the famous Prudence Crandall case in Connecticut, he noted that no final opinion had then been handed down upon it. Indeed, no precedent was to be found in any work of reference known in 1857, though one has since been discovered: in 1793 the Federal circuit court in Connecticut had decided that a free Negro of Massachusetts possessed the right to sue. Of the other judges, John McLean and Benjamin R. Curtis firmly asserted that a free Negro *was* a citizen, while the four others avoided the broad abstract question. Justice John A. Campbell, for example, held that Dred was a slave and hence not a citizen; but he skirted what seemed to him the academic issue whether the man, had he been a freeman, would have possessed citizenship. It was an important fact that only three judges found that no Negro, even when free, could be a citizen—that is, that the Federal courts were closed to all such persons. If five or more judges had so held, the case would have been halted then and there. As matters stood, it had to be pushed one step further.

This step was to determine whether Dred Scott's residence at Rock Island and Fort Snelling had freed him from bondage. In most of the Missouri cases bearing on this point the removal of the slave to free soil had been with a view to *permanent* domicile, something quite different from Dred's temporary sojourn. A majority of judges, led by Taney, held that the status of the Negro with respect to freedom or slavery was fixed, not by the law of areas in which he held transitory residence, but by that of the State in which he lived when the question was raised. As Judge Campbell put it: "The claim of the plaintiff to freedom depends upon the effect to be given to his absence from Missouri, in company with his master, in Illinois and Minnesota, and this effect is to be ascertained by reference to the laws of Missouri." The action of the Missouri Supreme Court was therefore upheld.

One justice, Daniel of Virginia, stated his opinion as to the controlling influence of Missouri law with vituperative emphasis. He pointed out that various slaveholding States had passed acts which limited the power of masters to set their slaves free. The arguments in behalf of Dred, he remarked, would permit any owner to emancipate his slave without reference to those legal restrictions; he need only take the slave to free soil and then bring him back: "At assumptions anomalous as these, so fraught with mischief and ruin, the mind at once is revolted." Judge McLean, on the other hand, held that the rule of interstate comity required Missouri to give due effect to the constitution and laws of Illinois. He noted that, as lately as 1851, the South Carolina Court of Appeals (following precedents in other Southern States) had recognized the principle that a slave when taken to reside in a free State lost his condition of bondage.

Since, of the nine judges, a majority concurred in holding that the Missouri law did control Dred's status, that he remained a slave, and that he therefore had no right as citizen to maintain a suit in a Federal court, the case might have been halted at this stage. Why go on to explore the constitutionality of the Congressional enactments making the Territory of Wisconsin and the other Territories free?

This, however, is precisely what the Court did. Only one justice, Nelson of New York, stopped short with the judgment that Dred had no right to come before the tribunal. Concurring with the verdict that the plaintiff was a slave, and that the Federal circuit court therefore had no jurisdiction, he halted at that point. Chief Justice Taney and the other seven associate justices went further. They dealt with the whole field of Congressional power. Six, including the Chief Justice, held that Congress had no right to exclude slavery from any Territory, and that the Missouri Compromise was therefore unconstitutional. (Of these six, Taney, Wayne, and Daniel held that a Negro like Dred could not be a citizen; Grier, Catron, and Campbell left the issue of citizenship untouched.) Two judges, Curtis and McLean, dissented from the decision *cum ira;* they argued that Congress had ample power under the Constitution to debar slavery from any Territory. The vagueness and ambiguity of the instrument gave full room for an honest difference of interpretation.

Taney's judgment on this constitutional issue was read by Americans with emotions varying from white-hot indignation in parts of the North to jubilant rejoicing in most of the South. Whenever new areas were acquired outside the limits of the United States, he reasoned, they were held for the common benefit of the people of the whole nation. The general government must act simply as trustee for the people, administering the areas for them until made part of the Union. It was undoubtedly necessary for Congress to establish some local government over the Territories, but it must not be on a discretionary or discriminatory basis as regards persons and property. The Georgian with his slave must have equality in the Territory alongside the Vermonter with his horse. He argued that what authority Congress did possess was derived, not from the clause empowering it to make necessary rules and regulations for the Territories (this being a mere emergency provision for the lands ceded to the Confederation), but from the power to create new States and to acquire land by treaty. It was therefore a power to acquire territory and prepare it for statehood; it was not a broad internal police authority. His language was emphatic: "No word can be found in the Constitution which gives Congress a greater power over slave property, or which entitles property of that kind to less protection, than property of any other description." Congress could not exclude slavery, for as Taney broadly construed it, this would violate the "due process of law" clause of the Fifth Amendment. It had "only the power coupled with the duty of . . . protecting the owner in his rights."

The five judges who concurred with Taney in holding the Missouri Compromise unconstitutional were Wayne, Daniel, Grier, Campbell, and Catron—Southerners, all but one. The position of James Catron of Tennessee was somewhat peculiar. While in his brief, crudely expressed opinion he joined the majority in pronouncing the Missouri Compromise restriction invalid, he declared that Congress was invested with a broad authority to make needful regulations concerning the Territories. Having hanged men under the power of Congress to pass laws for the western domain, he was anxious to insist that Congress and he had acted properly. He held, in short, that the national government had large powers—but not quite large enough to permit the interdiction of slavery. Justice Daniel once more used improper language. Some groups, he wrote, in attempting to exclude slavery from Territories, had "asserted a power in Congress, whether from incentives of interest, ignorance, faction, partiality, or prejudice, to bestow upon a portion of the citizens of this nation that which is the common property and privilege of all—the power, in fine, of confiscation." This, like his use of the terms "iniquity" and "absurdity," was undignified name-calling.

To sum up, three Southern judges declared that no Negro of

slave ancestry could be entitled to citizenship; five Southern judges, with Nelson of New York, decided that Dred's status depended upon the laws of Missouri; five Southern judges, with Grier of Pennsylvania, maintained that any law excluding slavery from a Territory was unconstitutional; and two Northern judges, McLean and Curtis, held that Dred was a citizen, that Missouri law did not control his status, and that Congress had a constitutional right to pass laws debarring slavery from any Territory.

The majority having made its decision, all territorial restrictions on slavery were dead; wherever the flag advanced into new regions, it carried slavery with it. The doctrine of squatter sovereignty seemed equally dead. So long as any area held the status of a Territory, its people were theoretically as helpless as Congress to bar out the slaveholders with their slaves. But what would be the actual force of the decision? Would all good citizens, as Buchanan had predicted in his inaugural, cheerfully submit to it, or would the Northern people, legislators, and courts, as several freesoil members of Congress had threatened in advance, disregard it? The answer was not left in doubt for a single day. The greater part of the North instantly rejected the judgment on the ground that, handed down by a bench overwhelmingly biased in favor of one section, one party, and one slaveholding interest, it had no moral validity, and would retain legal validity only until a truly national bench overruled it.

The storm of anger which instantly swept the North emphasized first and foremost the moral argument. Freesoilers believed that the fathers of the republic, anticipating a sentiment of the civilized world which by 1857 had become well-nigh irresistible, had regarded slavery as an evil which must eventually wither and die. It was therefore important to circumscribe and weaken it. The Constitution ought to be interpreted in the light of this basic principle; instead, it had been interpreted in such wise as to diffuse and strengthen slavery. Greeley called for the creation of an enlightened public opinion to place all departments of the government in "the hands of men who love the Constitution and the Union much, but Liberty, Eternal

Justice, and the Inalienable Rights of Man, still more." A number of editors raised the cry that if the Constitution recognized no difference between slave property and other property, then a State legislature was as powerless as Congress or a territorial legislature to deprive any slave owner of the full use of his property. The Lemmon case, an appeal from the New York appellate court involving the status of a slave carried into that State, was pending. The Supreme Court, said these alarmists, had now indicated what would be its decision. Let its doctrine be established by law, and Toombs's reputed boast that he would yet call the roll of his slaves under Bunker Hill Monument might be realized. Meanwhile, William Cullen Bryant was denouncing Taney's decision as morally intolerable:

> Hereafter, if this decision shall stand for law, slavery, instead of being what the people of the slave States have hitherto called it, their peculiar institution, is a Federal institution, the common patrimony and shame of all the States, those which flaunt the title of free, as well as those which accept the stigma of being the Land of Bondage: hereafter, wherever our jurisdiction extends, it carries with it the chain and the scourge—wherever our flag floats, it is the flag of slavery. If so, that flag should have the light of the stars and the streaks of morning red erased from it; it should be dyed black, and its device should be the whip and the fetter.
>
> Are we to accept, without question, these new readings of the Constitution—to sit down contentedly under this disgrace—to admit that the Constitution was never before rightly understood, even by those who framed it—to consent that hereafter it shall be the slaveholders' instead of the freemen's Constitution? Never! Never!

The Northern revulsion against Taney's judgment was deepened by several passages which suggested a certain harshness of outlook. In building a historical foundation for his doctrine that Negroes were ineligible to citizenship and hence could not sue, he, like Daniel, exaggerated the public antipathy to Negroes in colonial days. History, he wrote, showed that far more than a century prior to the adoption of the Constitution they had been regarded as "beings of an inferior order, and altogether unfit to associate with the white race, either socially or politically; and so far inferior that they had no rights which the white man was bound to respect." The black man might be reduced to slavery, bought and sold, and treated as an ordinary article of merchandise. "This opinion at that time was fixed and universal in the civilized portion of the white race." A substantial inferiority had indeed existed. Charles R. Ingersoll had said in the Connecticut legislature in 1787 that Negroes in that State were "universally regarded as a servile, subject, exceptional class, in no sense fitted for . . . American citizenship." Yet Taney painted the situation too blackly. All the chief British colonies contained free Negroes who held property, made contracts, sued and were sued. Many Negroes served valiantly in the Revolution, Taney's own Maryland gladly accepting their services. Many were highly respected. As for the opinion of the "civilized portion" of mankind, everyone knew that in 1773 Lord Mansfield had forever established the rule that no Negro could be held to slavery within the realm of England; and that Jefferson's first draft of the Declaration of Independence had contained a reprobation of slavery which was omitted only in deference to Georgia and South Carolina.

In another unhappy passage, Taney asserted that the decision to abolish slavery in the Northern States had not resulted from any changed opinion upon the Negro, but from the fact that the North had found slave labor unsuited to its climate and productions. This was an untenable simplification of a complex process, its emphasis on materialistic elements doing injustice to salient moral considerations. A truer statement would be that moral opposition to slavery, increasingly strong in both sections during the Revolutionary period, was promoted in the North but checked in the South by economic factors. The contribution of reformative idealism to Northern emancipation was decisive; the labors of John Woolman, Anthony Benezet, and Franklin in America and of Granville Sharp, Wilberforce, and Clarkson in Britain had nothing to do with dollars or pounds. Numerous followers of these reformers were actuated by justice and philanthropy to the detriment of their pockets. Taney also remarked that Northern unregeneracy was illustrated by the continued activity of slave-traders plying from Northern ports, their traffic being "openly carried on and fortunes accumulated by it, without reproach from the people of the States where they resided." It was well known that the few Northerners who engaged in the slave trade after 1800 were held in bad repute, and their business had sullied the name of their descendants.

Next to the moral argument, indignant Northerners emphasized a belief that the decision constituted a flagrantly improper intrusion into the political domain. Men declared that while the supreme bench must sometimes touch political issues, a body of judges so predominantly Southern and sympathetic with slaveholding culture had no right to present a decision so manifestly sectional and partisan. Had they vindicated their impartiality by a decision adverse to their personal predilections, a different view might have been taken of their course. But in a great national crisis, said freesoilers, they had stooped, with political motives, to an act which all too obviously favored their own half of the country. Bryant's *Evening Post* on March 7, and James Watson Webb's *Courier* on March 13, set up the cry of "political conspiracy"; it spread throughout half the Northern press; and its wide acceptance is indicated by the fact that Abraham Lincoln soon took it up. A political motive was believed even where the idea of a conspiracy was rejected.

Throughout the North and West, the dissenting opinions of Curtis and McLean (particularly Curtis's, which contained much the greater panoply of historical and legal facts) exercised a profound influence. They had weaknesses of evidence and logic. But taken together, they offered a large body of evidence to rebut Taney's findings on Negro citizenship and on Congressional power.

Nothing could be more erroneous, urged Curtis, than this denial of the Negro's historic status. The Constitution spoke of "citizens of the United States at the time of adoption" of the instrument. It was therefore clear that citizens of the several States under the Confederation were citizens of the United States under the Constitution; and it was a fact that in 1787 free native-born Negroes of five States (New Hampshire, Massachusetts, New York, New Jersey, North Carolina) were not merely citizens, but held suffrage rights on equal terms with white men. Curtis cited the opinion of Judge William Gaston of North Carolina that free Negroes had voted in his State for years until a constitutional amendment deprived them of the ballot. Both McLean and Curtis pointed out that under the Treaty of Guadalupe Hidalgo the United States had given citizenship to persons of color in the lands annexed from Mexico. It had done the same, they argued, in treaties covering Louisiana, Florida, and the Cherokee and Choctaw domains. Nor was it true, asserted Curtis, that the Constitution was made exclusively for white people. Its preamble declared that it was to secure to the people of the United States the blessings of liberty, and "people" certainly included the free Negroes voting in five States.

As for Congressional power over slavery in the Territories, McLean and Curtis offered arguments based both on theory and on precedent. In theory, McLean contended that the power to acquire carries the power to govern; that Congress had always exercised this authority; and that if it deemed slavery injurious to any Territory, it had a right to prohibit it. In this argument he was able to cite Chief Justice Marshall, who had described the right of governing as "the inevitable consequence of the right to acquire." It necessarily followed, he believed, that when the United States gained a new area by conquest or purchase, Congress might govern it in any manner and for any length of time it saw fit, so long as it remained a dependency external to the Union. Curtis laid down the same doctrine still more emphatically. Chief Justice Taney's contracted interpretation of the powers of the general government was inconsistent, he held, with the nature and purposes of the Constitution. That instrument gave Congress authority "to dispose of and make all needful Rules and Regulations respecting the Territory or other property" of the nation; it could deal *both* with jurisdiction and soil; and so long as the laws were "needful" (that is, not arbitrary, capricious, or unnecessary), their scope could be left to Congressional discretion.

In citing precedents, Curtis found that Congress had passed

two classes of acts. In eight distinct instances, beginning with the first Congress and coming down to 1848, it had excluded slavery from various Territories. In six distinct instances, beginning with the first Congress and coming down to 1822, it had recognized slavery in a Territory and contained it therein. These laws had been signed by seven Presidents, including all who were in public life when the Constitution was adopted. This fact, he believed, should have much weight in interpreting the Constitution, while it was difficult to resist the force of the acts themselves. (When the Missouri Compromise became law, all the Southern Senators, a large majority of Southern Representatives, and the whole executive branch deemed it constitutional. President Monroe, as J. Q. Adams's diary shows, propounded to the Cabinet—Adams, Calhoun, Crawford, McLean, and Wirt—the question of power and they unanimously concurred with him as to its existence.) Indeed, for a half-century the Congressional power was hardly challenged.

If it could be shown by the Constitution itself that when it gave Congress authority to make all needful rules and regulations slavery was excepted, then, said Curtis, he would give due weight to that fact; but no such demonstration was possible. He must find something more than Taney's theoretical reasoning to make him believe that the Constitution did not mean *all* when it said all; especially as the Court had repeatedly balked efforts to introduce exceptions not found in the Constitution. Under the power to regulate commerce, Congress had embargoed all ships, thus prohibiting the use of a special kind of property belonging mainly to citizens of the Northeastern States; yet the Court had held this constitutional. If the power to govern commerce extended to an indefinite prohibition of the use of vessels, did not the power to make all needful rules respecting the territory of the United States extend to a prohibition of slavery?

Would the prestige of the Court, which for sixty years had been gathering dignity and influence, override all opposition? "Mr. President," Senator Cass had exclaimed in the Senate two years earlier, "it is an impressive spectacle, almost a sublime one, to see nine men . . . establishing great principles essential to public and private prosperity and to the government; whose influence is felt throughout the whole Union, and whose decrees are implicitly obeyed. It is the triumph of moral force." Yet Cass knew that the interpretation of the Constitution was a human process, and that the conclusions of the nine judges must in the last analysis harmonize with the will of the people, or they would be swept aside; he acknowledged this fact when he said that the Court "lives and breathes upon public confidence," and that "it cannot carry into effect a single decree without calling upon the other departments of government to aid it." For two main reasons all Republicans and many freesoil Democrats were quite unwilling to acknowledge the finality of the decision; one being the biased composition of the Court, the other the widespread suspicion of some political maneuvering or even conspiracy behind its decision.

Northern spokesmen had for years repeatedly declared that public confidence in the Supreme Court was impaired by the lack of balance in its membership. Of the nine judges who heard the Dred Scott case, five, including the Chief Justice, were Southerners, and four Northerners. Of these four, Grier of Pennsylvania was as pronouncedly Southern in his sympathies as Buchanan. So far as sectional inclination went, the Court stood six to three. As for party affiliation, seven of the nine were Democrats, McLean was a Republican, and Curtis still called himself a Whig. The Court plainly had an excessive party and sectional bias. Representative Stanton of Ohio, early in 1857, had introduced a resolution calling on the House Judiciary Committee to inquire into an equalization of the population and business of the judicial circuits. As critics pointed out, the seventh circuit (Ohio, Indiana, Illinois, Michigan), with four and a half million people, had more white inhabitants than three Southern circuits combined.

The bias would have been excessive even had the times been perfectly calm. But the Court had been called upon to decide the constitutionality of the Missouri Compromise restriction just when President Pierce, Attorney-General Cushing, and Secretary Jefferson Davis were condemning that law as a monumental error, and just when President-elect Buchanan and the Southern leaders were hailing the late election as a sweeping verdict against any restrictions.

The character of the judges, whose attainments ranged, as always, from consummate ability to mediocrity, offered no guarantee that party and sectional pressure would be withstood. Of the intellectual power and profound learning of the Chief Justice no question could exist. Strength of mind and elevation of spirit were stamped upon Taney's face. Tall, thin, bent with his eighty years, his skin a parchment yellow, his features deeply furrowed, his hair drooping over his high forehead, his plain black garb ill-brushed, his long arms and bony fingers giving him a spidery look as he took nervous notes, he was not an attractive figure. Yet fire dwelt in his eyes, and intensity marked his movements. From the time in 1836 when Henry Clay had violently denounced his appointment, political opponents had spoken of him harshly. Counsel familiar with the Court, however, paid tribute to his spotless character, his sagacity, his vast legal erudition, his serene dignity as presiding officer, and his painful conscientiousness in holding the scales of justice even between litigants. Deploring slavery, he had long since freed all his bondsmen. A devout Catholic, he made it a daily custom to implore heaven for guidance. Even hostile editors admitted that in the sincerity of his convictions and his intellectual authority, he was no unworthy successor of John Marshall; while "affectionate reverence" was the term used by Judah P. Benjamin for the feeling which he inspired among friends. To his trenchant power as a political thinker, later generations would do full justice.

It could nevertheless be said that, penetration and not breadth being his chief mental attribute, he sometimes displayed a narrow stubbornness; that he was strongly molded by his early Calvert County environment, the tobacco-planting, slaveholding tidewater strip of Maryland, and was deeply sympathetic with Southern ways and manners; and that his conduct as a judge had not been untinged by partisanship. As a member of Jackson's Cabinet, helping make war upon the

Bank of the United States, he had developed an anti-monopolist feeling which expressed itself on the bench in a desire to restrain mercantile and financial concentrations. The tendency of his decisions was to a strict construction of national powers conferred in the Constitution, and to a protection of the States in a full and unfettered use of their retained authority. His judgment in the Charles River case was one of several which almost caused Justice Story to resign, and inspired James Kent's indignant protest. Even sympathetic biographers admit that his opinion in one case involving the Bank and his own previous action as Attorney-General went to the verge of impropriety.

It might be noted that, in the famous Prigg case, he and Justice Daniel had stood together in holding that States could pass laws for the surrender of escaped slaves, but not laws which impaired the master's right to recover them. A champion of human rights in the economic field, he had an agrarian instinct, a feeling for the rural South as against the wealthy, partially industrialized North, which was bound insensibly to color his judicial thought. He felt that the South, and with it the Union, were in imminent danger.

Of the four other judges from slaveholding States, John A. Campbell, only forty-six this year, was easily the ablest, and had gained national reputation as an attorney before Pierce lifted him to the Supreme Court. The son of an eminent Georgia lawyer, he grew up in the same aristocratic town as Toombs—Washington—and graduated from the University of Georgia. Removing to Montgomery, Alabama, he distinguished himself by studious tastes, a remarkable memory, and undeviating regard for principle. His charge to the grand jury in New Orleans in 1854, denouncing William Walker and other filibusters, was a long-remembered exemplification of his courage. Genial, gentle, and philosophical, a close and accurate reasoner, he was never strongly partisan. He labored nearly to the last against secession, although he believed it a right. Unhappily, his three Southern associates had a less rigid impartiality.

James M. Wayne of Georgia, an intelligent, hard-working, and in no way brilliant man, who bore his sixty-seven years sturdily and who had been a member of the Court since Jackson's Presidency, was deeply attached to the Union; a fact proved in 1861 when, unlike Justice Campbell, he stuck to it. But he was also sternly positive in defense of Southern institutions. His specialty was admiralty law. Another judge of Jacksonian antecedents, John Catron of Tennessee, was a big, forthright, awkward frontier lawyer who spoke his commonsense (and commonplace) mind in a booming and unmelodious voice. A shrewd politician, he had won his place on the bench by helping Jackson in his Bank contest, and a politician he remained. There was much that was likeable in a rough western way about Catron; he had shouldered a rifle at New Orleans and had resented insults to his honor with duelling pistols. The stamp of Nashville, not as the Athens of the South but as the capital of slaveholding Tennessee, with her old interest in western expansion, was upon him.

Equally picturesque was Peter B. Daniel, a tall, thin, sharp-visaged, fidgety Virginian of aristocratic family, who had studied law under Washington's Attorney-General, Edmund Randolph, and married his daughter. While he had a fine library, read widely, and cultivated music, he made few pretensions to legal learning. He was simply an old-school gentleman of taste and logical intellect. His weakness lay in his fanatical temper, for if Wayne was an extremist in defending slavery, Daniel was a bigot. He told his grandnephew, Moncure D. Conway, that the antislavery men were "monsters," and his language in the Dred Scott case was so intemperate that his friend W. W. Seaton gravely rebuked him in the *National Intelligencer*. The portrait of Daniel reveals a wild gleam in his eye, an intolerant set about his mouth.

These five members from the slaveholding region constituted a majority of the Court. Of the two judges from the Middle States, Samuel Nelson of New York was the more easily appraised. He was a conservative up-State Democrat who, while chief justice of the State Supreme Court, had been raised to the national tribunal by Tyler. Plodding, blunt, honest, and hard-working, he was perfectly trustworthy. His interest was in technical questions of maritime, patent, and international law rather than in broad constitutional issues. While his views might be limited, he stuck to them without regard for politics, personalities, or public opinion. The other, Robert C. Grier of Pennsylvania, one of Polk's appointees, had of late been ceaselessly attacked in his own section as a fickle tool of slavery. Like Taney (class of 1795) and Buchanan (class of 1809), he was a graduate of Dickinson College (class of 1812) at Carlisle. During recent years his zeal in upholding the Fugitive Slave Law had evoked Southern praise and freesoil wrath. "He succumbs to touch and returns to shape upon its removal," wrote James S. Pike of this rotund, cheerful jurist. "He is ardent and impressible." A neighbor and friend of Buchanan, he was eager for the success of the Administration and the party. It was to Grier that the President-elect had written just after his triumph the previous fall that he meant to destroy the dangerous slavery agitation, strengthen the Democratic Party, and thus restore peace to the distracted nation.

Grier's pliability was coupled with an inadequate instinct for propriety and dignity. The Buchanan Papers contain some curious letters showing that at this very time Grier's family affairs were embarrassed; indeed, he was always heavily burdened, for he had toiled hard to support his mother and help educate ten younger brothers. To mend his circumstances, he was anxious to install a relative as clerk of the circuit court in Philadelphia, a position held by an efficient party lieutenant, George Plitt. The justice first asked Buchanan to give Plitt another office, which the President coldly refused to do. Grier then brought pressure upon Plitt to resign. The clerk declined. "You and I and the public too," he wrote Grier, "if aware of all the facts, would know that by resigning I should make myself party to an apparent traffic in official trusts, which . . . the President, when it was hinted to him, promptly rebuked." Yet Grier persisted, and in the face of a memorial signed by numerous members of the Philadelphia bar brought about Plitt's removal. This improper act was much resented. Grier, to be sure, had certain good qualities; a former head of Northumberland College, he was broadly cultivated, while his Civil War record was to prove creditable. But he was a weak man.

Altogether, it is not strange that countless Northerners regarded the Dred Scott decision as the political stroke of a sectional, proslavery majority of judges. Many press reports were highly colored. Describing the panel on March 6, some Northern journalists pictured them as guilt-haggard conspirators. The general air of the majority, wrote Pike of the *Tribune,* was one of "nervous exultation over their attempt to garrote the free States." He presented a series of caustic vignettes of the Southern members. Daniel, he wrote, was a palsied, fretful old gentleman in glasses, with the politics of a Virginia slaveholder and abstractionist who still swore by the resolutions of 1798. Catron's errors would more often spring from obtuseness than from original sin. Campbell was more Southern than the extreme South from which he hailed. Wayne, who had shown his ill temper by uttering loud comments while Curtis read his judgment, would dispute the right of any Northern man to an opinion on slavery or its relations. But Pike's sharpest barbs were reserved for Taney. Not content with saying that the inverted step, narrow forehead, sunken eyes, and "sinister expression" of the Chief Justice made him look like a man of malign disposition, he impugned his honor. Reverdy Johnson, he declared, had overcome the opposition in the Senate when Jackson appointed Taney head of the Court, and Taney was duly grateful. Hence the eagerness of the slavery men to hire Reverdy Johnson to argue the Dred Scott case!

While such calumny was deplorable, Northern insistence that the one-sided decision would shortly be rectified by a truly national court was perfectly defensible. Freesoil men held that the decree was valid insofar as it affected Dred Scott, but not in its more sweeping pronouncements, and that as soon as a freesoil President could change the list of judges, the Court would restore the old reading of the Constitution. Every Republican editor caught up the cry. "The remedy," stated the Chicago *Tribune,* "is union and action; the ballot box. Let free States be a unit in Congress on the side of freedom. Let the next President be Republican, and 1860 will mark an era kindred with that of 1776." The Springfield *Republican,* Albany *Journal,* and other sheets pointed out that the judgments of the Court were always reversible. If the Court had affirmed the constitutionality of the Alien and Sedition Acts, the people would nevertheless have annulled them and paid back the penalties exacted under them. The Court had pronounced the Bank of the United States constitutional, but the people had made a contrary decision. The tribunal of final jurisdiction was the American nation massed at the polls.

Declaring that six million whites of the South had more weight in the Supreme Court than sixteen million people in the free areas, the New York *Tribune* called for a reapportionment; "Make the judicial districts equal, let judges be fairly selected therefrom, and the Dred Scott decision will soon be overthrown and effaced."

The conviction of Republicans upon the bias of the Court was enhanced by their belief that more "national" nominations to the bench had been defeated mainly by Southern votes. President Tyler had nominated John C. Spencer and Chancellor Reuben Walworth, both New Yorkers of high standing and both Whigs, but the Senate had refused confirmation. When Polk had nominated George W. Woodward of Pennsylvania, he had been rejected because of his alleged nativist views, because of the dislike of Simon Cameron, then a Democrat, and because some Senators feared Woodward would be hostile to slavery. Fillmore had nominated George E. Badger of North Carolina, a Whig, twice a Cabinet member, and a distinguished Senator. The Democratic press had deluged him with abuse, one editor terming him worse than an abolitionist because he believed the Wilmot Proviso constitutional, and the Senate blocked him. Had these four men gone into the Supreme Court, its character in 1857 would have been very different.

While charges against the Court's impartiality were serious, those against its probity were far graver. The theory that the majority decisions had originated in a conspiracy between Buchanan and Taney was bitterly asserted by several newspapers, and caught up by Republican politicians. Eminent leaders soon adopted it. In a resounding speech of March 3, 1858, Seward declared that before entering office Buchanan had approached or been approached by the Supreme Court; that his reference to the decision in the inaugural was proof of a coalition between Court and President "to undermine the national legislature and the liberties of the people"; and that the plot culminated in dishonorable "whisperings" between Buchanan and Taney just before the new President took his oath.

Taney was revolted by this charge. He long afterward told his first biographer that if the scoundrel Seward had been chosen President in 1860, he would have declined to administer the oath of office to him. That Seward wronged the Chief Justice, in bringing so harsh an accusation, there can be no doubt. While there had been a most improper exchange of views between the President-elect and two associate justices, there had certainly been no collusion between Taney and Buchanan. But, setting aside the misstated charge of conspiracy, we must still ask why the Court entered so unnecessarily upon the dangerous question of Congressional power in the Territories. When it was decided that Missouri law controlled Dred's status, it was beside the point to explore the validity of the Missouri Compromise. Did the Southern members of the Court wantonly intrude upon this political terrain, or did the fault lie elsewhere? Conflicting evidence requires the closest possible analysis.

Let us review what had happened. From the moment Congress met in December, 1856, and found the Court ready to hear argument, Southern and Democratic pressure was brought upon the judges to make a clear-cut decision on the Compromise. Alexander H. Stephens, a close friend of his fellow-Georgian Wayne, vigorously urged a broad judgment on this controverted issue. He wrote his brother Linton in mid-December that he was active and hopeful. The Washington correspondent of the New York *Express*, a Know-Nothing organ which prided itself on the best capital intelligence in the country, stated that a comprehensive decision was expected by those who knew the situation. "The Democracy is especially anxious that the bench should relieve them from the territorial issues of the slavery question, and it is understood are bringing whatever influence they may to bear upon the court." On New Year's Day, another of its correspondents added that some of the judges had made up their minds on the territorial issue. "Their opinion has found partial expression in the Dred Scott case, and you will find that, before six months shall have expired, the unconstitutionality of territorial legislation upon the question will be regarded as settled, both by the North and the South." The Washington *Union*, precentor of the Administration press, simultaneously prophesied that the Court would find the Compromise restriction unconstitutional by a vote of seven to two, McLean and Curtis dissenting. It and other Democratic sheets were patently anxious for a sweeping decision.

When reargument began in mid-December, the Chief Justice had carefully framed the two main questions to be treated *de novo*: (1) Whether a Negro of Dred's position and lineage could be a citizen of the United States and entitled to sue, and (2) Whether Congress had constitutional authority to exclude slavery from the Territories. It was noteworthy that counsel dealt with the whole range of issues. Reverdy Johnson, with much undignified gibing at "Sambo" and "Cuffee" combined with sarcasm, partisan prejudice, and appeals to Southern emotion, covered the widest possible ground. He held that slavery, as a beneficent institution, should be perpetual and should be given the right to expand. On Dred's side, Montgomery Blair argued the right of the Negro to citizenship, and George Ticknor Curtis the right of Congress to prohibit slavery in the Territories. Indeed, Curtis, the first of whose two learned volumes on *The History of the Origin, Formation, and Adoption of the Constitution of the United States* had appeared three years earlier, furnished a searching examination of the use Congress had made of its authority to devise "all needful rules and regulations" for the Territories. Geyer also argued the constitutionality of the Missouri Compromise. Press reports and editorial comment covered the whole subject, and with Democratic papers confident and Republican journals apprehensive, the public gained the impression that a broad decision impended.

Alexander H. Stephens, who was in touch with Justice Wayne, thought that such a decision was about to be rendered. On New Year's Day he wrote a friend that he felt a deep solicitude over the judgment. "From what *I hear sub rosa* it will be according to my own opinions upon every point as abstract political questions. The restriction of 1820 will be held to be unconstitutional. The Judges are all writing out their opinions I believe *seriatim*. The Chief Justice will give an elaborate one." Montgomery Blair, who was on the alert to pick up every grain of news, also expected a sweeping decision. He informed ex-President Van Buren on February 5 that it seemed to be the impression that the Court would decide against Dred, and also against the power of Congress over the Territories.

At this point an extraordinary correspondence began between the President-elect and Judge Catron. Buchanan, aware that he would be expected to say something about popular sovereignty in his inaugural, and that any explicit statement would anger either the Cass-Douglas or the Southern wing of the party, wished with characteristic caution to fall back on the Supreme Court. He wrote his old Jacksonian friend on February 3, asking whether he might say that the Court would soon decide the question. Catron immediately replied (February 6) that it rested with Chief Justice Taney to move in the matter, and that so far he had said nothing to him about it. A conference might have been held earlier, he thought, but for the prostration of Judge Daniel by the tragic death of his beautiful young wife, whose clothing had accidentally caught fire. This delay was really unnecessary, for Daniel "will surely deliver his own opinion in the case, *at length*." Probably Catron knew how profoundly Daniel's feelings were stirred. He promised to keep Buchanan informed. Four days later, February 10, he wrote again:

> The Dred Scott case will be decided next Saturday [that is, would be discussed in conference on Saturday, February 14] but it is not at all probable that you will be helped by the decision in preparing your Inaugural. Some of the judges will

not touch the question of [Congressional] power, others may, but that it will settle *nothing*, is my present opinion.

No opinions can be expected to be announced before the end of this month.

Catron went on to make it plain that he himself believed the Missouri Compromise unconstitutional, simply because the Louisiana Purchase had guaranteed slavery in that region. His letters must have provoked Buchanan. They made it evident that Daniel would surely express his fanatical opinions at length, that other judges might touch the Compromise issue, and that Catron himself had fixed views on the subject—but that he doubted whether the decision would settle the matter. On February 14, however, Glancy Jones, who operated his own listening post in the capital, sent Buchanan a different view. "The Supreme Court will give their decision soon and the reasoning of the opinion will cover Squatter Sovereignty. To anxious inquirers on this subject in your inaugural I have answered I believe you would rest on the decision of the Supreme Court."

What, meanwhile, was the Court actually doing? Rules of secrecy and judicial reticence envelop the subject in a murky haze through which we can peer but dimly, and dogmatic assertions on the critical point are impossible. It appears that when conferences began on or about the fourteenth, the majority wished to stop short with the decision that after Dred's return the Missouri law determined his status as slave, and he had no right to sue in a Federal court. Judge Nelson was deputed to prepare the majority opinion on the subject, and did so; the question of Congressional power would lie untouched. It also appears that various members contested this majority action, and a series of stormy debates began. What members? Catron had mentioned Judge Daniel's wish to express himself *at length*; evidence exists that Judge Wayne, pressed by Stephens, had already begun to write a broad opinion. Indeed, Judge Campbell later stated that several opinions had been begun before the first conference, and that Wayne shortly urged Chief Justice Taney to write a full decision instead of letting Nelson pen a brief judgment.

"The instruction of the majority, in reference to the preparation of this opinion," writes Campbell, "was to limit the opinion to the particular circumstances of Dred Scott; and Mr. Justice Nelson prepared his opinion, on file, under this instruction, to be read as the opinion of the Court. Subsequently, and before it was read, upon a motion of Mr. Justice Wayne, who stated that the case had created public interest and expectation, that it had been twice argued, and that an impression existed that the questions argued would be considered in the opinion of the Court, he proposed that the Chief Justice should write an opinion on all of the questions as the opinion of the Court. This was assented to; some reserving to themselves to qualify their assent as the opinion might require."

If we accept this statement, Wayne apparently convinced Taney, Catron, and Campbell that a broad verdict was needed —Daniel already taking that view. But Judge Grier, as a Northerner who had been under heavy fire for "subservience," was reluctant to act. If he held to his position, the Compromise restriction would be declared unconstitutional by five slave State judges. This, from the Southern point of view, was undesirable; at least one Northern judge should join the others. Something must be done!

For the Southern majority, Catron took action. Resuming his correspondence with Buchanan, he asked him to bring pressure upon his close friend Grier. Writing February 19, he stated that the omens were better, that the case had been before the judges several times since Saturday the fourteenth, and that Buchanan could safely pass responsibility to the Court. "You may say in your inaugural that the constitutionality of the Compromise is now before the tribunal," he wrote, "and you may add, 'It is due to its high and independent character to suppose that it will settle and decide a controversy which has so long and uselessly agitated the country, and which *must* ultimately be decided by the Supreme Court'." But would the President-elect please lend a hand? "A majority of my brethren will be forced up to this point by two dissentients. Will you drop Grier a line, saying how necessary it is, and how good the opportunity is, to settle the question by an affirmative decision of the Supreme Court, the one way or the other? He ought not to occupy so doubtful a ground as the outside issue—that admitting the constitutionality of the Missouri Compromise law of 1820, still, as no domicile was acquired by the Negro at Fort Snelling, and he returned to Missouri, he was not free. He has no doubt about the question on the main contest, but has been persuaded to take the smooth handle for the sake of repose." Catron knew that Grier readily yielded to manipulation.

Buchanan was quite ready to act. In fact, he had a special reason for doing so; for if Catron stuck to what was apparently his original position, that the Missouri Compromise was void merely because of the Louisiana Purchase treaty, then only a minority of four judges (Taney, Wayne, Daniel, Campbell) would declare that Congress had no power over slavery in the Territories in general. The President-elect sent Grier a letter, since lost, which urged him to join in quashing the slavery agitation. Grier replied on February 23 with all the expected complaisance. He had at once shown Buchanan's letter to Taney and Wayne, he wrote. "We fully appreciate and concur in your views as to the desirableness at the time of having an expression of the opinion of the Court on this troublesome question."

Indeed, he explained, they had already reached this conclusion. At first, Nelson had been commissioned to write an opinion leaving the difficult issues of citizenship and Congressional power untouched. "But it appeared that our brothers who dissented from the majority, especially Justice McLean, were determined to come out with a long and labored dissent, including their opinions and arguments on both the troublesome points, although not necessary to a decision of the case. In our opinion both the points are *in* the case and may be legitimately considered. Those who hold a different opinion from Messrs. McLean and Curtis on the power of Congress and the validity of the Compromise Act feel compelled to express their opinions on the subject."

Grier was anxious, he continued, that no line of latitude should seem to have determined the Court's decision; anxious, too, that the majority opinion should have a general unity of view. Conversing with Taney, he had agreed to concur with him, while he had also agreed to labor with Wayne to get Daniel, Campbell, and Catron to do the same. He feared that some Southern members might throw out extreme views. But at any rate, six judges would declare the Missouri Compromise unconstitutional. "We will not let any of our brethren know the *cause of our anxiety* to produce this result." This missive greatly relieved Buchanan and Catron. But they continued under some anxiety. As late as February 21, eleven days before the inauguration, Buchanan was writing Catron again to urge prompt action, and two days later Catron was replying that he had hoped to have the opinion delivered before the third of March, that most of his colleagues were ready, and that "I want Grier speeded."

What does all this come to? On the letters of Grier and Catron many writers have founded a dogmatic statement that the dissenters, McLean and Curtis, forced a broad decision; but hastily written letters usually give but a partial view of the truth. One curious contradiction in these epistles is evident at a glance. Catron asked Buchanan to induce Grier to support a sweeping judgment; Grier wrote Buchanan that he would try to get Catron to agree to one! The two men did not clearly understand each other. For half a dozen reasons . . . we may doubt their accuracy in placing the main responsibility for the broad decision upon McLean and Curtis; for this oversimplifies a very complex transaction.

Rosy hopes of benefit and prestige from the decision danced before the Administration's eyes. The truculent Douglas would have to "cave in"; Republicans would find themselves battling the Constitution and the Union. "There was but one thing needful to give to the result in the presidential contest the force of an absolute and final settlement of the sectional issue," exulted the Washington *Union*. "That thing was the judgment of the Supreme Court in confirmation of the Democratic doctrines which had received the popular endorsement. . . . The people have decided that sectional agitation must cease, and the highest judicial authority has declared that the people have decided in accordance with the Constitution." The attacks of

Republicans on the decision it stigmatized as "the last dying fit of fanatical sectionalism."

In the minds of Buchanan, Taney, Wayne, and wishful-thinking leaders of the Southern Democracy, a certain confusion existed. The Supreme Court "settled" great national questions. When it handed down its decision in *Marbury* vs. *Madison,* the right of judicial interpretation was "settled"; men ceased to contest it. When it spoke in *Gibbons* vs. *Ogden,* the jurisdiction of the national government over navigation was "settled"; thereafter none denied it. When it decided the Dartmouth College case, the sanctity of certain contracts was "settled"; acceptance was general. It was natural to believe that when the Court gave explicit judgment on the position of slavery in the Territories, that too would be settled. Good citizens would cease to hold an adverse view. Multitudes of Republicans would say, resignedly: "Well, I had thought we possessed some ground for believing slavery could be excluded from the Territories. I see now that it cannot. We shall have to pull our party over to the tariff, or some other new dogma."

The fact that a deep and insuperable difference existed between a demand that individuals should abandon a legal theory, and a demand that a great party should abandon a basic conviction, escaped these observers. Men could be persuaded by the logic of the Court to give up an interpretation which touched only property interests or the mechanics of government. They could not be persuaded to give up a party doctrine upon which they believed the whole destiny of the republic—nay, its very position as the hope of mankind—depended. Points of law could be determined by a decision from the Capitol basement; main lines of national development could not. Even had the Court in 1857 been a body of Olympian majesty, its purity unquestioned, millions of Republicans would have said: "Some issues can be decided only at the polls—only by the masses."

Thomas Hart Benton, now dying of cancer, expressed this conviction with characteristic vigor. Filled with indignation, he was determined to give his last energies to a long and minute exposé of the errors of the Court. He objected to its decision, he wrote, not so much because it was mistaken as because it violated a great principle. Recalling the failure of two efforts in Congress in 1848–49 to pass a bill carrying the Constitution (and slavery) into the Territories, he exclaimed: "And this is what the Supreme Court has decided—the judicial power deciding a political question!—and in a way which the political power had twice repulsed!"

The wave of denunciation that swept across the North and West was long in subsiding. Lincoln dealt with the decision in a widely reported speech in Springfield on June 12, 1857, notable for its appeal to first principles. The position of the slave, he declared, had grown worse. Masters had largely been prevented from emancipating them. Provisions had been written into State constitutions to prevent legislatures from abolishing slavery. The Supreme Court now decided that Congress could not keep slavery out of the Territories. Once the Declaration of Independence had been held sacred, but now it was assailed, construed, and hawked at until its framers would not recognize it—and all to make the bondage of the Negro universal and eternal. "All the powers of earth seem rapidly combining against him. Mammon is after him, ambition follows, philosophy follows, and the theology of the day is fast joining the cry. They have him in his prison-house; they have searched his person and left no prying instrument with him. One after another they have closed the heavy iron doors upon him; and now they have him, as it were, bolted in with a lock of a hundred keys, which can never be unlocked without the concurrence of every key—the keys in the hands of a hundred different men, and they scattered to a hundred different and distant places; and they stand musing as to what invention, in all the dominions of mind and matter, can be produced to make the impossibility of his escape more difficult than it is." He appealed to the rightful meaning of the Declaration. Its authors intended to apply it not to Americans and Britons alone, but to all peoples—they contemplated a progressive improvement in the condition of all men everywhere:

They meant to set up a standard maxim for free society, which should be familiar to all, and revered by all; constantly looked to, constantly labored for, and even though never perfectly attained, constantly approximated, and thereby constantly spreading and deepening its influence, and augmenting the happiness and value of life to all peoples of all colors everywhere.

The New York legislature adopted savagely condemnatory resolutions. After declaring that the Court had lost the respect and confidence of the State, it announced that New York would never permit slavery within its borders in any form, under any pretext, or for any space of time. Any slave brought to New York would instantly become free, and any person trying to hold a slave, even in transit, would be liable to imprisonment for two to ten years. A committee of the Pennsylvania legislature reported that the decision was a gross misconstruction of the Constitution, inoperative on any point save Dred Scott's own status. John A. Andrew assailed the Court in a speech to the Massachusetts legislature which became famous; and the Massachusetts, Maine, Connecticut, and Rhode Island houses all acted to condemn the decision. So did the Vermont legislature, a committee terming the majority judges "tyrants." Much of the press and pulpit did not hesitate to hit below the belt. The New York *Tribune* called Taney jesuitical, thought it fitting that he sunk his voice to a whisper, and spoke of his "atrocious" doctrine that Negroes had no rights which white men were bound to respect—though what he had actually said was that before 1787 this doctrine was universal. Personal liberty legislation received a strong impetus.

Copies of Benton's book, his final testament to the American people, were soon sown broadcast. "I will die upon the truth and justice of what I wrote," exclaimed the old Roman, who confessed that the annulment of the Compromise "is the heaviest political blow that ever fell upon my heart." Another telling indictment was presented by George Robertson, former chief justice of Kentucky, who had been a Congressman when the Compromise passed. In three articles in the *National Intelli-*

*gencer* he arraigned the majority decision and rebuked the Court. Such a tribunal, he wrote, could retain public esteem only by showing rare learning and complete impartiality—"and by never tampering with political questions or any others which its duty does not require it to decide."

This antagonism to the judgment of the Court never subsided. It soon crystallized, for Republicans and Douglas Democrats alike, in a simple refusal to accept the decision as binding upon anyone save the poor black man whose plea had evoked it. Lincoln, speaking for Western freesoilers, declared that he would refuse to obey it "as a political rule." Benton crisply remarked that such political decisions could not be enforced. "No mandamus can be directed to Congress and the people; no process of contempt can issue against them." This was true. When the Republicans took control of the government, the decision was set aside quietly, completely, and forever.

Events soon made it clear that Chief Justice Taney and his associates felt themselves upon the defensive. His half-inaudible decision had been very imperfectly reported by the press, and early and complete publication of the judgment was impatiently awaited. The custom was that judges should file their opinions with the clerk immediately after the delivery, whereupon they became accessible to anyone who applied and paid the costs of copying. The press soon carried reports, however, that Taney's judgment was being drastically revised. The New York Assembly committee, in reporting its condemnatory resolutions, stated that it had been unable to obtain authenticated copies of any of the majority decisions.

Meanwhile, behind the scenes, a remarkable controversy was taking place between Taney and Justice Curtis. Filing his opinion with the clerk, Curtis gave a copy to a Boston journal for publication, and left for his vacation in Pittsfield. Learning there that Taney's opinion had been revised and materially altered, he wrote the clerk for a copy. This was refused him, the clerk stating that Taney had directed that nobody should be allowed to see his opinion until it was published in *Howard's Reports*. The fact was that three majority judges, Taney, Wayne, and Daniel, had agreed on a rule, after their colleagues left Washington, which sealed up the Court's judgment on Dred Scott until published in the term volume.

Curtis then applied directly to the Chief Justice for permission to see the opinion. He received a reply tinged with acerbity. Taney censured Curtis for the publication of his opinion, which, along with McLean's, had been widely used by assailants of the Court; he spoke of the use of such documents by "political and partisan newspapers, for political and partisan purposes"; he objected strongly to a proposed pamphlet issue of Curtis's and Taney's opinions, implying that Curtis would take the profits "for his own emolument"; and he showed himself hurt because Curtis had announced from the bench that he regarded Taney's judgment on Congressional power as extrajudicial and not binding. Curtis made a vigorous rejoinder. He denied any connection with the scheme of pamphlet publication, censured the arbitrary rule laid down by the three judges, and deplored the delay in publication. Above all, he implied a strong criticism of Taney's course in revising his opinion after its delivery. Stung by this, the Chief Justice affirmed that he had not altered one statement of fact or principle in his opinion, but had merely inserted some new proofs and authorities. When Curtis saw the document, however (*19 Howard* appearing at the end of May), he took a different view, commenting that Taney had added at least eighteen printed pages, with new factual and theoretical matter, in rebuttal of Curtis's dissent.

Filled with disgust, Justice Curtis announced his resignation in September. His ostensible reason was the inadequacy of his salary; his real compulsion sprang from the fact that he could not again feel that confidence in the Court and that willingness to labor harmoniously with its members which were essential to a just discharge of his duties. He should have sat through one session more, declared his friends, to prove that no intimidation by slave State members could shake the firm seat of a judge of the Supreme Court.

The significance of Taney's tart replies to the more polite letters of Curtis lies in their revelation of the bitterness of the Chief Justice over the public reception of his decision. His feelings were lacerated by the hostile analyses of his argument, the Northern denunciation of the "pro-slavery judges," and above all, the painful fall in the prestige of the Court. He soon realized, moreover, that the majority opinions had not strengthened slavery in the Territories by one iota, that they were rejected as sharply by the Cass-Douglas wing of the Democracy as by the Republicans, and that they had thrown oil and not water on the flame of sectional dissension. Would not posterity arraign him as critically as had the mass opinion of the North?

The novelist G. P. R. James, British consul in Richmond, found Taney sunk in depression when in May the Chief Justice visited that city on circuit duty. The two, as old friends, spent a number of evenings together. Domestic affliction, in the recent death of his wife and the loss of a daughter by yellow fever, had contributed to the melancholy of the aged jurist. The sad state of the nation, however, weighed most heavily upon his spirits. He spoke of the evils of the spoils system and rotation in office, and of the bad effect of the frequent election of all officers, great and small, so that public servants became too timid to do their duty. He feared that a bloody national convulsion impended. As James wrote to Lord Clarendon of the Foreign Office:

> He believes that the unity and power of the Democratic Party have alone saved the Union from being torn in pieces by two conflicting factions—North and South—and that the growing dissolutions in that Party must end in arraying North and South in actual hostility against each other.
>
> The Chief Justice expatiated largely upon the anarchical tendencies evident in various parts of the United States— upon the organized riots in Baltimore, the anomalous condition of New York, the apathy of the Magistracy, the system of lynching, the Filibustering spirit in all Southern cities, the fanaticism of the North, the corruption in Congress—even, as he asserted, in the Senate; and the disregard of law, and want of respect for authority, evident everywhere.
>
> This, he said, might all be amended, and probably would be, did not the evils arise from sources, not only still acting,

but daily increasing in force, and so deeply fixed in the new constitutions of the various States, and in the minds of men, that there was no hope of their peaceful removal.

Their conversation touched upon the recent decision:

> A war on the subject of Slavery between the North and South, he thought very probable, and not remote; and he spoke freely of his late decision in the Dred Scott case, saying that he was fully aware, at the time he pronounced it, of the dangerous consequences which might ensue, but that he was on the Bench to announce the law and the Constitution, and not to make them; he was disinterested, too; for nobody could either promote or displace him, and all his own slaves he had emancipated twenty years ago.

Taney must undoubtedly be credited with high and patriotic motives; but no man is ever as impartial as he thinks, and he, as much as any Chief Justice in our history, had been shaped by a special environment and a distinct set of allegiances. He wrote ex-President Pierce late in the summer that he felt an abiding confidence that his decision would stand the test of time and the sober judgment of the country. This statement, itself a disclosure of uneasiness, has not been justified by events. Instead, the verdict of history has been enunciated by one learned jurist and endorsed by another: "The Dred Scott decision cannot be, with accuracy, written down as a usurpation, but it can and must be written down as a gross abuse of trust by the body which rendered it." The same authority remarks that its worst result was simply that it dealt a shattering blow to the influence of the judicial branch, so that during neither the Civil War nor Reconstruction did the Supreme Court play anything like its due role of supervision. But this is erroneous: the worst result was to appear in 1858–60 in the fateful Southern demand that the Democratic Party should be placed upon a Dred Scott platform. The party should be moved, that is, from the old position that Congress had no right to legislate slavery *out* of the Territories, to the new position that it must protect slavery *in* them.

Not one of the results expected from the decision appeared. It did not affect Dred Scott. It did not strengthen slavery in a single Territory. It did not unite the Democratic Party. It did not discomfit the Republicans. But it did give Southern extremists a judicial basis for that positive-protection demand which contributed so much to rend the Democracy and the nation in twain.

As for President Buchanan, he may have read with satisfaction the editorial in the Philadelphia *Pennsylvanian* which dogmatized: "There are certain points which are settled and beyond the reach of the fanatics of the nation. . . . The decision is a closing and clinching confirmation of the settlement of the issue." He may have helped John Appleton or Jeremiah Black write the leader in the Washington *Union* which sang a requiem over the slavery quarrel: "We believe it is settled, and that henceforth sectionalism will cease to be a dangerous element in our political contests. . . . Of course, it is to be expected that fanaticism ceases to be a formidable enemy, when it seeks to measure strength with the Union-loving spirit of the people, sustained or confirmed by the great arbiter of constitutional opinions." How completely these statements misread the situation the next stormy year was to show. Taney, who knew his Milton, could have pondered over applicable lines:

> Chaos umpire sits,
> And *by decision more embroils the fray*
> By which he reigns; next him high arbiter
> Chance governs all.

## For Further Reading

The best guide to the literature on the coming of the Civil War is Thomas J. Pressly, *Americans Interpret Their Civil War* (1954). A good text with an excellent bibliography is James G. Randall and David Donald, *The Civil War and Reconstruction* (2d ed., 1961).

The leading Revisionist views may be found in George Fort Milton's *The Eve of Conflict* (1934), in the first volume of James G. Randall's *Lincoln the President* (1945), and in three works by Avery O. Craven: *The Repressible Conflict* (1939), *The Coming of the Civil War* (1942), and *The Growth of Southern Nationalism* (1953). Similar in emphasis to these works are three studies of the immediate decisions (or nondecisions) leading to war: Roy F. Nichols, *The Disruption of American Democracy* (1948), dealing primarily with Buchanan's presidency; David M. Potter, *Lincoln and His Party in the Secession Crisis* (1942), covering the 1860–1861 winter; and Kenneth M. Stampp, *And the War Came* (1950).

Biographies of some of the leading figures shed light on forces contributing to the divisive atmosphere of sectionalism: see, for examples, David Donald's brilliant *Charles Sumner and the Coming of the Civil War* (1960); P. S. Klein, *President James Buchanan* (1962); Roy F. Nichols' study of Pierce, *Young Hickory of the Granite Hills* (1931); Oswald G. Villard, *John Brown* (1910); on Douglas, see Milton's book cited above and G. M. Capers, *Stephen A. Douglas* (1959); and the various works on Lincoln mentioned later in this volume. In addition to Nevins' account of the Dred Scott case, see Vincent Hopkins, *Dred Scott's Case* (1951), C. B. Swisher, *Roger B. Taney* (1935), and Stanley I. Kutler, *The Dred Scott Decision* (1967). A sound study on events immediately preceding the attack on Fort Sumter is Dwight L. Dummond, *The Secession Movement* (1931), and for the Fort Sumter crisis itself, see Richard N. Current, *Lincoln and the First Shot* (1963).

# Lincoln
# the Liberal Statesman

## James G. Randall

To say that more has been written about Abraham Lincoln than any other American considerably understates the case. Every conceivable aspect of the sixteenth President's life and career, from his habits of dress and his wit to his religion and the influence of his literary style on American writing, has been examined. Much of this literature can most accurately be described as hagiography, but Lincoln has not escaped debunking, notably in an extremely hostile biography written by Edgar Lee Masters in 1931. The axiom that no one ever knows enough history has at times been challenged, but it is hard to deny that it seems impossible for readers to ever learn enough about Lincoln. Full-length studies include the ten-volume biography by his personal secretaries John G. Nicolay and John Hay and six colorful but somewhat cluttered volumes by Carl Sandburg.

Much of the interest in Lincoln lies in the difficulty of understanding his motives. His law partner, William H. Herndon, once described him as "a profound mystery—

*Source:* James G. Randall, *Lincoln the Liberal Statesman* (New York: Dodd, Mead & Company, Inc., 1947), pp. 175–206. Copyright 1947 by Dodd, Mead & Company, Inc. Reprinted by permission of the publisher.

an enigma—a sphinx, a riddle.... You had to guess at the man after years of acquaintance and then you must look long and keenly before you guessed or you would make an ass of yourself." This quality of mystery and controversy is underscored by such titles as *Myths After Lincoln, The Lincoln Nobody Knows, The Lincoln Legend.*

Revisionist historians have observed that Lincoln's greatness was not universally recognized by his contemporaries. Savagely attacked throughout his administration in the North as well as the South, his apotheosis began only after his assassination. As Sandburg wrote, "A tree is best measured when it's down." The legend of the President as a nonpartisan man who stood above the factions, determined to bind up the wounds of the nation, served the political and psychological needs of the Reconstruction era. Lincoln's murder caused many to forget just how controversial a figure he had been; controversy surrounded his entire career. A good example is his role in the crisis over Fort Sumter. Did the President maneuver Jefferson Davis into firing the first shot, thus uniting the North in a determination to crush the rebellion? Southern historians have drawn a picture of a wily and unscrupulous Lincoln tricking the unwary Confederates so as to pin on them the stigma of first blood. This position rests chiefly on the extraordinary contention that "the Confederate government could not, without yielding the principle of independence, abate its claims to the fort." Quite true, but there is another side to this coin. How could Lincoln accept Confederate claims to Sumter without violating his duty to preserve the Constitution and the territorial integrity of the United States?

Another dispute concerns the true nature of Lincoln's relations with the Radical Republicans. Were they a menace to his administration? In recent years, the interpretation of the radicals as a united, purposeful group of fiery extremists, harassing the President and obstructing the war effort, has given way to a more balanced treatment. Troublesome the radicals assuredly were, but on the essential issues they usually supported the President. Lincoln once summed up his attitude to them in these words: "They are utterly lawless—the unhandiest devils in the world to deal with—but after all their faces are set Zionwards."

Another problem remains more or less up in the air. No scholar has successfully solved the puzzle about what part the President played in the selection of Andrew Johnson as his running mate in 1864. He has been variously portrayed as unconcerned about the vice presidential nominee, or hostile to Johnson, or actively working behind the scenes for his nomination.

In recent years, the most debated area of Lincoln historiography concerns Negro emancipation. Where did the Liberator really stand on slavery? As a young man Lincoln supposedly promised to "hit slavery hard," if he ever got the chance, and he told a Cincinnati audience in 1842 that "Slavery and oppression must cease, or American liberty must perish." But his later career shows that he certainly was not an abolitionist. At the war's beginning he put the preservation of the Union as his primary goal; although he believed that slavery had to be put "into the path of ultimate extinction," he would have apparently accepted the South back into the Union with slavery intact. Convinced that the sudden and total freeing of the blacks would be harmful to all concerned, he favored a gradual emancipation with fair compensation to the owners. Even the Emancipation Proclamation affected slavery only in states or districts "then in rebellion against the United States"; in other words, in precisely those areas where the federal government could not exert its influence. It did not directly strike at the peculiar institution in the loyal border states or in occupied areas of the Confederacy. The abolitionists strongly criticized the limitations of the act, and it may well be true to say, as some have, that Lincoln was a reluctant emancipator, but it is hardly fair to charge him with racism as some others have.

In the following selection, James G. Randall, whose four-volume *Lincoln the President* is the fullest and most profound of the modern biographies, states the case for Lincoln as the exemplar of the liberal democratic statesman. A deep concern for human rights and detestation of the evil practice of slavery animated his life and put him ahead of his time. But he tempered his innate idealism with traditional American pragmatism, distinguishing between what was ideal and what was at any given time possible. Not blaming the South for slavery more than the North, the famous proclamation was not Lincoln's preferred solution of the slavery issue, for he wished the North, through compensated emancipation, to share with the South the burden of liberation. But the time had come when to win the war, Northern antislavery opinion demanded Negro freedom. With his firm sense of public mood, Lincoln acted—and in acting insured the ultimate triumph of the Union.

To write of Lincoln's fundamental views requires a good deal of caution. It is the commonest thing to see the mind of Lincoln fitted into a preconceived pattern. Sometimes this is done by an elastic or strained interpretation of what he actually said, sometimes by pure conjecture as to what he "would have" said or done on some matter far beyond his time. Writers look into the body of Lincoln's utterances, or skim the surface, for the most diverse purposes. Obviously, not all the Lincolns we have presented to us can be genuine.

Lincoln has been presented to us as a conservative. In an able and eloquent paper his political philosophy has been analyzed in terms of expediency with more than a touch of opportunism. There is validity in thinking of him as conservative if one does not leave it there, but conservatism in the usual sense did not by any means encompass the horizon of his thought. There was, of course, moderation in his preference for orderly progress, his distrust of dangerous agitation, and his reluctance toward ill digested schemes of reform. More especially, he was conservative in his complete avoidance of that type of so-called "radicalism" which involved abuse of the South, hatred for the slaveholder, thirst for vengeance, partisan plotting, and ungenerous demands that Southern institutions be transformed overnight by outsiders. One of the tragic mistakes which Southerners made in an era of incredible blundering was to suppose that this type of intolerant radicalism was typical of the North. Antislavery ideals had their noble aspects. Only the best leadership could have adequately promoted them; but, historically speaking, abolitionist excess was not the sentiment of any substantial Northern element. That was shown even in war time by the congressional election of 1862.

It was because of Lincoln's more tolerant attitude toward the South that he was nominated by the Republican party in 1860 at a time when even the conservative Seward was rejected under the mistaken impression that he was too radical. It needs to be understood, however, that the word "radical" in the days of the Civil War and reconstruction was not a generic term. It had a meaning not discernible in the word itself. It was a specific designation of a particular group—Stevens, Chandler, Wade, *et al.*—whose dominance in the Federal government set the stage for one of the most abusive periods of American history. These men, considered realistically and taken as a group, were the opposite of liberal. As indicated in an earlier essay, they were in fact reactionary. This was evident from their opposition to civil rights, their denunciation of the Milligan decision of the Supreme Court, their denial of autonomy to Southerners, their extreme partisanship, and their friendliness toward exploitive capitalism.

One can ignore this, or deny it. A fabricated, rose-colored portrait of these radicals can be presented, but only if one distorts history. Thaddeus Stevens of Pennsylvania, for example, had, and still has, a reputation for egalitarianism and sympathy for the common man. He has been called the "Commoner" and has superficially been accepted as such. It is a different matter if, in studying this complex personality, one looks at the record instead of the stereotyped portrait. Stevens's dominance over the House of Representatives in Lincoln's day was arrogant, factional, and dictatorial. As Richard Nelson Current has pointed out, he "was not only the embodiment of Pennsylvania capitalism himself but also a go-between for others of that ilk, one whose function it was to convert the votes of the many into the policies of the few." Treating his rise to political power in prewar times, Mr. Current writes: "Lacking the humanitarian impulse, he stood stubbornly for 'vested rights' as against what he called 'the wild visions of idle dreamers,' 'the revolutionary and agrarian folly of modern reformers.'" His "Commoner" label was a handy thing. The reputation of the alleged friend of the people served perfectly to rake in thousands of votes, while maneuvers behind the scenes made use of these votes for special interests that were exclusive and predatory.

It is clear from convincing masses of contemporary evidence —including voluminous unpublished sources known to specialists—that these men who opposed Lincoln were "radical" in the sense of being drastic or violent, not in the sense of being liberal. To combat such men was in truth a mark of liberalism. In Lincoln's case particularly it should be so understood, from earlier stages of rampant sectionalism, on through the wartime days of radical intrigue, and down to the ugly and menacing deadlock by which the vindictives wrecked Lincoln's program for the postwar years.

In all such matters Lincoln emerges as a moderate, but that made him none the less a liberal. Liberalism is associated with democracy and democracy requires moderation. It is among enemies of democracy, as we know by bitter experience in our day, that we find violence, unbridled extravagance of statement, torture, terrorism, fanaticism, and criminal atrocities. Lincoln believed in planting, cultivating, and harvesting, not in uprooting and destroying. He believed in evolutionary democratic progress.

It is possible to take his economic views and, by a superficial showing, argue Lincoln's "conservatism" with reference to such matters as the national bank or the protective tariff. His favoring of the bank—the famous "Bank of the United States" so productive of discord in the Jackson era—was due largely to his attachment to the Whig party. As to the tariff, nearly everything he said on that subject could be classified under the head of tiresome or labored economics. Some of Lincoln's writings or speeches show that he either missed the point as to the working of the tariff or permitted himself to indulge in those meaningless verbalisms or homely illustrations which were characteristic of protectionist politicians; in Lincoln's case, however, there seem to have been twinges of conscience which coarser men lacked. Speaking at Pittsburgh on his presidential journey in February 1861 he related the tariff question to the lack of "direct taxation" and remarked that it "is to the government what replenishing the meal-tub is to the family." These phrases would apply to a tariff for revenue rather than for the protection of manufacturers. Yet his remarks on that occasion were supposed to be an endorsement of the Republican protectionist position.

After reading Lincoln's papers and speeches generally, with their clarity and pithy effectiveness, one turns to this Pittsburgh speech with a sense of let-down or disappointment. Trying to fit himself into the Republican tariff pattern, the more so because of his Pennsylvania audience (where among dominant party men the tariff was a specialty and questions concerning slavery unimportant), he fell into a lameness of statement and a confession of ignorance that were quite uncharacteristic. Republican protectionism was not his forte. Indeed his private correspondence shows that he had doubts on this subject which he did not wish to become public. The party was making a strong appeal to manufacturers, but Lincoln did not want to repel men who believed in freedom of trade or who disliked excessive favors to special groups. One suspects, not without reason, that Lincoln had an un-Republican fondness for freer trade himself.

The subject of the tariff is an example to show the manner in which Lincoln's "conservatism" can be overstated or superficially presented. What is needed is something deeper than superficial indications. It is partly a matter of the use of terms. What does "conservatism" mean? If it means caution, prudent adherence to tested values, avoidance of rashness, and reliance upon unhurried, peaceable evolution, Lincoln was a conservative. If, however, the dignified word "conservative" comes to us with an alloy as with the word "politics," if it has a reactionary connotation, if it casts an aura of respectability over tendencies that are exploitive and unprogressive, or if it signifies indifferent apathy toward human problems, then one can say with complete confidence that Lincoln was no conservative.

To think of Lincoln's conservatism is to think of selected facets of his policy. But the deeply searching mind of Lincoln had more in it than static acquiescence. It had motivating sympathy, awareness of social needs, enthusiasm for effective democracy—qualities appropriately denoted by the word liberal. If in procedure he wanted to be sure of his ground, in the content and purpose of his program he wanted liberal causes to succeed. If his conservatism was a kind of brake or saving common sense, liberalism was his vital spark.

The surest way to judge him is by those statements in which he appeared at his unhampered best. In expounding the protective tariff for the special benefit of manufacturers he fumbled and limped; but, as William H. Herndon said, it was far different when he dealt with fundamental human rights. In one of Herndon's manuscripts we have this description: "If he was defending the right—if he was defending liberty—eulogizing the Declaration of Independence, then he extended out his arms . . . as if appealing to some superior power for assistance and support; or that he might embrace the spirit of that which he so dearly loved. It was at such moments that he seemed inspired, fresh from the hands of his creator. Lincoln's gray eyes would flash fire when speaking against slavery or spoke volumes of hope and love when speaking of Liberty—justice and the progress of mankind."

It would not be going far wrong to say that the liberal credo was the key to Lincoln's views of man and the state. His basic ideas were those of Thomas Jefferson. He owed little to Hamilton who wanted a government to please the moneyed interests. Human rights meant more to him than profits. He was not content with lip service to the Declaration of Independence. He took its doctrines seriously in their stress upon equality of men. He cherished Anglo-Saxon muniments of civil justice. On one occasion he spoke out for woman suffrage far ahead of his time. Believing as he did in the broadening of political rights, he did not stop there but urged that such "rights" be carried forward in governmental achievement and human betterment.

His thought went out to the less privileged, to the "prudent, penniless beginner." The grasping rich who gained by the misfortunes of their fellow men, or who thought of war as an opportunity for profiteering, had his contempt, but repeatedly he expressed the wish that every poor man should have a chance.

Just how far Lincoln "would have" gone in extending the functions of government, and in using the government to promote the welfare of the country, is difficult to say; but there is ample evidence that his philosophy of man and the state did not begin and end with *laissez faire*. He vigorously favored what were called "internal improvements"—that being the term used in his day for large appropriations by the Federal government for various kinds of public works all over the country. He also favored such expenditures by the states. In the late 1830's when Illinois was launching upon a grandiose program for improvements in every county Lincoln was one of the most active legislative promoters of the plan. In Congress ten years later he argued elaborately in favor of such governmental expenditures. In this argument he took up, point by point, the objections of those who urged that such a system would "overwhelm the treasury," would provide merely local benefits with the use of general funds, and would be unconstitutional. He summed up the position of his opponents in the phrase "Do nothing at all, lest you do something wrong." This, he said, applied "as forcibly to . . . making improvements by State authority as by the national authority; so that we must abandon the improvements of the country altogether, by any and every authority, or we must resist and repudiate the doctrines of this message [an anti-internal-improvement veto message by President Polk]." Lincoln plainly stated he favored the latter alternative.

Warming to his theme, Lincoln showed that improvements in the 1820's had by no means overwhelmed the treasury, even in "the period of greatest enormity." He showed that "No commercial object of government patronage can be so exclusively general as to not be of some peculiar local advantage." Then he added: ". . . if the nation refuse to make improvements of the more general kind because their benefits may be somewhat local, a State may for the same reason refuse to make an improvement of a local kind because its benefits may be somewhat general." Such an argument "puts an end to improvements altogether." In this we have a typical Lincolnian argument. We recall the circuit lawyer in Illinois, analyzing the position of the opposing side and exposing the weakness of that position. He dealt with the constitutional objection at some length by quoting Kent and Story, clinching it with the following conclusion: ". . . no one who is satisfied of the expediency of making improvements need be much uneasy in his conscience about its constitutionality." Summarizing his whole position, he said: ". . . let the nation take hold of the larger works, and the States the smaller ones; and thus, . . . what is . . . unequal in one place may be equalized in another, extravagance avoided, and the whole country put on that career of prosperity which shall correspond with its extent of territory, its natural resources, and the intelligence and enterprise of its people."

On other matters Lincoln showed how far he was from the concept of a do-nothing government. He favored government help for the promotion of education. He earnestly advocated an elaborate scheme of state-enacted emancipation with Federal sponsorship and compensation. It was under him that the department of agriculture, destined to become one of the most active of government agencies, had its beginnings. As President he signed the homestead act of 1862, a measure of far-reaching government aid to the rural home maker. By that measure Uncle Sam gave away a vast amount of land in order to encourage a democratic system of individual land tenure. The act did not accomplish all that was hoped, because of exploitive tendencies in the post-Lincoln decades, but it assuredly did not proceed on the fundamental assumption that government should forever let the nation's economy alone. Lincoln's disapproval of that do-nothing theory was expressed in a fragment on government attributed to the year 1854. "Government [he said] is a combination of the people of a country to effect certain objects by joint effort. . . . The legitimate object of government is 'to do for the people what needs to be done, but which they can not, by individual effort, do at all, or do so well, for themselves.' There are many such things . . . ."

In any survey of Lincoln's beliefs and thought-patterns it is important to emphasize the supreme quality of tolerance. Innocent of that holier-than-thou attitude which made extremists of his day particularly irritating, he realized that slavery was a moral question—an institution which he hated—yet at the same time he recognized the moral sense of the Southern people. In personal matters he would deftly put in the tolerant touch. Writing in 1840 to a man who imagined he had been attacked and insulted, he was careful to assure the gentleman: "I entertain no unkind feelings to you . . . ." Any personal altercation he considered regrettable. Often in his correspondence one finds the conscious effort to avoid wounded feelings. He summed up the matter as follows:

> When the conduct of men is designed to be influenced, persuasion, kind, unassuming persuasion, should ever be adopted. It is an old and a true maxim "that a drop of honey catches more flies than a gallon of gall." So with men. If you would win a man to your cause, first convince him that you are his sincere friend. Therein is a drop of honey that catches his heart, which, say what he will, is the great highroad to his reason, and which, when once gained, you will find but little trouble in convincing his judgment of the justice of your cause, if indeed that cause really be a just one. On the contrary, assume to dictate to his judgment, or to command his action, or to mark him as one to be shunned and despised, and he will retreat within himself, close all the avenues to his head and his heart; and though your cause be naked truth itself, transformed to the heaviest lance, harder than steel, and sharper than steel can be made, and though you throw it with more than herculean force and precision, you shall be no more able to pierce him than to penetrate the hard shell of a tortoise with a rye straw. Such is man, and so must he be understood by those who would lead him, even to his own best interests.

It is worth while to linger a moment on this passage if one would understand Lincoln. In large part it is a key to his public and private relations. The emphasis is upon friendly approach, upon showing a man that you are his friend. You do not win a man by showing that he is wrong and you are right, by seeking to "command his action" or by setting him down as one to be despised. Your effort should not be to dictate his thought or coerce his judgment. The heart is "the great high road to reason." Gain access to a man's heart first; after that you may convince his judgment. Make sure that your own cause is just, but remember that if a man retreats "within himself" he will not be won over even by the purest truth. Your success does not depend only on the hardness of your lance, the precision or force of your throwing. You might wish it otherwise. You might prefer that naked truth and rightness of clear reasoning should come first and emotions be disregarded, but such is man. You must know what manner of animal he is. You must deal with human nature. If you are to lead you must understand those you are seeking to lead.

Lincoln was not justifying the idea that emotion rather than reason should take command in the formation of a man's attitudes. On other occasions he stressed the importance of clear thinking. In the passage before us he was not hedging on the bedrock value of solid judgment. He did not say that reason was of secondary importance, but that the heart was the "high road to reason." To get acceptance of a position based on tested thinking was his purpose, but he did not want the accomplishment of that purpose prejudiced by the wrong approach. He wanted truth to prevail, but he was thinking in terms of human relations, in which tact and winsome understanding were, by his observation, trump cards.

This attitude is the opposite of the fanatic. Such a man may be righteous, but his righteousness tends in the direction of the witch burner. Those who oppose him are evil; they must be destroyed, or at least suppressed. In that suppressive crusade one's language becomes extravagant; zeal overreaches itself; the lance of argument is thrown as if the Almighty himself were hurling a thunderbolt to strike down the evil doer. One's own motives are pure; the opponent must therefore be a sinister person; there must be no compromise with him. You withdraw from him. You spurn his friendship. Your speeches and articles are presented not so much to your opponent; he is hopeless; they are presented to your own audience; your opponent is treated as a third person. The more you can put him in the wrong the better you are pleased. You stand at Armageddon and you battle for the Lord, but you are the recruiting officer who enlists the Lord's services. Public affairs must be viewed in terms of clash, struggle, and crisis, rather than adjustment. To state these contrasting attitudes is to show that Lincoln stood not with the fanatic but with the friendly persuasive statesman.

Lincoln's liberal minded tolerance was evident in his friendly attitude toward foreigners. One must recall the factors working against such tolerance in his day. Men who came from other lands—they came in immense streams in the 1850's—were confronted with difficult conditions. America beckoned but Americans often repelled.

It is not sufficient to say that hostility to foreigners was prevalent in that period. It was rampant. The nativism of that time was characterized by an assumption of racial superiority and a policy of exclusiveness in favor of old-stock Americans. It is amazing how far this movement extended, particularly within the Whig party, in which Lincoln was a vigorous leader. On the political front the evasive nickname for these nativists was "Knownothing"; as of 1856 theirs was the "American" party; before that party was formed they had gone so far in organization on the state level as to control some of the key commonwealths. When the Whig caucus of the New York legislature met in February 1855 it was stated by the *Evening Post* that of the eighty senators and assemblymen present "sixty at least" of these Whigs had taken the Knownothing oath and joined the order. The mysterious secrecy of the order and the unblushing casuistry of their reasoning enabled them to pay as much or little attention to these oaths as they chose. If it became necessary for political purposes to evade their pledges they could absolve themselves with the greatest of ease. Lines of retreat were prepared in their rear. They could even deny membership. Their "principles," which "smell mouldy and unwholesome in the dark and damp," were not often ventilated.

In Massachusetts, by the election of 1854, the Knownothing party elected the governor (Henry Joseph Gardner), all the state officials, "all but two members of the legislature and every member of Congress from Massachusetts." According to George F. Hoar, Gardner played the game of flattery and demagoguery, using men "who were odious or ridiculous among their own neighbors, but who united might be a very formidable force." He rose to power by organizing "the knave-power and the donkey-power of the Commonwealth." Two names will illustrate the powerful hold which this anti-foreign group had upon leading men of that period—Samuel F. B. Morse, one of the most outstanding nativist propagandists of his time, and Millard Fillmore, ex-President of the United States, who became the candidate of the American party in 1856.

Lincoln was like Fillmore in Whig allegiance; he was like both Fillmore and Morse in ancestral American background; he was, however, firm and outspoken in his opposition to nativism. Writing to his friend Joshua F. Speed in 1855, he said: "I am not a Know-nothing; that is certain. How could I be? How can anyone who abhors the oppression of negroes be in favor of degrading classes of white people? . . . When the Know-nothings get control . . . I shall prefer emigrating to some country where they make no pretense of loving liberty . . . ."

He vigorously opposed anti-alien tendencies in Massachusetts. He was careful to say that he had never been in an American or Knownothing lodge. In 1858, in a slightly known message to a committee of Chicago Germans, he offered the following sentiment: *"Our German Fellow-Citizens:*—Ever true to *Liberty,* the *Union,* and the *Constitution*—true to Liberty, not selfishly, but upon *principle*—not for special *classes* of men, but for *all* men . . . ." He made a contract with Theodore Canisius for the control of a German-American newspaper at Springfield. In a letter to Canisius in 1859 he wrote: "Understanding the spirit of our institutions to aim at the elevation of men, I am opposed to whatever tends to degrade them. I have some little notoriety for commiserating the oppressed negro; and I should be strangely inconsistent if I could favor . . . curtailing the . . . rights of white men, even though born in different lands, and speaking different languages from myself."

As President he showed the same tolerance. When General Grant issued an order expelling "all Jews" from the lines of his military department early in 1863 (the purpose being to exclude peddlers), Lincoln revoked the order. It was explained to Grant that he did this because the order "proscribed an entire religious class, some of whom are fighting in our ranks." These are but a few examples; others could be added. Lincoln's Americanism was not a matter of prejudice, of witch hunting, or hatred directed against particular groups or classes of men.

It is instructive to compare Lincoln's record as to Knownothingism with that of the alleged equalitarian and "Commoner," Thaddeus Stevens. Lincoln was clear cut against the Knownothings and against anti-foreign intolerance. Stevens courted the nativists; the roping in of their votes appealed to his politician mind. When the Republican national convention in 1856 indirectly condemned nativism by a declaration in favor of "liberty of conscience and equality of rights," Stevens tried unsuccessfully to have these words withdrawn. Realizing that the Knownothings were politically powerful in Pennsylvania, he did not want to alienate their support and for this reason he favored the colorless McLean of Ohio for presidential candidate instead of Frémont, who was not a Catholic, but against whom the cry of Catholicism had been raised. After the presidential nomination of 1856 had been made, including Fillmore for the "Americans," Stevens (as we learn from reading the biography by Richard Nelson Current) worked hard to enlist the support of Knownothing editors for the Republican ticket. In this he succeeded, not without a brazen use of money. He himself stated that he "expended

$4,000 in securing presses." One "American editor," he said, "was to change his course and have $350." Mr. Current remarks: "Old Thad was the sort who believed an honest man to be one who, once bought, would stay bought. . . ." All this was in 1856, but the day was to come when Lincoln as President, in his unhappy relations with Congress, would have to deal with the domineering and intriguing Stevens as Republican leader (or boss) in the House of Representatives.

Lincoln's broad tolerance was shown in his speech on temperance. He had nothing of the self-righteous unction so common among temperance reformers. Far from denouncing the drunkard, he showed that in his growing years intoxicating liquor was "a respectable article of manufacture and merchandise." "From the sideboard of the parson [he said] down to the ragged pocket of the houseless loafer, it was constantly found." To berate habitual drunkards as utterly incorrigible was repugnant to his sense of human decency. He considered such an attitude "fiendishly selfish." It was "like throwing fathers and brothers overboard." He himself was not a drinker, but taking drunkards as a class he believed that "their heads and their hearts will bear an advantageous comparison with those of any other class." Proneness to this vice he believed characteristic of generous people. As to those who had not fallen victims to drink, he thought they might have been spared "more by the absence of appetite than from any mental or moral superiority." It should be added that Lincoln spoke vigorously for temperance. The point emphasized here is his manner of doing so. Temperance in his judgment was not promoted by any type of intolerance, nor by unfriendliness toward "a large, erring, and unfortunate class of . . . fellow-creatures."

Lincoln repeatedly spoke in terms of friendliness to labor. Hard work had been his portion in pioneer days. While very young, as he states in his autobiography, he "had an ax put into his hands . . . and from that till . . . his twenty-third year he was almost constantly handling that . . . useful instrument." More than once he identified himself with workingmen. He referred to himself as a "penniless boy, working on a flatboat at ten dollars per month." At New Haven, Connecticut, on

March 6, 1860, he said: "I am not ashamed to confess that twenty-five years ago I was a hired laborer . . . ." With no thought of denying legitimate profits, he disliked the concept of labor being in a dependent position with reference to capital. One can quote several passages on this point. The following is typical:

> The world is agreed that labor is the source from which human wants are mainly supplied. . . . By some it is assumed that labor is available only in connection with capital—that nobody labors, unless somebody else owning capital . . . induces him to do it. . . . They further assume that whoever is once a hired laborer, is fatally fixed in that condition for life; . . . . That is the "mud-sill" theory. But another class of reasoners [Lincoln associated himself with this group] hold . . . that . . . these assumptions are false, and all inferences from them groundless. They hold that labor is prior to, and independent of, capital; that . . . capital is the fruit of labor, and could never have existed if labor had not first existed; that labor can exist without capital, but that capital could never have existed without labor. Hence they hold that labor is the superior—greatly the superior—of capital.

These words having been uttered in 1859, Lincoln returned to the theme in the same words in his first annual message to Congress in December of 1861, where he spoke unfavorably of "the effort to place capital on an equal footing with, if not above, labor." Speaking now from the presidential chair, he said: "Labor is prior to, and independent of, capital. . . . Labor is the superior of capital, and deserves much the higher consideration." Fairness toward both labor and capital was his aim. He said: "Capital has its rights, which are as worthy of protection as any other rights. Nor is it denied that there is, and probably always will be, a relation between labor and capital producing mutual benefits. . . . No men living are more worthy to be trusted than those who toil up from poverty. . . . Let them beware of surrendering a political power . . . which, if surrendered, will surely be used to close the door of advancement against such as they, and to fix new disabilities and burdens upon them, till all of liberty shall be lost." He did not want laborers "tied down" or "obliged to work under all circumstances." He wanted labor peace, but he favored the right to strike.

It is not to be supposed that Lincoln had any antagonism toward capital. That was not the point. "[W]hile we do not propose any war upon capital [he said], we do wish to allow the humblest man an equal chance . . . with everybody else." Often he recurred to this idea of equality of opportunity. Remarking that his own lot was "what might happen to any poor man's son," he said: "I want every man to have a chance—and I believe a black man is entitled to it—in which he can better his condition . . . ." It was to produce such a result that he favored the cause of the Union. Describing it as "a people's contest," he declared: "On the side of the Union it is a struggle for maintaining in the world that form and substance of government whose leading object is to elevate the condition of men—to lift artificial weights from all shoulders; to clear the paths of laudable pursuit for all . . . ."

In the dark days of the war it gave Lincoln heart for his task to believe that labor's welfare would be promoted by the cause for which he struggled. One of his finest presidential papers was his letter to the workingmen of Manchester, England, in response to a laudatory address which had been sent to him at the time of the New Year, 1863. When honorary membership in the Workingmen's Association of New York was tendered to him in 1864 he indicated his grateful acceptance in a speech especially directed to the cause of labor. Repeating his comments as to labor and capital already given in his message to Congress of December 1861, he showed the breadth and international application of his principle in these words: "The strongest bond of human sympathy, outside of the family relation, should be one uniting all working people, of all nations, and tongues, and kindreds. Nor should this lead to a war upon property, or the owners of property. Property is the fruit of labor; property is desirable; is a positive good in the world. That some should be rich shows that others may become rich, and hence is just encouragement to industry and enterprise. Let not him who is houseless pull down the house of another, but let him work diligently and build one for himself, thus by example assuring that his own shall be safe from violence when built."

Lincoln is known, as much as anything else, for a basic Americanism. At the outset of his presidency he showed the utmost fervor in emotionally underlining "our national fabric, with all its benefits, its memories, and its hopes." Here was national pride historically buttressed, reason enlivened by feeling, present loyalty linked with folk memory. He once said: "I love the sentiments of those old-time men . . . ."

Yet these thoughts were qualified. They were not naively simple. He did not forget national shortcomings. They brought a sense of humility, though he believed that the United States had the best government in the world. He said as a young man: "We find ourselves in the peaceful possession of the fairest portion of the earth . . . under . . . a system of political institutions conducing more essentially to the ends of civil and religious liberty than any of which the history of former times tells us." That this was not thoughtless boasting was shown by other statements in which he warned against lawless and antisocial tendencies into which his countrymen were prone to fall.

Not oratorical exaggeration, but clear-headed logic, characterized his thinking on American institutions. The pillars of the national temple, he thought, should be "hewn from the solid quarry of sober reason." Passion would be our enemy. "Reason—cold, calculating, unimpassioned reason—must furnish all the materials for our future support and defense." Lincoln's head and heart were in balance. His emotions might glow, but his well considered judgment would take command. In reading his writings one finds a constant blend of stirring inspiration with steady reflection.

There is, perhaps, a kind of earth-bound quality in the philosophy of most Americans. Ready pragmatism is more to their liking than the unballasted flights of the mystics. America is of the West, not the East. This attitude of hard practicality—of impatience for "success" and "results"—is impressively evident in scientific achievement, industrial organization, managerial talent, and technological accomplishment. Sometimes, however, the same quality—or a coexisting quality—is expressed in a careless and unambitious acceptance of things as they are so far as governmental and social institutions are concerned, sometimes in impatience toward those who sincerely labor to improve social conditions. Faults of American democracy as imperfectly practised—rampant partisanship, interracial maladjustment, uninspired "politics," pressure lobbying, congressional inefficiency, and deadlocked government—are too often endured with indifference. The public conscience is never dead, but it is often dormant, inarticulate, or frustrated. The active electorate may be only a fraction of the people. Appeals to prejudice, sometimes on a shockingly low level, may carry an election. The "anti-" agitator (anti-labor, anti-Negro, anti-British, etc.) may win by a kind of default—that is, by the absence of an outstanding candidate to represent the more intelligent element. American democracy has not been in danger from those who would "subvert" it nearly so much as from those who give it superficial adherence and lip service while ignoring its pressing problems.

Lincoln had given thought to certain aspects of this problem, or related problems, as they arose in his time. His Americanism was no mere badge or slogan. He was never the professional patrioteer. Our democracy, he urged, is in danger from within; its threat is a kind of "suicide." In addressing the Young Men's Lyceum at Springfield in 1838, he specified contemporary factors that caused him great distress: "the increasing disregard for law which pervades the country," the breakdown of that "strongest bulwark of any government"—namely, "the attachment of the people," and the tendency of the "best citizens" to become alienated from a government that permits abuses to exist.

In Lincoln's attitude toward these matters of law and order one finds the kind of liberalism that is deeply thoughtful rather than superficially optimistic. He faced unpleasant facts. Speaking of mob rule he said that the process went on "from gamblers to negroes, from negroes to white citizens, and from these to strangers, till dead men were seen literally dangling from . . . trees upon every roadside." The thought that men should be impatient of government disturbed him. Bad laws, he thought, ought to be repealed, but while on the books they "should be religiously observed." To give up enforcement of laws because people resisted, disobeyed, or disregarded them he considered highly unfortunate.

He pleaded for eternal vigilance in this matter. "There is no grievance [he said] that is a fit object of redress by mob law." Government in former days had "many props"; in his day he feared that the fruits of government achievement, having been appropriated, were less appreciated. Democracy was an experiment. The very impulse to make the experiment succeed was a stay, a prop, and a chance for deathless distinction. The game having been caught and the crop harvested (at least in the attainment of independence), he hoped that the constant, day-by-day preservation of democratic standards would be as much of an object as their early establishment. To this end he said:

> Let reverence for the laws be breathed by every American mother to the lisping babe that prattles on her lap; let it be taught in schools, in seminaries, and in colleges; let it be written in primers, spelling-books, and in almanacs; let it be preached from the pulpit, proclaimed in legislative halls, and enforced in courts of justice. And, in short, let it become the political religion of the nation; and let the old and the young, the rich and the poor, the grave and the gay of all sexes and tongues and colors and conditions, sacrifice unceasingly upon its altars.

In such warnings and pleadings there was sternness in Lincoln's tone. He did not burble about democracy. To describe him briefly, he could be called a tough minded, liberal realist. He was, of course, a man of ideals. His leadership would not have been worth much otherwise. But it is in fact our liberals who have been the tough minded men. It is only a misconception to suppose that liberals have been soft minded, nor is it true that they have been removed from practical reality. Sometimes we call the wrong ones "realists." Foolish and uncritical acceptance of stereotyped ideas or slogans is not unknown among "conservatives." Sometimes those who oppose liberal views, or who have appeased reactionaries, have fallen prey to arguments or blandishments which are shockingly unreal and flimsy.

In the matter of Negro rights Lincoln's position must be viewed in relation to the background of his time. He opposed intermarriage of the races, resenting the very suggestion. Such intermarriage, however, was not an issue. It was only a bogey or scarecrow intended to mislead and becloud the less intelligent popular mind. Lincoln was cautious as to political and social equality, though he vigorously objected when the Supreme Court issued its opinion in the Dred Scott case to the effect that a Negro, even though a citizen of a state, could not be a citizen of the United States. In the debate with Douglas (1858) he did not favor Negro voting, but that is not to say that he was opposing any actual movement to establish Negro suffrage; there was no such movement. It is more to the point to note that as the nation's leader he became increasingly liberal and that in the latter part of his presidency he took a more advanced position as to the franchise. Writing on March 13, 1864, to Michael Hahn, governor of Federally occupied Louisiana, he asked "whether some of the colored people may not be let in—as, for instance, the very intelligent, and especially those who have fought gallantly in our ranks. They would probably help, in some trying time to come, to keep the jewel of liberty within the family of freedom."

Often he praised the colored soldiers and emphasized their vitally important contribution to the Union cause. He showed friendliness to the Negro. He wanted him treated as a man. He confessed a sensitiveness on this subject. He could not bear to see Negroes sold at auction, nor strung together "like so many fish upon a trot-line." He argued: "If the negro is a man, why then my ancient faith teaches me that 'all men are created equal,' and that there can be no moral right in connection with one man's making a slave of another." He added: ". . . no man is good enough to govern another man without that other's consent."

The following passage, which seems to have been but slightly quoted, illustrates Lincoln's sympathy for human beings held in bondage:

> ... In those days [i. e., earlier days of the republic] our Declaration of Independence was held sacred by all, and thought to include all; but now, to aid in making the bondage of the negro universal and eternal, it is assailed and sneered at and construed, and hawked at and torn, till, if its framers could rise from their graves, they could not at all recognize it. All the powers of earth seem rapidly combining against him. Mammon is after him, ambition follows, philosophy follows, and the theology of the day is fast joining the cry. They have him in his prison-house; they have searched his person, and left no prying instrument with him. One after another they have closed the heavy iron doors upon him; and now they have him, as it were, bolted in with a lock of a hundred keys, which can never be unlocked without the concurrence of every key—the keys in the hands of a hundred different men, and they scattered to a hundred different and distant places; and they stand musing as to what invention, in all the dominions of mind and matter, can be produced to make the impossibility of his escape more complete than it is.

To make Lincoln out as a practical contender for full equality would be unhistorical, however strong might be the impulse of liberals so to represent him. Very few in his day, in any part of the country, were contenders for complete equality to be applied in their own localities. Even Kansas, famous for antislavery emphasis, proved in many of its laws and social attitudes to be an anti-Negro state. The Negro suffrage amendment did not come until five years after Lincoln's death; the full observance and implementing of that amendment has never come. There were things Lincoln could do and things he could not. There was, as he said, the "argument of necessity." On moral grounds, he favored the ideal of equal rights. He believed that an ideal, though unrealized at the time, could point the way toward future reality. He would not deny the humanity of the Negro. He spoke eloquently of a "sense of justice and human sympathy continually telling you that the poor negro has some natural right to himself." He spoke in stinging denunciation of "those who deny it and make mere merchandise of him."

Racial bigotry did not control Lincoln's mind. Slavery was legal in his day, till by the hand of war and constitutional amendment it was abolished. Bad laws, he felt, ought to be observed till repealed. Despite many difficulties presented in a slaveholding nation, and in a Northern society that fell far short in interracial relations, he did what he could in his own day to elevate the status of the Negro, to present his case at the bar of humanity, and to urge his claim for sympathy and fair treatment. Lincoln was no Don Quixote. He had to deal in practical terms. Gradualism was essential in his method. He had elements of conservatism as well as liberalism. Steps to elevate the race could not all be taken at one jump. The country had far to go on that road; it still has far to go. No man of genuine feeling can contemplate without painful emotion the long story of the Negro's ordeal, nor deny to him the credit that attaches to his record as faithful servant and loyal soldier. It is in the Lincoln tradition to give the Negro his just place in American social history and to recognize his values in American folklore and culture. These values appear in a hundred varied forms, from strutting cake walk and hilarious minstrelsy to those deeply melodious spirituals through which, rather than through degrading self pity, the age-long memories of a submerged people find undying expression.

Elsewhere the author has treated Lincoln and slavery, and that treatment will not be repeated here. Before the presidency his approach was quite different from that of the abolitionist. During the presidency the working of his policy was, or seemed, slow. It did not always seem like kingdom come. It was hedged in by circumstances, by the paramount urgency of the Union, by political factors, constitutional restrictions, congressional non-coöperation, border-state reluctance, regard for Southern property rights, the need for proper timing, military considerations, and attention to the realities of Southern home economy. To some his emancipation proclamation had a ringing, messianic fervor; to others it seemed a terroristic invitation to a war of races (a mistaken concept); to still others is appeared utterly futile.

It is essential for the present purpose to note elements of Lincoln's liberalism in his attitude toward human bondage. He kept saying that slavery was an evil, however much its eradication might be impeded by the Constitution, by state rights, or by the existing state of society. His humane sympathy for the slave was combined with that readiness to understand Southern conditions which was ever his characteristic. Though he confessed that he found no easy answer to the problem of doing away with slavery, he looked forward to such an answer in the future and in the meantime he wanted to resist its spread. He wanted no slavery in the territories and he wanted Illinois kept free. Recalling that we once considered it "a self-evident truth" that all men are created equal, he deplored the degradation of the public conscience to the point where, having "grown fat," we called "the same maxim 'a self-evident lie'" and made the "Fourth of July . . . a great day—for burning firecrackers."

Frequently he showed that he did not want sectional strife because of slavery—that was not the intention of his house-divided speech—but with equal frequency he showed that in his concept slavery was morally wrong. Tolerant though he was, he wanted no apathetic indifference where moral wrong existed. Though not a hater of men, he said:

> This declared indifference . . . for the spread of slavery, I cannot but hate. I hate it because of the monstrous injustice of slavery itself. I hate it because it deprives our republican example of its just influence in the world; enables the enemies of free institutions with plausibility to taunt us as hypocrites; causes the real friends of freedom to doubt our sincerity; and especially because it forces so many good men among ourselves into an open war with the very fundamental principles of civil liberty, criticizing the Declaration of Independence, and insisting that there is no right principle of action but self-interest.

In the same vein, in the year of his nomination for the presidency, he said: "We think slavery a great moral wrong, and while we do not claim the right to touch it where it exists, we wish to treat it as a wrong in the Territories, where our votes will reach it. We think that a respect for ourselves, a regard for future generations and for the God that made us, require that we put down this wrong where our votes will properly reach it. We think that species of labor an injury to free white men—in short, we think slavery a great moral, social, and political evil, tolerable only because, and so far as, its actual existence makes it necessary to tolerate it . . . ."

If he envisaged "irrepressible conflict," it was not that he preached the need of war between North and South, but rather that ideas were in conflict. "Now these two ideas—the property idea that slavery is right and the idea that it is wrong—come into collision, and . . . produce that irrepressible conflict which Mr. Seward has been so roundly abused for mentioning." He added: "Now I don't want to be misunderstood. . . . I don't mean that we ought to attack it where it exists." If he saw a snake in the road he would seize the nearest stick and kill it; but if it were in bed with his children or his neighbor's children, he would be cautious. "If there was a bed newly made up, to which the children were to be taken, and it was proposed to take a batch of snakes and put them there with them, . . . no man would say there was a question how I ought to decide!"

He deplored as fallacious the assumption that " 'In the struggle between the white man and the negro' . . . either the white man must enslave the negro or the negro must enslave the white." This sort of contention he regarded as a misleading catch phrase. "There is no such struggle [he said]. It is merely an ingenious falsehood to degrade and brutalize the negro. . . . This good earth is plenty broad enough for white man and negro both, and there is no need for either pushing the other off."

In the phraseology of the Constitution he noted that references to slavery were "ambiguous, roundabout, and mystical"; never was the institution mentioned directly by the word "slavery" or "slave." Why didn't they use the word? "They expected and desired that the system would come to an end, and meant that when it did the Constitution should not show that there had ever been a slave in this good free country of ours." Historically, the name of Lincoln is the one most prominently associated with the abolition of slavery in the United States. Contemporary limitations and legal complexities of his policy are not commonly understood in the popular mind, but it is with valid and well earned distinction that he remains the Emancipator.

No problem of modern civilization is more urgent than reorientation of outlook and of policy in the matter of war making. The pledges that have been made in establishing the United Nations, and the principles that have been implemented in the Nuremberg trial, have placed war makers in the category of criminals. In terms of international commitments as they now exist, there is no honorable way by which one nation, by its own unilateral action, may *begin a war*. By principles now solemnly declared there are only two conditions in which one of the United Nations can be honorably at war— by defense against attack, or by action envisaged by the United Nations charter. Such action could legitimately be taken only to check an aggressor. Perhaps the full implications of existing commitments are yet to be realized, but aggressive war, as shown at Nuremberg, is a recognized crime—indeed the highest of crimes.

For this reorientation, and for the revulsion toward war which it involves, one may rightly invoke the spirit and also the words of Lincoln. Nothing was more foreign to his nature than the character of the warlord. He dared to speak out against President Polk for the conduct of his administration at the beginning of the Mexican War. In his Mexican speech he said that "a nation should not, and the Almighty will not, be evaded." As to Polk he said: "he feels the blood of this war, like the blood of Abel, is crying to Heaven against him."

Though many historians would be less severe on Polk, these words of Lincoln may now be seen to have a timeless importance as a denunciation of war itself. It is in this sense that one may now read in this same speech Lincoln's stinging reference to "the exceeding brightness of military glory,—that attractive rainbow that rises in showers of blood—that serpent's eye that charms to destroy." In the *Trent* affair, by reasonable international adjustment instead of warlike truculence, he produced tremendous international as well as American gain. Earlier in that year, 1861, in the July 4 message to Congress, he wrote eloquently that "ballots are the rightful and peaceful successors of bullets." He added, in a context which showed that he was thinking of a world-wide principle, that success in the appeal to ballots instead of bullets would "be a great lesson of peace: teaching men that what they cannot take by an election, neither can they take it by a war; teaching all the folly of being the beginners of a war."

Though primarily interested in popular rights on these shores, Lincoln showed a vigorous sympathy for democracy in other lands. He declared that when he saw a people borne down by tyranny he would do all in his power to raise the yoke. He showed both his lack of isolationism and his sympathy with movements for free institutions in Europe in connection with the Kossuth affair. Here was a question of liberalism abroad which was too hot for the American state department, but it was a subject on which Lincoln did not hesitate to express himself.

Louis Kossuth was a revolutionary leader in Hungary, a defiant opponent of the conservative Metternich, and a spearhead of the movement which culminated in the anti-Hapsburg declaration of Hungarian independence in April of 1849. In September of that year a meeting was held in Springfield, Illinois, to express sympathy for the cause of Hungarian freedom. Lincoln was the spokesman of a committee of four to voice the sentiments of the meeting. The resolutions which he reported extended to the revolting Hungarians "our highest admiration . . . our warmest sympathy . . . [and] our most ardent prayers for their speedy triumph and final success." Success did not come. In that mid-century period liberal revolutionary aims were aflame in many parts of Europe, but they were quenched and reaction lived on. Had these aims succeeded as Lincoln hoped—had Austria-Hungary and the German states (to mention examples) been able to use and encourage, instead of ruthlessly suppressing, their democratic-minded elements—a colossal amount of future grief would have been avoided. Lincoln was no specialist on European matters, but there was more than localism and nationalism in the wide reach of his democratic thought.

In writing a eulogy a man may give a key to his own sentiments. If one is studying Lincoln's thought and faith he cannot ignore the elaborate eulogy of Henry Clay which he delivered in the Illinois state house in 1852. There is much of Lincoln's own ideal in the following statement:

> Mr. Clay's predominant sentiment, from first to last, was a deep devotion to the cause of human liberty—a strong sympathy for the oppressed everywhere, and an ardent wish for their elevation. With him this was a primary and all-controlling passion. Subsidiary to this was the conduct of his whole life. He loved his country partly because it was his own country, and mostly because it was a free country; . . . he burned with a zeal for its advancement . . . because he saw in such the advancement, prosperity, and glory of human liberty, human right, and human nature. He desired the prosperity of his countrymen . . . chiefly to show to the world that free men could be prosperous.
>
> Mr. Clay's efforts in behalf of the South Americans, and afterward in behalf of the Greeks, in the times of their respective struggles for civil liberty, are among the finest on record, upon the noblest of all themes, and bear ample corroboration of what I have said was his ruling passion—a love of liberty and right, unselfishly, and for their own sakes.

It is obvious that no man could have uttered those words with such a glow of enthusiasm and with such genuine appreciation unless he himself had been a man of liberal views. If in that period Lincoln had been conservatively apathetic toward human liberty in other lands, his eulogy of Henry Clay would either have omitted such a passage entirely or he would have presented it without enlisting his own ardor and with less emotional emphasis.

When Lincoln thought of self-government he thought not alone of America, but of the human race. In a passage of unusual literary embellishment he referred to "our political revolution of '76" as having "given us a degree of political freedom far exceeding that of any other nation of the earth." "In it," he said, "the world has found a solution of the long-mooted problem as to the capability of man to govern himself. In it was the germ which has vegetated, and still is to grow . . . into the universal liberty of mankind." In speaking of temperance he hailed it as "a noble ally . . . to the cause of political freedom; with such an aid its march cannot fail to be on and on, till every son of earth shall drink in rich fruition the sorrow-quenching draughts of perfect liberty." He linked the factor of moral self-control with governmental self-rule. "How nobly distinguished that people who shall have planted and nurtured to maturity both the political and moral freedom of their species." In eulogizing Washington he spoke of the might of his name "in the cause of civil liberty, . . . [and] in moral reformation." His bond of sympathy for John Bright, treated in another essay, shows that his view of democracy was international, not nationalistic; cosmopolitan, not provincial.

This world view as to democracy was so strongly underlined by Lincoln that it is fair to regard it as the pivotal factor in his political philosophy. At Gettysburg, with the ghastliness of the war before his eyes and with the butchery still in progress, he spoke not of immediate issues or war problems; nor did he show even a trace of bitterness. The Gettysburg occasion as he viewed it was a high challenge. To meet this challenge, nothing less would serve than a concept so fundamental that it offered a key to the age in which he lived, or rather to the whole sweep of American history in a setting of world history. It was the exaltation of the theme—democracy as a world factor—that gave serenity and timeless significance to this dedicatory vignette. In phrases that were unforgettable he paid tribute to the dead. Then he associated the deepest of patriotic emotions with his dominant political idea—that is, the imperative obligation to make democracy succeed and thus prove to other nations that the American experiment of government by the people is no failure.

Early in the war he said to John Hay that he considered that to be the central idea in the struggle—"the necessity that is upon us, of proving that popular government is not an absurdity." Addressing Congress on July 4, 1861, he pointed out that the issue "embraces more than the fate of these United States." It was, he said, a question of concern "to the whole family of man." With an eye to that larger meaning he wrote to Congress, December 1, 1862: ". . . we cannot escape history. We . . . will be remembered in spite of ourselves. . . . In giving freedom to the slave, we assure freedom to the free . . . . We shall nobly save or meanly lose the last, best hope of earth."

Lincoln had rough sailing in his administration. He had a war to wage on a tremendous scale, with inadequate equipment and faulty organization. More than that, he had a mission to perform—not only to lead a nation to victory at arms, not only to save the Union cause, but to shape that cause in terms of adequate ideals and human values. He did not end with ingrowing thoughts of America. He looked to far horizons. Substantially to advance the cause of free government in the world was his fundamental goal.

In struggling toward this goal he had to endure inefficiency, factional bickering, repeated Union defeat, shameful greed and profiteering, defection behind the lines, and alarming division within his own party. There were times when the military machine, because of the inefficiency of central army control at Washington, almost broke down. His cabinet was an ill-assorted group of men who distrusted each other and were targets of constant attack by Congress or the newspapers.

We think of Lincoln rising to meet the fearful responsibilities of state, and that he did; but a typical picture of the time would show him trying unsuccessfully to dodge a horde of office seekers crowding through his door or waylaying him on the street. It is hard to see how he found time for his larger duties, considering the unending pressure of those who wanted a high judicial office, but who might be willing to serve their country as deputy collector or second assistant paymaster. Military men brought him not merely their problems, but also their petty jealousies. If he told Secretary Stanton to do a thing, it might be that the secretary would do the opposite, or perhaps nothing at all. Lincoln is said to have remarked that he had "not much influence with this administration," meaning his own. Whether or not he said it, the statement had significance. He had to endure the intrigues of cabinet members, and the interference of congressmen whose committee on the conduct of the war was a factor in Union failure and an instrument of inquisitorial abuse.

In meeting these conditions Lincoln became a practitioner of government as a human art. He somehow held his cabinet together. He had a way with governors. In 1862 it might almost have been said that the governors "ganged up" on him. There was a conclave of state executives whose purpose was to criticize and perhaps to do something worse. Some of the papers referred to it as a conspiracy to force the President to resign. The governors met at Altoona, then in Washington; but they found it was Lincoln who held the trumps. They came to assail him, but the interview was so managed that it left Lincoln in command. He had a way with senators. He did not have their coöperation, but he avoided an explosion. A group of Republican senators descended upon him in December 1862 breathing threats; but by shrewdness and tact he turned this senatorial upheaval into a triumph of presidential prestige. He had a way with visiting delegations. He would listen, or perhaps he himself would do the talking, he would tell an amusing story, would bow them out, and act on his own larger judgment. In an age of confusion he kept a clear head. He took the broader view. He saw enduring values, was impatient of unenlightened politics, and refused to surrender to cynicism.

Undoubtedly an important element in Lincoln's statesmanship was mastery of language. Somewhere back in early self-training there was a study of the forms and substance of speech not for their own sake, not just to win applause, but because Lincoln had an object to accomplish, a message to convey, and he realized the effectiveness of the written and spoken word in reaching and controlling men's minds. With Lincoln as with Woodrow Wilson the art of language was a means to an end. In stating a law case, Lincoln had a knack of brushing away technicalities and getting at the core of the subject. Few men could match him in the prairie years as a stump speaker. The people delighted to hear him. Most of the speeches common in his day were rhetorical and florid after the manner of Sumner; they were one with the fashion plates which showed elaborately dressed women and grandiloquently attired men. But Lincoln's speech was not like the Godey fashion plate; it had little in common with Sumner's rhetoric. There was in his diction something suggestive of the King James version of the Bible, something also of Shakespeare, and much that was just Lincoln. What made him a master of words was fitness to the occasion, a readiness of epigram, a cogency of speech that served well in place of adornment, a sense as to how adornment itself should be used, and the ability to take the simplest words and give them the greatness of inspired dignity.

At his second inaugural he made no effort to review the events of his administration, but delivered a brief address which ranks among his greatest papers. He refused to blame the South for the war, and counseled his countrymen to judge not that we be not judged. "With malice toward none"; he said, "with charity for all; . . . let us strive on to finish the work we are in; to bind up the nation's wounds; . . . to do all which may achieve and cherish a just and lasting peace. . . ." In the cacophony of war the note he struck was that of conciliation, of friendliness, of peace and charity. He avoided the language of contemporary preachers, but in his life and utterance he gave sincere expression and devotion to the Christian faith.

He could turn a trick by a good humored story. Your self-important soul, or your strutting dictator, does not often smile. In Lincoln the priceless element of humor was an index to the shape and quality of his mind. To his overburdened spirit,—amid strain and fatigue so overwhelming that, as he said, the remedy "seemed never to reach the tired spot"—laughter was a saving blend of play, restorative relaxation, and mental hygiene. It supplied a sense of proportion. At times it was a refreshing pause. On a very solemn occasion in a cabinet meeting when the emancipation proclamation was coming up, he got a big laugh out of Artemus Ward, much to the digust of his humorless secretaries. He liked Petroleum V. Nasby (David Locke). His humor was down to earth, yet in point and originality it was above the level of his time. His stories, verbal sallies, and quips of expression are a rich part of the American tradition. In treating Lincoln's laughter alongside his religion, Carl Sandburg shows that, in enjoying fun, he was no mere joker or buffoon. The man of backwoods pioneer origin must have courage, and humor is part of that courage. "This side of him [writes Sandburg] was momentous in one respect at least. It had brought him to folk masses as a reality, a living man. . . . Did he truly have something of the cartooned figure of Uncle Sam, benign, sagacious, practical, simple, at times not quite beyond taking a real laugh for himself and the country? Whatever the elements of this trait, it rested on American material, connected with an immense variety of American circumstances and incidents, and had become inevitably associated with Lincoln's name and personality."

Lincoln's greatness arose from a combination of qualities in a balanced personality. One could never define his conduct as springing from mere automatic reaction. It came rather from informed study and mature reflection. Mere slogans and stereotypes did not impress him. He was a simple man—he was unpretentious in manner and straightforward in expression—but he was never naïve. He could be enthusiastic with practical common sense. He attained a position of lofty eminence and moved among the great without making other men feel small. He was a sturdy individual; this, however, should be understood not as a denial of needful social coöperation, but rather in the Robert Burns sense of emphasis upon human worth. He could assert himself without becoming a dictator. He had ambition, but without selfishness. He had that largeness of soul that we call magnanimity. If a colleague, a subordinate, or a cabinet member were attacked, he would take the blame upon his own shoulders. Sometimes he would write a letter as an outlet for overwrought feeling, think it over, realize that it might wound the recipient, and then withhold it.

He encouraged the North without abusing the South. Though a war leader he wanted no perpetuation of war attitudes in peace time. He opposed the abuses of militarism. It is of present significance that in 1848 he had uttered a crushing denunciation of what would now be called "preventive war." The "war mind" never possessed him. His main feeling toward the war was deep regret that the avoidable tragedy had happened, a sense of mystery as to the ways of Providence, a realization that the scourge was as much a punishment of the North as of the South. He wanted the war to end with the surrenders. As the men after Appomattox went back to their plowing, he wanted healing and restoration. Coarser men took the saddle and Lincoln's plan of reconstruction was defeated, but Lincoln would have brought the South back if possible without bitterness and without treating Southerners as inferiors.

The Lincoln record is no mere success story of a railsplitter who became President, a prairie lawyer who reached world fame. One might wonder just how he became to the majority of his countrymen the embodiment of the American genius. Perhaps the inner source of his strength has not been fully plumbed. It might be hard to answer where and how he learned statecraft, but statesmen even yet will do well to take him as guide and mentor. In each new recurring crisis—in colossal wars that have shaken the world—men continue to carry the appeal to the spirit of Lincoln. Only in poetry does his ghost stalk at midnight, but his inspired words and the rugged vigor of his ideals seem today to have a greater vitality than during the vexed years of his presidency.

## *For Further Reading*

Of the several collected editions of Lincoln's works, the definitive is Roy P. Basler, ed., *The Collected Works of Abraham*

*Lincoln* (9 vols., 1953-1955), while Paul M. Angle and Earl S. Miers, eds., *The Living Lincoln* (1955), is an excellent short selection of the writings. For books about Lincoln, Jay Monaghan, ed., *Lincoln Bibliography 1839-1939* (2 vols., 1945), is very nearly complete for the dates given, but Paul M. Angle, *A Shelf of Lincoln Books* (1945), is more discriminating.

The major biographical treatments are the old, uncritical but still useful John G. Nicolay and John Hay, *Abraham Lincoln: A History* (10 vols., 1890); the imaginative, often confusing but nonetheless rewarding Carl Sandburg, *Abraham Lincoln: The Prairie Years* (1926), and *Abraham Lincoln: The War Years* (1939); and James G. Randall's scholarly and Revisionist *Lincoln the President* (4 vols., 1945-1955), the final volume completed by Richard N. Current. Among the many older shorter biographies, Lord Charnwood, *Abraham Lincoln* (1917), is considered the best, although now superseded by Benjamin P. Thomas, *Abraham Lincoln: A Biography* (1952), which is more convincing than Reinhard H. Luthin, *The Real Lincoln* (1960), an able study written from the Revisionist point of view. Controversial aspects of Lincoln's career are discussed by David Donald, *Lincoln Reconsidered* (1956), and Richard N. Current, *The Lincoln Nobody Knows* (1958), while the changing course of Lincoln historiography can be traced in Roy A. Basler, *The Lincoln Legend* (1935), Benjamin P. Thomas, *Portrait for Posterity* (1947), and David Donald, *Lincoln's Herndon* (1948).

Studies dealing with limited aspects of Lincoln's life and career that deserve mention include John J. Duff, *A. Lincoln: Prairie Lawyer* (1960); Don E. Fehrenbecher, *Prelude to Greatness: Lincoln in the 1850's* (1962); Reinhard H. Luthin, *The First Lincoln Campaign* (1944); David M. Potter, *Lincoln and His Party in the Secession Crisis* (1942); T. Harry Williams, *Lincoln and the Radicals* (1941); James G. Randall, *Constitutional Problems Under Lincoln* (rev. ed. 1951); Colin R. Ballard, *The Military Genius of Abraham Lincoln* (rev. ed. 1952); Jay Monaghan, *Diplomat in Carpet Slippers* (1945); and Lloyd Lewis, *Myths after Lincoln* (1929).

# The War Ends

## Bruce Catton

Once regarded as the last of the old-fashioned, romantic wars, the American Civil War has gradually been perceived as the first of the modern ones. The size of the conflict was staggering by nineteenth-century standards. At least two million men, perhaps more than two and a half million, served in the Union armies, about 900,000 in the Confederate forces. Of these, 700,000 died and 400,000 were wounded, these losses occurring in a total population of thirty-one million in 1860. Put another way, these statistics become more comprehensible; the mortalities are more than all other American wars from the Revolution to Vietnam combined. Material costs are almost impossible to calculate; to military expenses must be added the value of destroyed homes and farms, shipping and railrods, not to mention the cost of pensions or interest on the federal debt which continued to be paid well into the twentieth century. Looked at from purely an economic viewpoint, the emancipation of the slaves alone wiped out $4 billion in capital, "the most stupendous act of sequestration in the history of Anglo-American jurisprudence."

When this gigantic struggle began the contending sides were not evenly matched. The free states enjoyed a huge superiority over the seceded slave states in the three

*Source:* Bruce Catton, *A Stillness at Appomattox* (New York: Doubleday & Company, Inc., 1953), pp. 349–380. Copyright 1953 by Bruce Catton. Reprinted by permission of the publisher.

essential ingredients of modern war: men, materials, and money. The North numbered twenty million people compared to only eleven million in the states of the Confederacy, and of this number, four million were slaves whose potential value to the Southern cause could not be effectively exploited because of fierce opposition to all proposals to free and arm the blacks. This manpower disparity would become crucial in the closing year of the war. The same story can be told for materials and wealth. Twenty-one thousand miles of railroads connected the Northern states, compared to nine thousand in the South; three quarters of all manufacturing establishments, skilled workers, and bank deposits were located in the North. Nor did the absence of factories give the South any kind of agricultural advantage, for it produced only a third of the national output of grain, beef, pork, and horses. To William T. Sherman, living in Louisiana during the secession winter of 1860–1861, the South's headlong rush into war seemed "a folly, madness, a crime against civilization." In a remarkably prophetic letter to a Southern friend, the future devastator of Georgia asked "where are your men and appliances of war. . . . The Northern people not only greatly outnumber the whites at the South, but they are a mechanical people with manufactures of every kind, while you are only agriculturists—a sparse population covering a large extent of territory, and in all history no nation of mere agriculturists ever made successful war against a nation of mechanics. . . . You are bound to fail."

Ultimately the Confederacy did fail, but the question arises, how was it able to survive as long as it did, indeed, how was it able to come so close to victory in the face of these overwhelming odds? Among other explanations that have been advanced are first of all morale, the strong will of the vast preponderance of the Southern people, no matter what they thought about slavery or the legality of secession, to defend their homes against the invaders. In addition, the South did not have to conquer the North to win the war; it had only to persevere in resistance. Many drew a parallel with the American Revolution. When Cornwallis surrendered, Britain still controlled most of the land area of the infant United States and almost all the major cities, but the war had become unsupportable for the English people and had to be ended.

Another important consideration was a distinct Confederate superiority in military leadership during the first two years of the rebellion. While Lincoln searched for a capable commander, experimenting with one general after another, the Confederacy enjoyed superb military leadership. The outstanding figure was Robert E. Lee, who had declined the command of federal forces. Ably supported by Stonewall Jackson, James Longstreet, J. E. B. Stuart, and others, Lee performed military miracles in the first two years of the conflict. Ability descended down through the entire officer corps, since a military career had been one of the most honorable of occupations in the antebellum South. The larger number of officers trained at West Point came from secessionist territory and followed their states into the Confederacy. In the ranks, also, the rebel armies enjoyed an early edge, for most Southern boys could handle a rifle and a horse. These were skills that thousands in the Union armies had to learn. But learn they did. By 1864, the Northern army had become the best trained, best equipped, and most powerful military force the world had ever seen. In Lincoln, Grant, and Sherman a leadership emerged that understood the advantages and potential of their superior forces and discarded outmoded concepts of strategy and tactics. Inevitably, the South was hammered into submission.

Bruce Catton, the most prolific and most popular of the modern historians of the war, writes of the foot soldiers, the volunteers, the bummers and bounty jumpers, the young boys and the graybeards who did the fighting. He has not neglected the general officers as his two stirring volumes on U. S. Grant attest, nor does he hesitate to make broad generalizations about tactics and strategy, but primarily he tells the story "of the kind of men who enlisted in 1861, the spirit with which they came forward, and strangely innocent ways in which the process of turning them into soldiers was undertaken." The following selection is taken from the final volume of

Catton's trilogy on the Army of the Potomac. This immensely readable series uses as its sources not only the official records of the rebellion and the memoirs of the commanders but also the often overlooked regimental histories, the diaries and letters of the common soldiers, which give "the homely and often almost incredible little touches which make those far-off soldiers suddenly come alive." Here he brings alive the last nine days of the war.

Major General Gouverneur Kemble Warren and his V Army Corps had been having a bad day. The corps had been in position, wet and uncomfortable, a little west of Hatcher's Run, presumably a trifle south of the extreme right flank of Lee's main line, and during the morning—while Devin's troopers were meeting Rebel infantry in front of Five Forks and were beginning their difficult withdrawal to Dinwiddie Court House—Warren sent one division forward to make a reconnaissance and find out just where the Rebels might be.

By ill chance this division began to advance just when Lee ordered a force of his own to move forward and pick a fight with the Yankees in order to protect the move which Pickett was making a few miles farther west. This force caught the Federal infantry division off guard and piled into it with savage vigor, and the Federals were driven back in disorder. In their retreat they ran through the bivouac of the second of Warren's three infantry divisions, and these troops were all gathered around smoky campfires trying to dry their clothing and their blankets, no one having alerted them to the fact that there might be action. So this second division was routed, too, and Warren had to send in his third division and call for help from the II Corps, over on his right, in order to restore the situation.

By evening he had won back the ground that had been lost, but his men had had a hard all-day fight, with painful losses; and now, just as they were collecting their wounded and trying to get snug for the night, there came these orders to make a forced march to join Sheridan.

It was a foul night to move troops. It was so dark, as one soldier said, that it was literally impossible to see a hand before one's face. The rain had stopped, but the roads were deep with mud, every little creek had overflowed, and there was a completely unfordable stream flowing straight across the principal highway that the troops had to use. Warren's engineers tore down a house and used the timbers to build a bridge, but construction work at midnight with everybody exhausted was slow work.

Warren had received conflicting orders about the routes he was to take, so that there was a good deal of wearing countermarching for some units, and there was much confusion about maps and place names. Also, at the time he got his marching orders Warren's skirmish line was in contact with the enemy, and he felt that he should use much caution in getting his men away. Some regiments started on time but most of them did not, nothing that could conceivably go wrong went right, and by five in the morning—the hour at which it had been hoped that the whole corps would be taking position at Dinwiddie Court House—two of his divisions were just beginning to move.

Sheridan was furious. He met the head of the infantry column in a gray dawn as the men came splashing up to the rendezvous, and he demanded of the brigadier commanding: "Where's Warren?" The brigadier explained that Warren was back with the rear of the column, and Sheridan growled: "That's where I expected to find him. What's he doing there?" The officer tried to explain that Warren was trying to make sure that his men could break contact with the Confederates without drawing an attack, but Sheridan was not appeased. Later, when Warren arrived, the two generals were seen tramping up and down by the roadside, Sheridan dark and tense, stamping angrily in the mud, Warren pale and tight-lipped, apparently trying to control himself.

Wherever the fault lay, the early-morning attack that had been planned could not be made. It was noon before the V Corps was assembled, and by that time the Confederates were gone. During the night Pickett had got wind of the Yankee move, and around daybreak he took his entire force back to the breastworks at Five Forks.

These works ran for a mile or more along the edge of the White Oak Road, and they faced toward the south. At their eastern end, for flank protection, the line made nearly a right-angle turn and ran north for a few hundred yards. With his men in and behind these works, and cavalry patrolling both flanks, Pickett seems to have taken it for granted that he was safe from assault for the rest of the day. With a few other ranking officers he retired to a campfire some distance in the rear to enjoy the pleasures of a shad bake.

As far as Sheridan was concerned, however, Pickett was in as much danger as he had been in before. There was still a wide gap between his force and the rest of Lee's army, with only the thinnest chain of cavalry vedettes to maintain contact, and in that gap Sheridan could see a dazzling opportunity. He had his cavalry maintaining pressure along Pickett's front, and he had a whole mounted division waiting in reserve, ready to go slashing in around the Confederate right at the proper time. If, while the cavalry held the Southerners' attention, he could drive 16,000 good infantrymen into the open gap and bring their entire weight to bear on Pickett's left flank, just where the Rebel breastworks angled back toward the north, the war would be a good deal nearer its close by nightfall.

The 16,000 good infantrymen were at hand, and a comparatively short walk would put them into position. They were dog-tired. They had fought all of the day before, and they had spent practically all of the night and morning on the march, and while Sheridan and Warren discussed battle plans they were catching forty winks in some fields near a little country church. When Warren at last came over to move them up to the jump-off line they were sluggish, and getting them formed was slow work, and it seemed to Sheridan—watching the afternoon sun get lower in the sky, and reflecting that the whole situation might be very different by tomorrow morning—that Warren was not doing much to make things go faster. But the men would fight well when the time came, because they considered themselves a crack outfit and they had a great tradition.

The V Corps was one of the famous units of the whole Federal Army. Fitz-John Porter had commanded it, and it had been McClellan's favorite corps, and in general orders he had held it up as a model for the other corps to emulate, which caused jealousies that had not entirely worn away even yet. (It caused War Department suspicions, too, and promotion for higher officers in this corps was harder to get, it was said, than in the rest of the Army of the Potomac.) The corps had been built around a famous division of Regulars, and in the beginning all of its ranking officers had been Regulars, mostly of the stiff, old-army, knock-'em-dead variety. Its discipline tended to be severe, there was strict observance of military formalities, and the Regular Army flavor endured, even though many of of the old officers and all of the Regular battalions had disappeared.

This was the corps which Sheridan now was preparing to use as his striking force. When Grant first sent the corps out to operate on Lee's flank, he did two curious things. He detached it from Meade's command and put it entirely under Sheridan, promising to do the same with the II Corps if Sheridan needed it—which was a bit odd, considering that Sheridan was simply the cavalry commander, while Meade commanded the Army of the Potomac—and he specifically authorized Sheridan to relieve Warren of his command, if it seemed necessary, and to put someone else in his place.

Grant's subsequent explanation of these acts was brief and vague, but what he was actually trying to do was to find a solution for the old, baffling command problem that had beset the Army of the Potomac from its earliest days.

Time and again the Army of the Potomac had missed a victory because someone did not move quite fast enough, or failed to put all of his weight into a blow, or came into action other than precisely as he was expected to do. This had happened before Grant became general in chief and it had happened since then, and the fact that Warren had been involved in a few such incidents was not especially important. What Grant was really shooting at was the sluggishness and caution that were forever cropping out, at some critical moment, somewhere in the army's chain of command. With the decisive moment of the war coming up Grant was going to have no more of that. Instinctively, he was turning to Sheridan, Sheridan the driver—giving him as much of the army as he needed and in effect telling him to take it and be tough with it.

Sheridan was the man for it. As Warren's brigades struggled into position Sheridan was everywhere, needling the laggards, pricking the general officers on, sending his staff galloping from end to end of the line. He rounded up the cavalry bands, which had made music on the firing line the evening before, and he put them on horseback with orders to go into action along with the fighting men when the advance sounded. It was four o'clock by now, and there would not be a great deal more daylight, and at last the infantry began to move. Sheridan spurred away to send the cavalry forward too. There was the peal of many bugles and then a great crash of musketry, and thousands of men broke into a cheer, and the battle was on.

A skirmisher trotting forward a few hundred yards ahead of the V Corps turned once to look back, and he saw what neither he nor any of his mates had seen in a dreary year of wilderness fighting and trench warfare, and he remembered it as the most stirring thing he had ever looked upon in all of his life. There they were, coming up behind him as if all of the power of a nation had been put into one disciplined mass—the fighting men of the V Corps, walking forward in battle lines that were a mile wide and many ranks deep, sunlight glinting on thousands of bright muskets, flags snapping in the breeze, brigade fronts taut with parade-ground Regular Army precision, everybody keeping step, tramping forward into battle to the sound of gunfire and distant music. To see this, wrote the skirmisher, was to see and to know "the grandeur and the sublimity of war."

It was grand and inspiring—and, unfortunately, there was a hitch in it.

Warren was sending his men in with two divisions abreast and a third division following in support, and by some mischance he was hitting the White Oak Road far to the east of the place where he was supposed to hit it. Instead of coming in on the knuckle of Pickett's line, he was coming in on nothing at all. His men were marching resolutely toward the north and the battle was going on somewhere to the west, out of their sight and reach.

The left division in the first line was commanded by General Ayres, a hard-bitten survivor of the original old-army set of officers, and the left of his division brushed against the left flank of Pickett's force and came under a sharp fire. Ayres spun the whole division around, brigade by brigade, making almost a 90-degree turn to the left—hot enough work it was, too, with Rebel infantry and cavalry firing steadily and the ground all broken—and as he turned the rest of the corps lost contact with him. The division that had been advancing beside him was led by General Crawford, who fell a good deal short of being one of the most skillful soldiers in the army, and Crawford kept marching to the north, getting farther away from the battle every minute. Most of the third division followed Crawford, Ayres's men were for the moment so entangled in their maneuver that they could not do much fighting—and, in sum, instead of crunching in on the Rebel flank with overpowering force, the V Corps was hardly doing more than give it a brisk nudge.

A confusing long-range fire, heavy enough to hurt, kept coming in from the left, and smoke fog was drifting through woods and fields. Warren had gone riding frantically on to try to find Crawford and set him straight, and entire brigades had lost touch with their corps and division commanders. One of these, presently, got into action, led by one of the most remarkable soldiers in the army, the hawk-nosed theologian turned general, Joshua Chamberlain of Maine.

Before the war Chamberlain had done nothing more militant than teach courses in natural and revealed religion, and later on in romance languages, at Bowdoin College. In 1862 he had been given a two-year leave of absence to study in Europe. Instead of going to Europe he had joined the army, and in a short time he showed up at Gettysburg as colonel of the 20th Maine Infantry, winning the Congressional Medal of Honor for his defense of Little Round Top. Since then he had been several times wounded—he had an arm in a sling today, as a matter of fact, from a wound received twenty-four hours earlier in the fight near Hatcher's Run—and he had twice won brevet promotions for bravery under fire. It was occurring to him now that since bullets were coming from the left there must be Confederates over that way, so he took his brigade over to do something about it.

Beyond a gully, Chamberlain could at last see a Confederate line of battle. He got his brigade into line, took it down into the little ravine, came out on the far side, and headed for the enemy. The fire was hot, now—and here, in the thickest of it, came Sheridan, riding up at top speed as always, his mounted color-bearer riding behind him. Sheridan pulled up facing Chamberlain, his dark face glowing.

"By God, that's what I want to see! General officers at the front!" cried Sheridan. He asked where Warren and the rest of the corps might be, and Chamberlain gestured toward the north, trying to explain what had happened. Sheridan interrupted, saying that Chamberlain was to take command of everybody he saw in the immediate vicinity and press the attack—and then Sheridan rode off fast, looking for Warren and the missing infantry.

All along the breastworks on the White Oak Road dismounted Yankee cavalrymen were attacking—looking, as a man who watched them said, with their tightly fitting uniforms, natty jackets, and short carbines, as if they had been especially designed for crawling through knotholes. Many of the carbines were repeaters, and at close range the troopers had terrific fire power, and a deafening racket went up from the narrow aisle in the woods. Around the angle Ayres's division and Chamberlain's brigade and fragments of other commands were still in some confusion, but they were beginning to get it straightened out now, and they were hitting the Confederates from flank and rear. Far to the north, the troops that had gone off at a tangent were at last wheeled around so that they could cut across the Confederates' rear.

Sheridan was all over the field. When a skirmish line met a severe fire, wavered, and seemed ready to fall back, up came Sheridan at a gallop, shouting to the men: "Come on—go at 'em—move on with a clean jump or you'll not catch one of 'em! They're all getting ready to run now, and if you don't get on to them in five minutes they'll every one get away from you!" An infantryman at his side was struck in the throat and fell, blood flowing as if his jugular vein had been cut. "You're not hurt a bit!" cried Sheridan. "Pick up your gun, man, and move right on!" The soldier looked up at him, then obediently took his musket, got to his feet, and staggered forward—to drop dead after half a dozen steps. Chamberlain came up to Sheridan once and begged him not to expose himself on the front line, promising that the rest of them would press the attack. Sheridan tossed his head with a grin which, Chamberlain felt, "seemed to say that he didn't care much for himself, or perhaps for me," and promised to go to the rear—and then dashed off to a sector where the fire was even hotter.

Finally the line was formed as Sheridan wanted it. In a boggy woodland, heavy smoke clouding the last of the sunlight, Sheridan looked down the shifting mass of soldiers, turned in the saddle, and called: "Where's my battle flag?" Up came his color-bearer. Sheridan took the flag from him, raised it high over his head, and went trotting along the front. The line surged forward and got up to the Rebel works, Sheridan put his horse over the breastworks, and the infantry went over in a riot of yelling jubilant men—and the Rebel flank was broken once and for all, and the men of the V Corps fought their way down the length of Pickett's battle line taking prisoners by the score and the hundred.

By this time Warren had Crawford's errant division far around to the Rebel rear, rounding up fugitives and cutting off the line of retreat, and Warren sent his chief of staff over to tell Sheridan about it. This officer found Sheridan on the battlefield and trotted up proudly. But the great fury of battle was on Sheridan. Warren's corps had been late getting to Dinwiddie and it had been late getting into position at Five Forks, and when it attacked two thirds of it had gone astray and Warren had gone with it; Sheridan did not in the least care whether the reasons for all of this were good or bad, and he did not want to receive any more reports from General Warren.

"By God, sir, tell General Warren he wasn't in that fight!" he shouted. The chief of staff was dumfounded. Warren had been doing his best, no one in the Army of the Potomac ever spoke that way about a distinguished corps commander—but Sheridan was clearly implacable, his face black, his eyes flashing. The officer managed to say at last that he disliked to deliver such a message verbally—might he take it down in writing?

"Take it down, sir!" barked Sheridan. "Tell him by God he was not at the front!"

Warren's man rode away, stunned. The next to come up was General Griffin, ranking division commander in the V Corps—Regular Army to his fingertips, rough and tough and gifted with a certain magnetism—a man, in fact, cut somewhat after the Sheridan pattern. Bluntly, Sheridan hailed him and told him that he was now in command of the V Corps. Then he sent a courier to find Warren and deliver a written message relieving him of his command and ordering him to report to General Grant at headquarters.

Pickett's force was wholly wrecked, by now, with the front broken in and victorious Yankees charging in from the flank and rear to make ruin complete. Yet Sheridan still was not satisfied. The enemy must be annihilated, all escape must be cut off, that railroad line must be broken, no one must relax or pause for breath as long as there was anything still to be accomplished. . . . He was in a little clearing in the forest, directly behind what had been the main Confederate line, and through the clearing went the road that led from Five Forks to the Southside Railroad, the railroad Lee had to protect if his army was to live; and just then there came up to Sheridan some now unidentified officer of rank, to report triumphantly that his command was in the Rebel rear and had captured five guns.

Sheridan gave him a savage greeting:

"I don't care a damn for their guns, or you either, sir! What I want is that Southside Railway!"

The sun was just disappearing over the treetops, and the clearing was dim with a smoky twilight. Many soldiers were in and about the road through the clearing, their weapons in their hands, conscious of victory and half expecting to be told that they had done a great thing and were very fine fellows.

Sheridan turned to face them, and he suddenly stood up in his stirrups, waving his hat, his face as black as his horse, and in a great voice he roared:

"I want you men to understand we have a record to make before that sun goes down that will make Hell tremble!"

He waved toward the north, toward the position of the railroad, and he cried: "I want you there!"

He turned and rode to the north. Meeting Griffin and Ayres and Chamberlain, he called to them: "Get together all the men you can, and drive on while you can see your hand before you!"

While the officers formed the men into ordered ranks and prepared to move on, a pale, slight man rode up to Sheridan and spoke to him quietly: General Warren, the written order clutched in his hand, asking Sheridan if he would not reconsider the order that wrecked a soldier's career.

"Reconsider, hell!" boomed Sheridan. "I don't reconsider my decisions! Obey the order!" Silently, Warren rode off in the dusk, and Sheridan went on trying to organize a force to break through to the railroad.

Actually, no more could be done that night. No more needed to be done. To all practical purposes, Pickett's forces had been wiped out. Thousands of prisoners were on their way back to the provost marshal's stockades, and there were so many captured muskets that Sheridan's pioneers were using armloads of them to corduroy the roads. Some of the Rebel cavalry elements which had got away were swinging about to rejoin Lee's army, but the infantry that had escaped was beaten and disorganized, drifting off to the north and west, effectively out of the war. Sheridan could have the railroad whenever he wanted to march his men over to it, and he might just as well do it tomorrow as tonight because the force which might have stopped him had been blown to bits. There was no need to put exhausted troops on the road before morning, and in the end even Sheridan came to see it. Cavalry and infantry went into bivouac where they were.

Around General Griffin's campfire the new commander of the V Corps talked things over with division and brigade commanders. These men were deeply attached to Warren.

They felt that his troubles today had mostly been caused by General Crawford, and it seemed very hard that Warren should be broken for mistakes and delays which had not, after all, affected the outcome of the battle. This was the first time in the history of the Army of the Potomac that a ranking commander had been summarily fired because his men had been put into action tardily and inexpertly. Sheridan had been cruel and unjust—and if that cruel and unjust insistence on driving, aggressive promptness had been the rule in this army from the beginning, the war probably would have been won two years earlier. . . .

As the generals talked, a stocky figure stepped into the light of the campfire—Sheridan himself.

He was in a different mood, now, the battle fury quite gone, and he spoke very gently: If he had been harsh and demanding with any of them that day he was sorry, and he hoped they would forgive him, for he had not meant to hurt anyone. But —"you know how it is; we had to carry this place, and I was fretted all day until it was done." So there was this apology for hot words spoken in the heat of action, and there was the general's thanks for hard work well done; and then Sheridan went away, and the generals gaped into the dark after him. General Chamberlain, who was one of the cricle, reflected that "as a rule, our corps and army commanders were men of brains rather than magnetism"; but Sheridan, now—well, "we could see how this voice and vision, this swing and color, this vivid impression on the senses, carried the pulse and will of men."

Several miles to the east, one of Grant's staff officers who had been with Sheridan this day finished a tiring ride over crowded, watery roads, and pulled up his horse by the open fire at Grant's headquarters. His fellow officers there crowded around him before he had dismounted, eager for news, and he shouted it to them in breathless sentences—complete victory, Rebels utterly routed, the way to Lee's railroad and Lee's rear wide open, roads all clogged with prisoners—and they shouted, tossed hats and caps in the air, slapped one another on the back, capering in wild enthusiasm; all but Grant himself, who stood in their midst impassive, cigar in his teeth, and as soon as he could make himself heard in the din asked the staff officer the question that seemed to be his private gauge for measuring a victory: How many prisoners? The officer said that the best estimate was about five thousand, and for a moment Grant looked pleased, almost enthusiastic. Then he went over to the telegraphers' tent, coming out a moment later to remark: "I have ordered an immediate assault all along the lines."

Great things might have been done on the flank, but the Army of Northern Virginia still lay directly in front, and from the moment he crossed the Rapidan River Grant's basic idea had always been, not to make that army retreat, but to break it. Now the time had come when it could be broken. Yet "immediate" did not actually mean "right away." Orders had to go from Grant through Meade and Ord to corps and division commanders. Artillerists had to frame and distribute orders to batteries and gun pits. Orders for the infantry had to filter down from army to corps to division to brigade and regiment; and it was likely to be dawn, or close to it, before the assault could really be made.

On the right, where the lines were close together and where the Confederate defenses were most tightly knit, Parke would send his IX Corps straight in from their trenches. Farther around, west of Fort Hell, the big push would be made by the VI Corps, with Ord holding his men ready to follow the moment there was a sign of success. In this part of the front the lines were a mile or more apart, and in the counterblow after Fort Stedman the Federals had taken the Confederate picket lines; so in here there was a little room to maneuver, and around midnight the men of the VI Corps filed out of their trenches to go into position.

General Wright had gone out ahead of them to pick the target. There was comparatively high ground here, and along part of the front there was no water in front of the Confederate works. There were five lines of abatis to be crossed, very stout and formidable, but the pickets had reported a singular fact: there was a pathway through these entanglements, used by enemy details which came out to get firewood or go on picket duty, and at night the Rebels kept a bonfire alight toward the rear in line with this pathway. If the Federals who formed on the higher ground would simply guide their advance on this bonfire, then, they would get through the abatis and up to the trenches.

Wright formed his corps wedge-shaped, with the third brigade of the second division as the thin end of the wedge—1,600 men in six veteran regiments, the rest of the corps in echelon to right and left. With the advance there would be a detail of gunners with rammers and primers, ready to turn captured guns on the defenders. It was understood that the advance would begin as soon as a signal gun was fired from Federal Fort Fisher, in the rear.

The night was bewilderingly dark, and there was a mist that made the gloom even thicker. The VI Corps these days was known as the army's high-morale outfit—the men had shared in the great Shenandoah Valley victories, and they were cocky about it—but they were glum and silent as they left their trenches and took their places. The high command might know that when Lee detached troops to operate under Pickett at Five Forks he left his main line so badly undermanned that it could at last be broken, but the infantry knew nothing of this. All that the veterans understood was that these terrible fortifications which they had learned to consider unconquerable were at last to be attacked, and they took it for granted that the hour of doom had arrived.

When company commanders read off the orders, soldiers here and there were heard to mutter: "Well, good-by, boys—this means death." As always, the men got ready for the fight in their different ways. Some scribbled hasty letters home, others threw away decks of playing cards, still others examined cartridge boxes and canteens to make sure that they were filled, a few put pipe and tobacco within easy reach. And tonight a good many did what they never did except when they figured they were about to be slaughtered. They wrote their names and addresses on slips of paper and pinned these to their uniforms, so that their bodies could be identified after the battle.

Huddled close to the ground in the creepy no man's land between the armies, utter darkness and graveyard silence all around, the men waited nervously for the signal gun that would send them on their way. But once again there had been a mix-up in the arrangements. What finally came, jarring and stunning them and seeming to pin them down by sheer weight of violence, was not the report of one cannon but the crash of a tremendous bombardment, with every gun and mortar in the Federal lines opening fire.

There were miles upon miles of gun positions, all the way from the Appomattox to the works near Hatcher's Run, and from every weapon in this crescent there came the most intense and sustained volume of fire the gun crews could manage. Never before, not even at Gettysburg, had the army fired so much artillery so fast and so long. The whole sky pulsed and shuddered with great sheets of light. Jagged flames lit the horizon as the Confederate guns replied. In the blackness overhead the battle smoke piled up in monstrous thunderheads, fitfully visible in the flash of exploding shell.

A gunner wrote proudly of "a constant stream of living fire" pouring from the flaming gun pits, and a front-line infantryman said that the very ground shook and trembled with the concussion. Miles away to the west, men in the V Corps said the sky was lighted up as if by aurora borealis. How long it all lasted, nobody ever knew. After a time men realized that the Confederate batteries had stopped firing, and then the crash of the Union guns seemed definitely lighter—and now, as the bombardment slowly tapered off, staff officers from corps headquarters were going to brigade and regimental commanders asking why the men were not moving: the signal gun had been fired, somewhere in the midst of all of this uproar, and the attack should have been made ten minutes ago.

Officers prodded men to their feet, and the smoky sky began to turn gray, although it was still too dark to see anything a hundred yards away, and presently the whole great wedge of infantry was moving. And then the guns stopped altogether, and there was silence on the battlefield, and in this silence an officer realized that there was a mysterious pervasive noise that seemed to be the sound of a deep, distant rustling, "like a strong breeze blowing through the swaying boughs and dense foliage of some great forest." He realized at last that this was the noise made by 14,000 soldiers tramping forward over soft damp ground.

Rebel pickets came to life and began to shoot, and then rolling volleys of musketry lit the main line of Confederate works, and the guns opened heavily. The VI Corps raised a cheer and began to run forward. The leading brigade lost sight of the path through the abatis, but the whole corps was running now, details with axes were smashing at the entanglements, sheer weight of numbers was breaking a dozen openings —and the tide flowed on, past the abatis and into the ditch, with the black loom of the fortifications rising just ahead.

Far to the rear, on the parapet of a Union fort, an army surgeon had been watching, and in the predawn gloom he could see a twinkling, flashing line of fire half a mile wide— the rim of the Confederate works, lit by musketry. As he watched he saw a black gap in the center of this sparkling line, and then there was another gap a little to one side, and then a third one, and as he watched these gaps widened and ran together, and suddenly the whole chain of lights was out and he knew that the line had been captured.

It was not done easily, for if the defenders were few they died hard, and there was hand-to-hand fighting along the works. Storming parties got over in squads, stabbing and clubbing muskets. There was no cheering—everyone was too much out of breath for that—but the men coming up in the support brigades realized that the trenches had been taken when they saw Confederate cannon reversed, firing toward the Confederate rear. In some cases Union infantry refused to wait for the parties of artillerists who had been sent over to work the captured guns, and tried to operate them themselves. The 11th Vermont claimed to have fired twelve rounds from one battery, overcoming the want of primers simply by discharging muskets into the vents of the loaded pieces.

Dawn came at last, and the whole line of works was black with Union soldiers. Beyond the line lay the Confederate camps, with eager parties of VI Corps hot-shots pushing on through them, every man for himself—some of them running on to reach the unguarded rear areas, some looking through tents and huts for loot, some just going, kept moving by the excitement of victory. Far to the right, the IX Corps had stormed the whole first line of deadly trenches but met stubborn resistance on the second line, and the sound of artillery and musketry rolled across the pine flats. On the left, the entire line of defense had dissolved. Ord's troops, and the II Corps, were breaking through on the west, cutting the defenders' organizations into fragments and driving these broken units before them. By twos and threes and by disorganized squads, the Federals broke clear through past the railroad to the edge of the Appomattox. In a chance encounter by a bit of wood, some of these killed the famous General A. P. Hill.

In the Confederate camps the VI Corps made merry. One man remembered seeing a burly buck private outfitting himself in the tinseled gray dress-uniform coat which some Confederate officer would never need again, and another soldier was wrapping a Confederate flag about his shoulders as if it were a toga. The whole corps was up, now, overflowing the trenches, scampering around among bombproofs and huts and tents, staring out over ground which no armed Yankee had previously seen. Up into their midst came a group of mounted men, Grant and Meade and Wright trotting over to reorganize the storming columns and make the break-through complete.

"Then and there," wrote a Connecticut soldier exultantly, "then and there the long-tried and ever faithful soldiers of the Republic *saw daylight!*" And the whole corps looked up and down the Petersburg lines—broken forever, now—and took in what had been done, and caught its breath, and sent up a wild shout which, the Connecticut man said, it was worth dying just to listen to.

The end of the war was like the beginning, with the army marching down the open road under the spring sky, seeing a far light on the horizon. Many lights had died in the windy dark but far down the road there was always a gleam, and it was as if a legend had been created to express some obscure truth that could not otherwise be stated. Everything had changed, the war and the men and the land they fought for, but the road ahead had not changed. It went on through the trees and past the little towns and over the hills, and there was no getting to the end of it. The goal was a going-toward rather than an arriving, and from the top of the next rise there was always a new vista. The march toward it led through wonder and terror and deep shadows, and the sunlight touched the flags at the head of the column.

For a long time the Army of the Potomac had wanted to enter Richmond, and it almost seemed as if that was the object of everything that it did, but when Richmond fell at last the army did not get within twenty-five miles of it—not until long afterward, when everything was over and the men were going home to be civilians again. Most of the army did not even get into Petersburg, which had been within sight but out of reach for so long. Instead the troops moved off on roads that led to the west, pounding along in hot pursuit of Lee's army—no victory was final as long as that ragged army still lived and moved.

Only the IX Corps entered Petersburg, and it did so chiefly because the town lay right across its path. It moved in on the morning of April 3 a few hours after the last Confederate soldiers had moved out. The corps came in proudly, flags uncased and bands playing, but the town was all scarred by months of shellfire, the cheers and the music echoed through deserted streets, and there seems to have been a desolate, empty quality to it all that made the jubilation sound forced and hollow. Officers and newspapermen who had breakfast in Petersburg hotels found the fare poor, as was natural in a starved beleaguered city, and noticed that the hotel proprietors would not accept Confederate money.

In the dwelling houses the blinds were all drawn, and here and there an expressionless face could be seen peering out through parted curtains. Men remarked that there was not a woman to be seen; only a few old men, and an occasional cripple, and of course an awed concourse of colored folk. One officer saw Grant standing in a doorway, gesturing with his cigar as he dictated orders to his staff, utterly matter-of-fact, displaying rather less emotion and pride than the ordinary brigadier would show at a routine review of troops, and looking "as if the work before him was a mere matter of business in which he felt no particular enthusiasm or care."

In refusing to allow the army to relax and celebrate Grant was simply following common sense. From his viewpoint he had not actually won anything yet. From the moment when he headed down to the Rapidan fords, eleven months and many thousands of lives ago, he had had just one idea in mind: to destroy Lee's army. Now Richmond had fallen, and so had Petersburg, but Lee's army still lived and if it was to be destroyed it must first be caught. It would never be caught by pursuers who let days or hours go to waste; not that army, led by that general. So the Army of the Potomac would keep moving, and if there was to be a celebration it could come later.

Beaten and reeling in flight, the Rebel army was still dangerous. Proof that its men still wanted to fight came this morning at the prisoner-of-war stockade. Nearly 5,000 of the men captured at Five Forks were herded together there, and the Federal provost marshal had them paraded and made a little speech to them, pointing out that their cause was doomed and inviting everyone to step up, take the oath of allegiance, and then go home and fight no more. Out of the 5,000 present, fewer than 100 moved out to take the oath—and they were bitterly derided by all the rest, who profanely denounced them as cowards and traitors.

So although the grim Petersburg trenches were empty and harmless, and troops from the Army of the James were in Richmond putting out the fires that threatened to destroy the whole city—the Confederate rear guard had fired arsenals and storehouses, and the flames had got out of hand—nothing had really been settled. The Army of the Potomac had not yet brought its adversary to bay, and it would have to march long and fast to do it.

There were certain advantages. Leaving Petersburg, Lee had gone north of the Appomattox River. Somewhere above that river he was picking up the troops that had come down from Richmond and was collecting the fragments that had been sent flying when Sheridan took Five Forks and the VI Corps broke the Petersburg line. With everybody assembled, he would try to join Joe Johnston in North Carolina, and to do that he would have to go west and south. The Army of the Potomac was nearly as far west as he was, and it was a good deal farther south. Properly handled it ought to be able to head him off because it had a shorter distance to travel.

The railroads were important. There were two lines that mattered: the familiar Southside Railroad, and the Richmond and Danville, which latter went slanting down into Joe Johnston's territory and bisected the Southside line halfway between Petersburg and Lynchburg. Lee's quickest route would put him on the Richmond and Danville at Amelia Court House, sixteen miles northeast of the point where the two railroads intersected.

If the Federals moved west by the shortest route, they should strike the Richmond and Danville road at or near the junction before Lee's people could get down there via Amelia Court House. If that happened, it would be impossible for Lee to meet Johnston. He would have only two alternatives: to stand and make a finish fight of it, a fight that could end in but one way, or to keep on going west in the hope that he could reach Lynchburg, where he might get supplies and win some sort of breathing space in the wooded folds of the mountains.

So the task was not to overtake his army but to get ahead of it. Every march was to be a forced march. Sheridan and his cavalry were leading the way. Meade and three infantry corps were following close behind, and Ord and three divisions from the Army of the James were moving on parallel roads just a little farther south. The men carried extra rations, for there would be no waiting for supply trains, and a thirty-mile hike—ordinarily a perfect prodigy of a march—would be considered no more than a fair day's work. Officers in the V Corps called out to the men: "Your legs must do it, boys!"

Spring had come, and the world was turning green and white and gold with new leaves and blossoms. The cramping misery of the trenches had been left behind, and men's spirits were so high that even dogtrotting along in the wake of the cavalry did not seem a bad assignment. The rank and file was not entirely clear about just what had happened, but it was clear that the Johnnies were on the run at last. Grant summed it up in a telegram to Sherman: "This army has won a most decisive victory and followed the enemy. That is all that it ever wanted to make it as good an army as ever fought a battle."

They might be victorious, but the men were still cagey. Midway of the first day out, excited staff officers rode down the columns shouting the news—Richmond taken, the Union flag flying over the Confederate capital! The veterans perked up, and then they remembered that they had been had before. When an especially hard march was to be made, staff officers often circulated false announcements of good tidings just to keep everybody stepping along briskly. So the men jeered at each bearer of good news, calling out: "Put him in a canteen! Give him a hardtack! Tell it to the recruits!" But pretty soon the bands began to play, and the colonels formally announced the news to their own regiments, and up and down the line of march the men began to realize that for once the good news was true.

"Stack your muskets and go home!" yelled one of Ord's men, when General Gibbon announced the fall of Richmond. As the army bivouacked that night, one veteran told another: "I feel better tonight than I did after that fight at Gettysburg."

Far out in front, fantastic outriders of victory, went Sheridan's scouts. Sometimes they rode dressed as Confederate officers or couriers, and sometimes they wore faded jeans and rode decrepit horses or mules with makeshift bridles and saddles, pretending to be displaced farmers or roving horse doctors. Either way, they visited Rebel picket posts, rode blithely through cavalry cordons, ambled alongside Lee's wagon trains, paused to chat in Confederate camps. Most of them got back alive, and they kept Sheridan informed about where the enemy's people were and where they were going to be next.

As they did all of this, riding under no man's control, they appear to have found unheard-of opportunities for loot. They visited farms and plantations and collected much food for themselves, they got new horses when they felt that they needed them, and (as other cavalrymen reported enviously) they were not always above helping themselves to more substantial valuables, taking cash and jewelry from planters' homes and leaving their victims quite at a loss to say just who had robbed them. They were a wild, lawless crew, carrying their own lives and other people's property in their naked hands, and they feared nothing in particular except the black scowl of Phil Sheridan.

They swarmed all around the head of the cavalry column, exploring the whole network of country roads and learning where every lane and cowpath led. Behind them came hard columns of questing cavalry, slashing through to nip at the flanks of Lee's moving army, driving Confederate troopers off the roads, harassing the plodding columns with quick thrusts and then pulling away fast to strike again a mile or two farther on. Back of these, in turn, came Sheridan and the main body of cavalry; and two days out of Five Forks Sheridan led his men into a country town called Jetersville, which place was important for two reasons—it was on the Richmond and Danville Railroad and Lee and his army had not yet reached it.

Sheridan sent one division west and north to see what was to be seen and to cause as much trouble as possible for the Confederacy. The rest he led northeast, and after a few miles his men ran into Rebel cavalry patrols and drove them back. Then Sheridan called a halt and had his men build breastworks, and a little later General Griffin came up with the V Corps and threw his men into line of battle beside them, and the rest of the infantry was not far away. Meade himself was coming up, in an ambulance. He had taken ill, from indigestion and general nerve strain, after the fall of Petersburg, but he was coming along with the army regardless. So here was the Army of the Potomac getting ready to fight its old antagonist, and for the first time in history its battle line was facing toward the northeast. It had won the race and if Lee was to go any farther south he would have to fight.

Lee's army was at Amelia Court House, half a dozen miles short of the spot where Meade's infantry was going into line. It could not stay there because it had used up all of its rations and there was nothing in Amelia Court House for it to eat, and after surveying the Yankee line carefully Lee concluded that his army was not strong enough to fight its way through. Since the army could not retreat—there were Yankees in both Richmond and Petersburg now—only one move remained on the board: to go west, cross country, and strike the western part of the Southside Railroad. Provisions could be brought up from Lynchburg by this line, and if the army moved fast and had luck there was an outside chance that it could still slip around the Federal flank and get south. Failing that, it might at least reach Lynchburg and try to survive there for a time. There was nothing else it could even try to do.

Sheridan did not believe it should be given any leeway. His whole instinct was to attack before anybody got six hours older, and he seems to have feared that Meade would be content to wait for Lee to start the fight. At any rate, Sheridan wanted the boss; so one of his scouts, dressed like a Confederate colonel, took a note which Sheridan scribbled on tissue paper, folded the tissue paper in tin foil, concealed that in a wad of leaf tobacco, and shoved the tobacco in his mouth—after which he went trotting off cross country to find U. S. Grant.

Grant was with Ord that day, a dozen miles away, and the scout reached him toward evening, narrowly missing getting shot by Ord's pickets as he came cantering in. So Grant got Sheridan's message, which described the situation, suggested that Lee's army might be captured, and urged Grant to come and take charge in person. With his staff and a small mounted escort Grant immediately set out, guided by the gray-uniformed scout, following rambling country roads in the dark—with his staff wondering uneasily just what would happen to the war if the little party should blunder into the Confederate lines by mistake. It was late at night when Grant reached Sheridan's tent, and nothing could be done with the troops until morning.

If Sheridan feared that Meade would sit down and wait for the fight to be brought to him, he was mistaken. Meade wanted to fight and he started the infantry toward Amelia Court House at dawn, but Lee was no longer there. He had put his tired, half-starved troops on the road for a night march, trying the last chance that was left to him, striking due west for the town of Farmville, on the Southside Railroad. When the flight was discovered Meade ordered pursuit, but Grant modified the order: let part of the infantry follow in Lee's rear, pressing him and making him stand and fight whenever it could, but let the rest follow the cavalry and get west as fast as possible, keeping always south of the Confederates. The idea still was to win a race, and if they could plant infantry across Lee's path just once more it would all be over.

So the foot race was on again and away they went, infantry and cavalry and the lumbering guns. It was April 6, and the Petersburg break-through was four days behind them, and some of the infantry units were doing thirty-five miles a day and more. In some ways it was like any other hard march—woods and swamps and wispy fields, muddy roads churned into quagmire by thousands of horses, a hard pull on the long hills and everybody too winded to say much. Yet now it was all different, because for all anyone knew the thing they had been marching toward for four years might lie just the other side of the next hill.

On every side there were multiplying signs of Confederate defeat, littering roads and fields like driftwood dropped by an ebbing tide: broken wagons and ambulances, guns with broken wheels, discarded muskets and blanket rolls, stragglers bedded down in fence corners or stumbling listlessly through the woods—and, every so often, "dropped in the very middle of the road from utter exhaustion, old horses literally skin and bones, and so weak as scarcely to be able to lift their heads when some soldier would touch them with his foot to see if they really had life." Every regiment had its congenital pessimists, as one soldier confessed, men who fought well but who always darkly prophesied ultimate Rebel victory; but now, this man said, "the utter collapse of the rebellion was so near that no one could fail to see it, and the croakers were compelled to cheer in spite of themselves."

Humphreys was driving the II Corps in on Lee's rear guard, and the day was a long succession of savage little fights wherever the Confederates could find a defensive vantage point. On other roads the other corps struggled to gain ground, and up ahead and along the way there was the cavalry—always the cavalry, with Sheridan sending galloping columns in to skirmish, wheel, and dash away again, forcing weary Southerners to halt, form line of battle, and then go on with their march. He had three divisions doing this, probing always for a weak spot, slowing down the enemy's march, relentless and seemingly tireless. In midafternoon he found, at last, the opening he was looking for.

Custer spied a Confederate wagon train winding through hill country, the bleak woods glistening from the spring rains, and he whistled his squadrons in on the dead run with sabers swinging. Confederate infantry fell into line to repel the attack, but up ahead a gap developed in the moving column and Custer's men went pouring through it, stopping the wagon train, cutting the traces and driving the teams away, sabering drivers, breaking wagon wheels with axes, and setting fire to the wreckage. More and more cavalry went into the gap, and Sheridan sent couriers back to bring up the infantry: here is a whole section of Lee's army cut off, come on up quick and we can bag the lot!

Nearest infantry was the VI Corps, which had marched all night and all day without food and was just filing into some fields to make coffee and eat bacon and hardtack when Sheridan's messengers came up. Down the lines went staff officers and colonels to tell the men the news: Sheridan is just ahead and he wants help, and we can all eat later perhaps. The men fell into ranks cheering and they stepped off eagerly, and before long they formed a battle line on a slope looking down to a little creek, on the far side of which there was a Confederate battle line. Sheridan rode up, and the VI Corps veterans who had followed him in the Valley pointed and told each other: "There's Phil! There's Phil!" and yelled their heads off. One of their officers mused: "The sight of that man on the field was more gratifying than rations, more inspiring than reinforcements."

On the horizon was the burning Confederate wagon train. Straight in front was a fair piece of the Rebel army, brought to bay at last, then dangerous as so many wounded panthers; and off to the left were four brigades of Yankee cavalry, moving forward at a walk as if passing in review, heading for the Confederate flank. For a minute or two everything seemed to hang in suspense, as if the army had gone to great pains to pose a dramatic picture. Then the wild high notes of the bugles sounded from end to end of the line, and everybody went forward on the run, cavalry and infantry alike, and there was a great shouting and the smoke from thousands of muskets banked up over the valley. Then the cavalry had broken through, and the infantry was tussling in the shallows, and suddenly there was no more Rebel battle line, nothing but groups of men throwing down their arms, cavalry ranging far and wide to round up fugitives, thousands of Confederates surrounded and surrendering—among them, picturesque one-legged General Dick Ewell, who had been Stonewall Jackson's lieutenant when the world was young. Far in the distance, Lee on a hilltop watched it all and told an officer beside him: "That half of our army has been destroyed."

There was exaggeration in the remark, but not a great deal. What remained of two Confederate army corps had gone to pieces, with thousands of men taken prisoner, only a few escaping through the woods. The rear guard hung on until dark and then the Confederates followed their last fading chance to the north side of the Appomattox River, burning the bridges behind them. If they could keep the Federals south of that still unfordable river and go on with desperate forced marches it might yet be possible . . . just barely possible . . . to get away and join Johnston, or reach the mountains, or find somewhere a chance to rest and refit and make the war go on a little longer.

Along the creek where they had won their triumph the Federals cheered and danced. Someone found barrels of Confederate paper money in a headquarters wagon not yet burned, and the men went scampering about with handfuls of it, tossing it in the air, using it to kindle fires, offering great bundles of it to the gloomy prisoners. All of the ground was covered with the debris of the broken army, and as the VI Corps moved away the men found the road for two miles so littered with discarded muskets that it was hard to move without stepping on them. A major of the 65th New York was mortally wounded when someone's horse trod on one of these muskets and caused it to go off and shoot him.

If the VI Corps found a few hours to relax, Humphreys kept the II Corps moving, and it got to one of the river crossings just as a Rebel rear guard was firing the last bridge. Barlow had the advance, and he sent his men down to the bridge a-running, fighting Confederate skirmishers and beating out the flames at the same time. In the end they saved the bridge and drove off the Confederate guards, and the whole army corps went pouring over to the north side of the river and pushed on to harry the rear of the Army of Northern Virginia and make any breathing spell impossible.

Two Confederate armies Grant had captured entire, in this war, and now the third and greatest of them was stricken, limping pathetically in its effort to get away from him. The increasing signs that the army was ready for destruction simply made Grant drive his own troops all the harder. Sheridan's cavalry ranged west, untiring, and Griffin's and Ord's troops followed as if the mounted men were pulling them on. North of the Appomattox, the II Corps continued to press the Confederate rear. Since this corps was miles away from the rest of the Union army, there was danger that Lee might turn suddenly and destroy it, and so Grant ordered the VI Corps to cross the river and march with Humphrey's men.

It was April 7 now, and Grant was in the little town of Farmville by the Appomattox. Evening had come, and the troops in Farmville had lighted bonfires all along the main street, and Grant was sitting on the veranda of the homely country hotel there when the head of the VI Corps came marching through on its way to the north side of the river. As they marched between the fires the men saw the unassuming little general on the porch, and they suddenly realized that this man was at last leading them to the victory they had dreamed of so long. They broke ranks briefly, seized brands from the bonfires and made torches, and then paraded past

Grant, waving the burning torches and yelling hysterically. Brigade bands materialized, and the VI Corps marched by to music. Men who had no torches waved their caps, and the corps went on out of the firelight into the darkness, crossing the Appomattox. After they had passed, Grant went inside the hotel and wrote a formal note to be delivered to Robert E. Lee under a flag of truce, inviting Lee to surrender.

Of this note the soldiers knew nothing. They knew only that in all of its existence the Army of the Potomac had never been driven as hard as it was being driven now. Wagon trains were left far behind, whole brigades and divisions marched without food, and every rod of the way the army dribbled stragglers. These stragglers found the foraging in this part of Virginia very good, since marching armies had not previously been here, but the land's plenty was of little help to the men who remained in the ranks. The army was moving too fast to bother with foraging details.

A soldier in the 20th Maine said that "we never endured such marching before," and another man in the V Corps remembered making a forty-two-mile march that went clear through from one sunrise to another. Whenever the column stopped for a five-minute rest, he said, men would drop in their tracks and go instantly to sleep, and when the column moved on many of the men who stumbled to their feet, shouldered their muskets, and went lurching down the road would still be sound asleep. The very utmost men could do was demanded of them now, and the only reality was the road itself.

It was a bad road to march on, like all the roads of war—deeply rutted, fouled by the march of the cavalry up ahead, by turns heavy with mud or deep with the dust that would make marching a gray choking agony. Yet this was the road the army had been marching toward from the very beginning, and many thousands of men had died in order that this road might at last be marched on; for this was the road to the end of the war, and on over the horizon to the unimaginable beginnings and endings that would lie beyond that. Also, and more intimately, it was the beginning of the long road home.

It was April 8, by now, and tomorrow would be Palm Sunday, and the land was rich and warm with spring. Below the Appomattox, that day, the road wound interminably through deep woods, so that dusk came down early. Ord's divisions were on the road, and all of the V Corps, together with much artillery, and the artillery was supposed to have the road while the infantry filed along on each side. But the road was very narrow, so that there was much crowding and confusion, and the men were very tired and quarrelsome, and some time after dark a tremendous fight broke out between infantry and artillery. Infantry complained that the gunners were driving their six-horse teams recklessly, forcing men off the road and causing injuries. Gunners declared that infantrymen were hitting artillery horses over the head with musket butts. Everybody was hungry, irritable, and half out of his mind with fatigue, and the yelling and cursing and hitting and general uproar went up from the dark lane for an hour or more.

When it was finally settled it was after midnight, and the troops were led off the road to make a supperless bivouac. They got very little rest—one regiment at the tail of the column complained that it was roused just fifteen minutes after it turned in—because couriers came riding in from Phil Sheridan, who was a few miles farther on, near a little place called Appomattox Court House. He had his cavalry squarely in front of the Rebel army, and he was writing that if the infantry could be there first thing in the morning they could probably wind the whole business up.

Sheridan's scouts had come to him earlier in the day with word that several freight trains with food had pulled in at Appomattox Station, a mile or so from the courthouse town, and that Lee's wagons would presently be alongside, loading up. Sheridan sent Custer off at a gallop, and Custer's division took the Confederates by surprise, seizing the trains just as they were ready to unload. There were former railroad men among the Yankee troopers, and these flung themselves from the saddle and raced for the locomotives, climbing into the cabs with much clumping of heavy boots and clanking of sabers. They threw out the Southern train crews, blew whistles and rang bells, and bumped the trains back and forth in aimless celebration until someone finally had them run the cars up the track a few miles so that they would be out of reach of any Confederate counterthrust.

Custer took the main body of his troops on past the station, seized a big wagon park and artillery train, and chased fugitives eastward along a road that led uphill through deep woods. He came out into the open just at dark, and saw a rude breastwork cutting across the highway with gray-clad infantry behind it. Beyond, many campfires put a soft red glow on the sky. They were the campfires of Lee's army—and Custer's cavalry was due west of them.

Sheridan came up soon after, with the rest of the cavalry. He sent hurry-up messages for the infantry, put half of his men in line, dismounted, facing the Rebel breastworks, and ordered the rest into bivouac near the railroad a mile to the south.

The road his cavalry was on was the main road to Lynchburg, which lay twenty miles to the west. Of all the world's roads, this was the only one that mattered now to the Army of Northern Virginia. If, when morning came, that army could knock the Yankees out of the way and march west on this road it might still hope to live for a while—a day or two, a fortnight, a few months. If it could not do that, it would cease to exist within twenty-four hours. Cavalry alone could not bar the way very long, but if the blue infantry came up in time then it would be taps and dipped flags and good-by forever for Lee's army.

Federal infantry was on the road in the dark hours before dawn, with very little sleep and no breakfast at all. The men were told that if they hurried this was the day they could finish everything, and this inspired them. Yet they were no set of legendary heroes who never got tired or hungry or thought about personal discomfort. They were very human, given to griping when their stomachs were empty, and what really pulled them along this morning seems to have been the promise that at Appomattox Station rations would be issued. Most of the men who made the march that morning, one veteran admitted, did so because they figured it was the quickest way to get breakfast. Even so the straggling was abnormally heavy, and there were regiments in the column which had no more than seventy-five men with the colors.

It was Palm Sunday, with a blue cloudless sky, and the warm air had the smell of spring. The men came tramping up to the fields by the railroad station with the early morning sun over their right shoulders, and they filed off to right and left, stacked arms, and began collecting wood for the fires with which they would cook the anticipated rations. The divisions from the Army of the James were in front, Ord and John Gibbon in the lead, and the V Corps was coming up close behind. Gibbon and Ord rode to a little house near the railroad where Sheridan had his headquarters, and Sheridan came out to greet them and explain the situation.

The Lynchburg Road lay about a mile north of cavalry headquarters. It ran along a low ridge, partly concealed by timber, with a boggy little brook running along a shallow valley on the near side, and a couple of miles to the east it dipped down to a little hollow and ran through the village of Appomattox Court House. In and around and beyond this village, with its advance guard holding the breastworks half a mile west of it, was what remained of the Army of Northern Virginia. Off to the east, out of sight beyond hills and forests but not more than six or eight miles away, was Meade with the II Corps and the VI Corps, coming west on the Lynchburg Road to pound the Confederate rear. In effect, the Federals occupied three sides of a square—cavalry on the west, infantry on the south, Meade and the rest of the army on the east. The Rebel army was inside the square, and although the north side was open that did not matter because the Confederates could find neither food nor escape in that direction. Their only possible move was to fight their way west along the Lynchburg Road.

So Sheridan explained it, warning the generals that he expected the Rebels to attack at any moment and that they had better get ready to bring their troops up in support.

While he was talking the sound of musket fire came down from the ridge. It was sporadic, at first, as the skirmishers pecked away at each other, but it soon grew much heavier and there was the heavy booming of field artillery. The big push was on, and Sheridan sprang into the saddle, ordering the rest of his cavalry up into line and telling the officers to bring their infantry up as fast as they could. Then he was off, and the generals galloped back to put their men in motion.

The hopeful little breakfast fires died unnoticed, nothing ever cooked on them, and the infantry took their muskets, got into column, and went hurrying north to get astride of the Lynchburg Road. The crossroad they were on led through heavy timber and the men could see nothing, but the noise of the firing grew louder and louder as they marched. Then, for the last time in their lives, beyond the trees they heard the high, spine-tingling wail of the Rebel yell, a last great shout of defiance flung against the morning sky by a doomed army marching into the final sunset.

The Federals got across the Lynchburg Road, swung into line of battle facing east, and marched toward the firing and the shouting. As they marched, dismounted cavalry came drifting back, and the troopers waved their caps and cheered when they saw the infantry, and called out: "Give it to 'em—we've got 'em in a tight place!"

In a clearing there was Sheridan, talking with Griffin and other officers of the V Corps; Sheridan, talking rapidly, pounding a palm with his fist; and the battle line marched on and came under the fire of Rebel artillery. One brigade went across somebody's farm, just here, and as the firing grew heavier a shell blew the end out of the farmer's chicken house, and the air was abruptly full of demoralized chickens, squawking indignantly, fluttering off in frantic disorganized flight. And here was the last battle of the war, and the men were marching up to the moment of apotheosis and glory—but they were men who had not eaten for twenty-four hours and more, and they knew Virginia poultry from of old, and what had begun as an attack on a Rebel battle line turned into a hilarious chase after fugitive chickens. The battle smoke rolled down over the crest, and shells were exploding and the farm buildings were ablaze, and Federal officers were waving swords and barking orders in scandalized indignation. But the soldiers whooped and laughed and scrambled after their prey, and as the main battle line swept on most of this brigade was either continuing to hunt chickens or was building little fires and preparing to cook the ones that had been caught.

The Confederates had scattered the cavalry, and most of the troopers fled south, across the shallow valley that ran parallel with the Lynchburg Road. As the last of them left the field the way seemed to be open, and the Confederates who had driven them away raised a final shout of triumph—and then over the hill came the first lines of blue infantry, rifles tilted forward, and here was the end of everything: the Yankees had won the race and the way was closed forever and there was no going on any farther.

The blue lines grew longer and longer, and rank upon rank came into view, as if there was no end to them. A Federal officer remembered afterward that when he looked across at the Rebel lines it almost seemed as if there were more battle flags than soldiers. So small were the Southern regiments that the flags were all clustered together, and he got the strange feeling that the ground where the Army of Northern Virginia had been brought to bay had somehow blossomed out with a great row of poppies and roses.

So the two armies faced each other at long range, and the firing slackened and almost ceased.

Many times in the past these armies had paused to look at each other across empty fields, taking a final size-up before getting into the grapple. Now they were taking their last look, the Stars and Bars were about to go down forever and leave nothing behind but the stars and the memories, and it might have been a time for deep solemn thoughts. But the men who looked across the battlefield at each other were very tired and very hungry, and they did not have much room in their heads for anything except the thought of that weariness and that hunger, and the simple hope that they might live through the next half hour. One Union soldier wrote that he and his comrades reflected bitterly that they would not be here, waiting for the shooting to begin, if they had not innocently believed that tale about getting breakfast at Appomattox Station; and, he said, "we were angry with ourselves to think that for the hope of drawing rations we had been foolish enough to keep up and, by doing so, get in such a scrape." They did not mind the desultory artillery fire very much, he said, but "we dreaded the moment when the infantry should open on us."

Off toward the south Sheridan had all of his cavalry in line again, mounted now with pennons and guidons fluttering. The Federal infantry was advancing from the west and Sheridan was where he could hit the flank of the Rebels who were drawn up to oppose that infantry, and he spurred over to get some foot soldiers to stiffen his own attack. General Griffin told Chamberlain to take his brigade and use it as Sheridan might direct. Men who saw Sheridan pointing out to Chamberlain the place where his brigade should attack remembered his final passionate injunction: "Now smash 'em, I tell you, smash 'em!"

Chamberlain got his men where Sheridan wanted them, and all of Ord's and Griffin's men were in line now, coming up on higher ground where they could see the whole field.

They could see the Confederate line drawing back from in front of them, crowned with its red battle flags, and all along the open country to the right they could see the whole cavalry corps of the Army of the Potomac trotting over to take position beyond Chamberlain's brigade. The sunlight gleamed brightly off the metal and the flags, and once again, for a last haunting moment, the way men make war looked grand and caught at the throat, as if some strange value beyond values were incomprehensively mixed up in it all.

Then Sheridan's bugles sounded, the clear notes slanting all across the field, and all of his brigades wheeled and swung into line, every saber raised high, every rider tense; and in another minute infantry and cavalry would drive in on the slim Confederate lines and crumple them and destroy them in a last savage burst of firing and cutting and clubbing.

Out from the Rebel lines came a lone rider, a young officer in a gray uniform, galloping madly, a staff in his hand with a white flag fluttering from the end of it. He rode up to Chamberlain's lines and someone there took him off to see Sheridan, and the firing stopped, and the watching Federals saw the

Southerners wheeling their guns back and stacking their muskets as if they expected to fight no more.

All up and down the lines the men blinked at one another, unable to realize that the hour they had waited for so long was actually at hand. There was a truce, they could see that, and presently the word was passed that Grant and Lee were going to meet in the little village that lay now between the two lines, and no one could doubt that Lee was going to surrender. It was Palm Sunday, and they would all live to see Easter, and with the guns quieted it might be easier to comprehend the mystery and the promise of that day. Yet the fact of peace and no more killing and an open road home seems to have been too big to grasp, right at the moment, and in the enormous silence that lay upon the field men remembered that they had marched far and were very tired, and they wondered when the wagon trains would come up with rations.

One of Ord's soldiers wrote that the army should have gone wild with joy, then and there; and yet, he said, somehow they did not. Later there would be frenzied cheering and crying and rejoicing, but now . . . now, for some reason, the men sat on the ground and looked across at the Confederate army and found themselves feeling as they had never dreamed that the moment of victory would make them feel.

". . . I remember how we sat there and pitied and sympathized with these courageous Southern men who had fought for four long and dreary years all so stubbornly, so bravely and so well, and now, whipped, beaten, completely used up, were fully at our mercy—it was pitiful, sad, hard, and seemed to us altogether too bad." A Pennsylvanian in the V Corps dodged past the skirmish line and strolled into the lines of the nearest Confederate regiment, and half a century after the war he recalled it with a glow: ". . . as soon as I got among these boys I felt and was treated as well as if I had been among our own boys, and a person would of thought we were of the same Army and had been Fighting under the Same Flag."

Down by the roadside near Appomattox Court House, Sheridan and Ord and other officers sat and waited while a brown-bearded little man in a mud-splattered uniform rode up. They all saluted him, and there was a quiet interchange of greetings, and then General Grant tilted his head toward the village and asked: "Is General Lee up there?"

Sheridan replied that he was, and Grant said: "Very well. Let's go up."

The little cavalcade went trotting along the road to the village, and all around them the two armies waited in silence. As the generals neared the end of their ride, a Yankee band in a field near the town struck up "Auld Lang Syne."

## *For Further Reading*

The principal source for the military history of the Civil War is that voluminous and indispensable set of volumes, *The War of the Rebellion: A Compilation of the Official Records of the Union and Confederate Armies* (128 vols., 1880–1901). An additional source that can be used very effectively with the above is the *Atlas to Accompany the Official Records of the Union and Confederate Armies* (new ed. 1958). Clarence C. Buel and Robert U. Johnson's *Battles and Leaders of the Civil War* (4 vols., 1887) preserves the recollections of the leading generals, North and South. Good reference tools are Frederick H. Dyer, *A Compendium of the War of the Rebellion* (new ed., 3 vols., 1960), and Mark M. Boatner, *The Civil War Dictionary* (1959).

Bruce Catton's *This Hallowed Ground* (1955) is an eloquent presentation of the Union side with strong emphasis on military history, while Clifford Dowdey, *The Land They Fought For* (1955), does a comparable job for the Confederacy. Douglas S. Freeman's famous works, *Robert E. Lee* (4 vols., 1949) and *Lee's Lieutenants* (3 vols., 1942–1944), cannot be disregarded by any Civil War buff, but his concentration on the Eastern theater of operations should be corrected by Frank Vandiver's *Rebel Brass* (1956). For the Northern command system, see T. Harry Williams, *Lincoln and His Generals* (1952), and Kenneth P. Williams, *Lincoln Finds a General* (2 vols., 1949–1959). Also concerned with Lincoln's role in the military operations is Colin R. Ballard, *The Military Genius of Abraham Lincoln* (new ed. 1952). On Grant, see J. F. C. Fuller, *The Generalship of Ulysses S. Grant* (new ed. 1958), and three volumes of a still uncompleted biography begun by the late Lloyd Lewis and continued by Bruce Catton: *Captain Sam Grant* (1950), *Grant Moves South* (1960), and *Grant Takes Command* (1969). William T. Sherman is the subject of two distinguished biographies, B. H. Liddell Hart, *Sherman: Soldier, Statesman, Realist* (new ed. 1958), and Lloyd Lewis, *Sherman, Fighting Prophet* (1932). The "biography" of the foot soldiers is the subject of Bell I. Wiley's *The Life of Johnny Reb* (1943) and *The Life of Billy Yank* (1952). An essential study is Fred A. Shannon, *The Organization and Administration of the Union Army 1861–1865* (2 vols., 1928).